Sujit Mukherjee

An Indian Cricket Century

Selected Writings

Edited and with an Introduction
by
Ramachandra Guha

Orient Longman

To
Keshava and Iravati

ORIENT LONGMAN PRIVATE LIMITED

Registered Office
3-6-272 Himayatnagar, Hyderabad 500 029 (A.P.), India

Other Offices
Bangalore / Bhopal / Bhubaneshwar / Chandigarh / Chennai
Ernakulam / Guwahati / Hyderabad / Jaipur / Kolkata
Lucknow / Mumbai / New Delhi / Patna

First Published by Orient Longman Private Limited 2002

ISBN 81 250 2204 X

Typeset by
OSDATA, Hyderabad 500 029

Printed at
Orion Printers, Hyderabad 500 004

Published by
Orient Longman Private Limited
3-6-272 Himayatnagar
Hyderabad 500 029

Contents

Acknowledgements

To Hind Pocket Books, Delhi, for "Double Trouble", "Magnifico", "V for Victory" from *The Romance of Indian Cricket* (1968).

To Orient Paperbacks, Delhi, for "Bombay Burning", "An Early Cricket Writer", "The Cardus Complex" from *Between Indian Wickets* (1976).

To Orient Longman, Madras, for "Behind the Stumps and Before" from *Playing for India* (1972); "Ten Feet Tall" from *Matched Winners* (1996).

To *The Telegraph,* Kolkata, for "An Abbasid Monarch".

To *Sportsweek's World of Cricket,* Mumbai, for "Imran's Ten: The Mystery".

To *National Sports,* New Delhi, for "One Magic Afternoon".

To Ravi Dayal Publisher, New Delhi, for "Father and Sons", "Military Manoeuvres", "Fulbright Fielder" from *Autobiography of an Unknown Cricketer* (1996).

To *Seminar,* New Delhi, for "Cricket by the Book".

To *Playfair Cricket Monthly,* London, for "Cricket in the Mother-Tongue".

To *Deccan Chronicle,* Secunderabad, for "Paigah Nawabs vs Vazir Sultans".

To *Outlook,* New Delhi, for "The All-ness of India".

Note on the Editor

With this collection, Ramachandra Guha completes a hat-trick of cricket anthologies. The first, *An Indian Cricket Omnibus* (1994), which he co-edited with T. G. Vaidyanathan, has a national spread and is the first of its kind; the second and much larger *The Picador Book of Cricket* (2001) is perhaps more international than any of its predecessors anywhere in the world; the third, the present volume, is a tribute to an old friend and mentor who has set exemplary if sometimes unattainable standards to the younger generation.

ABBREVIATIONS

ACC	Associated Cement Company of India
AIR	All India Radio
Am. Lit.	American Literature
b	bowled
Bombay CA	Bombay Cricket Association
c	caught
CCBI	Cricket Control Board of India
CCI	Cricket Club of India
IMC	Indian Military College
INCA	Indian National Cricketers Association
INCLA	Indian National Comparative Literature Association
l-b-w	leg-before-wicket
MCC	Marylebone Cricket Club
NCC	National Cadet Corps
NDA	National Defence Academy
NICA	North India Cricket Association
n.o.	not out
NWFP	North West Frontier Province
RSI	Rajendra Singhji Institute
SJOC	Silver Jubilee Overseas Cricket
st	stumped
SX	St Xavier's School, Patna
WISCA	Western India States Cricket Association

Introduction

The game of cricket has always attracted the attention of men known for more general contributions to literature or scholarship. C. L. R. James, the author of the finest book ever written on the game, was also a novelist, political pamphleteer and historian. In America, that largely cricket-innocent land, James is remembered as the author of *The Black Jacobins* – a pioneering work on slave revolts – rather than as the author of *Beyond a Boundary*. Likewise, Alan Ross is known to others as a poet, travel writer and literary editor, yet we Indians know him more as the biographer of K. S. Ranjitsinhji and the editor of *A Cricketer's Companion*. His compatriot Edmund Blunden made his mark on poetry too, but in his spare time wrote *Cricket Country*, a charming evocation of the sport's place in English culture.

In this distinguished company falls the name of Sujit Mukherjee. Now Mukherjee has had at least five careers. The first is as a teacher of English literature at the universities of Patna and Poona. The second is as a literary historian, as the author of *A Passage to America,* a richly detailed account of Rabindranath Tagore's visits to that land, and more recently of *Forster and Further,* a suggestive analysis of novels written on Indian themes by foreigners. A third career is of a translator, who has rendered into English several classic stories and novels originally written in his native Bangla. A fourth is as a publisher, who in a long and distinguished career at Orient Longman promoted works by Indian historians, novelists and essayists.

These other sides to the man might not have been known to the *India Today* reviewer who, some years ago, wrote of Sujit Mukherjee that he was a sure contender for the best Indian cricket-writer slot. Mukherjee has indeed had a long-standing engagement with cricket, this running parallel to his other interests. Before he commenced teaching at Patna College he had already played in the Ranji Trophy for Bihar. He even played the game in Philadelphia, where he was a Fulbright scholar. He put away his whites thereafter, but his interest in the sport never dimmed. He read about it, he wrote about it, and on occasion he broadcast about it.

Sujit Mukherjee is that rare bird, a first-class cricketer who is also a first-rate writer. This combination of skills and experience finds full expression in his five books on the game. Here, expert knowledge is conveyed in lucid prose, the mixture further enriched by the author's understated wit and love of irony. There are other Indians who write well and love cricket but do not understand its finer points; yet others who may have played at the highest level but cannot effectively convey, in words, what they have learnt or seen. Only Sujit Mukherjee is not limited in one or other respect. Moreover, his literary training and sensibility allow him to evocatively capture the drama and character of cricket at the highest level.

The first of Mukherjee's cricket books was *The Romance of Indian Cricket* (1968), where, as he put it, he recalled his own boyhood heroes by "laying my tribute at their buckskin-shod feet". The essays in this book focus on the first, formative years of Indian cricket, on men such as Nissar and Amar Singh, Merchant and Hazare, Mankad, Modi and Amarnath.

Reviewing the book in the *Sun Herald* of Melbourne, Ray Robinson wrote that Mukherjee "handles English like a master". Robinson was himself one of the acknowledged masters of cricket writing, but while Mukherjee valued his praise he cherished as much the reactions of his old Patna colleagues. A fellow Bihari wrote of how, en route to an All-India Ophthalmological Conference, he picked up this "wonderful book" at Nagpur railway station, and finished it before his train reached Bombay. Best of all were the comments of Father Kevin N. Cleary, S. J., who had taught Sujit Mukherjee both cricket and English at St. Xavier's, Patna. His old master thought *The Romance of Indian Cricket* "very readable, excellently presented, stamped with the mark of a cricketer who knows his game". The teacher took the book to class, displayed it to his students and said, "There you are! This man did all his homework as a boy and now you see what a great man he is!"

Four years after *Romance,* appeared *Playing for India,* a wide-ranging analysis of all who had been capped for the country in test cricket (a revised edition was published in 1988). The Englishman Ronald Mason, like Mukherjee a literary historian-cum-cricket writer, commented that the book was written "with a shrewd eye for character and irony as clearly as for addition and subtraction". Third in line was *Between Indian Wickets* (1976), in which portraits of famous cricketers sit alongside reflections on crowd behaviour, literature and language. This book, noted the respected cricket writer K. N. Prabhu, completed a hat-trick for the author: it was "as good as those that have gone before..."

For some time thereafter cricket took a backseat to the publisher and translator. However, in the year 1996 two further books appeared under his name. One was *Matched Winners,* a set of paired analyses of modern greats, such as Venkatraghavan and Chandrasekhar, Bedi and Prasanna, Engineer and Kunderan. The other was *Autobiography of an Unknown Cricketer,* which recalls, with warmth and whimsy, a long life's love affair with cricket. To quote the historian Sarvepalli Gopal, the author "communicates an infectious love of cricket as a sport in stimulating and light-hearted prose of quality". Yet, as the editor and columnist M. J. Akbar noted, Mukherjee's autobiography was not about cricket alone: "it is about an education, a lifestyle, a state of mind, a moment of history and, since the years bridge the transfer of power, a shift in mood".

Books on the subject of cricket can be divided into five distinct genres. The first genre is what I call the 'romantic evocation', where the style of the writer is more manifest than the technique of the cricketer. This kind of cricket writer lays more stress on the personality of the player rather than on his distinctive achievements; he also sets character in its wider cultural context. The second genre may be termed 'the methodical reconstruction'; here, closer attention is paid to batting or bowling techniques, to the scrutiny of a career in the round, and to specific innings or spells or matches. The third genre is that of the autobiography, where cricketers great or small recall their life in the game. The first three genres, at their best, qualify as 'literature'. The other two genres do not. These are, respectively, the statistical compendium and the ghosted autobiography of the great star.

Now what is notable about the ouevre of Sujit Mukherjee is that he has worked in all genres of cricket literature. The title of *The Romance of Indian Cricket* places it firmly in the category of 'romantic evocation'; so do its contents, its loving recollections of cricketers and characters from the past. Both *Playing for India* and *Matched Winners* fall into the second category, 'methodical reconstruction': the focus being more sharply on cricketing matters, on the rise and fall of individual careers and their place in the overall history of Indian cricket. Then there is his autobiography. Of all the memoirs that have been published under the names of our cricketers this is the only one known not to have used a 'ghost'. It is the finest of Indian sporting autobiographies, and bears comparison with the best of such works from other parts of the world: with Bernard Hollowood's *Cricket on the Brain* and Arthur Mailey's *1066 And All That.*

These three genres of cricket literature are all handsomely represented in *An Indian Cricket Century*. The book brings together what, in my opinion, are Sujit Mukherjee's most enduring essays on cricket. The first section includes tributes to great Indian cricketers, from Vijay Merchant to Sunil Gavaskar; it also contains appreciations of two famous Pakistanis. The second section carries three sketches of cricket as played in somewhat unlikely locations. The final section collects meditations on a variety of themes such as cricket's relation to literature, nationalism and violence. An *Indian Cricket Century* draws on all of Mukherjee's books, as well as on uncollected periodical essays. Some chapters were first written in the 1960s, while the most recent was commissioned for the Millennium Special Issue of *Outlook* magazine.

An Indian Cricket Century is the product of a fruitful meeting of cricket and literature. We have here a treasure trove of insight, information and remembrance, conveyed in stylish prose. The book presents the distilled reflections on our national obsession of our finest cricket writer. At the present time, when there is much cynicism about the future of the sport, this book will allow the lover of cricket to happily escape from the contaminated present into a purer past.

II

I first met Sujit Mukherjee more than twenty years ago, in a large, airy hall in New Delhi's Pragati Maidan. The Third World Book Fair was on, and he was presiding over the Orient Longman exhibition. I was introduced to him by his daughter, who went to the same college as I, and knew of my passion for cricket. I had already read – and re-read – Mukherjee's books. So I listened as he spoke, spoke of the curious fact that the two best books on Indian cricket had been written by Australians—E. L. Docker's *History of Indian Cricket* and Richard Cashman's *Patrons, Players and the Crowd.* (These are indeed good books, but so were his own. His modesty would not permit him form mentioning, either, that he was instrumental in the publication of Cashman's work.)

Later that winter we watched, together, a day or two of an absorbing Ranji Trophy semi-final. Delhi were playing Karnataka, at the Ferozeshah Kotla. After the home side were dismissed for a score in the region of 300, the match really depended on how many G. R. Vishwanath would get. Delhi's hopes rested on the great Bishan Bedi getting him out early. This did not happen, but when Vishy had proceeded in silken fashion to 70 not out Bedi took the new ball, in a last, desperate throw of the dice. In Mohinder Amarnath's first over, Vishy played his trademark square-cut, for four. Mohinder now bowled an inswinger fuller in length, but the batsman pivoted, opened up and stroked the ball past mid-on. "Hazare", exulted Sujit Mukherjee, "only Hazare could play the on-drive like that."

While a student in Delhi, I cultivated Mukherjee for his range of cricketing reference and his ability to link the past with the present. As I have said, he had other work outside cricket, so when he was asked to revise and update *Playing for India* he suggested that I help him. I agreed, but shortly thereafter went away to Calcutta to do a Ph.D. In that city I became, inevitably, a Marxist, and gave up my interest in cricket. A decade later I returned to a job in Delhi. Mukherjee lived in the same town, but I was too ashamed to get in touch. He heard of this, and sent a message through a mutual friend, the writer Mukul Kesavan. "Tell him I have revised the book myself", ran the message. "He has no further reason to feel guilty. Give him a kick on the butt, and ask him to come and see me."

I called, and went over. By now I had been abandoned by the Marxists, and returned to cricket. Between 1989 and 1995 I had many lovely *adda*s with the Mukherjees in their Hauz Khas flat. They are indeed a remarkable couple, each eminent in their field (Meenakshi is perhaps India's best-known literary scholar and critic), each combining learning and achievement with a rare lack of malice and a deep interest in the doings of the young. In those *adda*s at Hauz Khas we spoke, of course, of cricket, but also of literature, history and Marxism. In the Mukherjees' home I met a range of unusual people, including Sujit's own regular whisky buddies, the Hindi novelist Rajendra Yadav and the Oriya playwright J. P. Das.

One evening, when I went over to Hauz Khas Sujit was alone. Meenakshi was out of town, and so were J. P. Das and Rajendra Yadav. We talked while Sujit poured himself a drink – I am a teetotaller – and then another. Suddenly, in the middle of his third whisky he asked me, in Hindi, "Kya tum off-spinner thé?" Yes, I answered, I did indeed bowl off-breaks. "Tab ham tumko aisé" – this said with a flick of the wrists and with a long stress on the first syllable, in the Bihari style – "hum tumko aiii-sé mid-wicket ke upar sé uttha deté"—this is how I would have lofted you for six over mid-wicket. In our now old acquaintance I have not heard him make another boastful remark. Alas, it can never be put to the test, for this lowly college off-spinner will never be able to bowl to that Ranji Troply batsman. I will not play cricket with Sujit Mukherjee, but I have been lucky enough to watch cricket with him, to talk to him about cricket, and above all to read him on cricket. So, with this book, can a new generation of cricket lovers.

Ramachandra Guha

Part I: True Greats

Double Trouble

It generally requires two persons in the blacksmith's workshop to conquer an obdurate piece of metal. One holds it with a pair of tongs and places it on the anvil; the other swings the heavy hammer against the helpless metal. Hour after hour the process goes on. For Mohammed Nisar and Lala Amar Singh, the hammer and the tongs of Indian bowling, the process lasted about seven years. During this period there was no batting in India or abroad that they encountered and did not tame. The power and velocity of one, the precision and tenacity of the other, raised them as a pair of opening bowlers to the world's highest class.

Their capacity for dual destruction was really discovered seven thousand miles from home, on the playing fields of England during India's first official cricket visit to that country in the summer of 1932. Prior to this they had achieved little, that too separately. It is strange that the fertile test cradle of inter-communal cricket seldom saw them at their best. At the end of their careers, Nisar had bowled some 325 overs in Quadrangular and Pentangular matches to claim 50 wickets; Amar Singh had bowled about sixty overs more for his bag of 39. Consequently, in 1932 they were just players of promise. Frank Tarrant coached them before they left for England and summed up saying Nisar was "a bowler of splendid physique" while Amar Singh was "the best bowler on the side".

Five months later, *Wisden* acknowledged Amar Singh's tour haul of 111 wickets at an average of 20.78 in no mean terms: "Better bowling than his in the second innings of the test match has not been seen for a long time and more than one famous old cricketer said afterwards that Amar Singh was the best bowler seen in England since the war." On this tour Nisar bowled about half the number of overs that Amar Singh did to top the averages with 71 wickets at 18.09. More than any two other cricketers of this seventeen-man side, they had succeeded in raising Indian cricket to international reckoning.

From the moment they began functioning together on the English tour (in the seventh match, against MCC at Lord's, to be exact), it was manifest that they constituted a formidable and double-edged spearhead. In the only test of that year, also at Lord's, they proceeded to confirm this impression indelibly; England won the toss and opened their innings with the dread Yorkshire pair of Holmes and Sutcliffe who had compiled their 555-run first-wicket partnership only ten days back. Within fifteen minutes of play Nisar whisked them both back to the pavilion, and when Lall Singh ran Wolley out at 19, consternation muttered in the English ranks. England rallied round to reach 259 before end of day, but not before Nisar had bagged 5 for 93 in twenty-six splendidly hostile overs. For the first time in India's test career the batting failed in the first innings and England built a match-winning lead in their second innings in spite of the dogged bowling of Amar Singh whose figures of 41/13/84/2 do not tell the real story. It was this bowling which made veterans like Walter Brearley and Arthur Gilligan wonder if they had seen a better bowler in England since the War.

Englishmen had a chance of revising their opinion when Jardine brought the first official MCC team out here in 1933–34, but Nisar claimed 5/90 in the first test at Bombay to quash all doubts about his calibre. At Calcutta they both failed, and Nisar did not appear in the final test at Madras. So Amar Singh was left to battle the elements alone, and this he did nobly with 44.4/13/86/7—to this day that test loot has not been exceeded by an Indian pace bowler. In six other matches against the visitors Amar Singh captured 38 wickets, which in addition to 14 in the tests, swelled his total bag to 52 wickets against the Englishmen alone. Playing for Nawab Moin-ud-dowlah's XI against the MCC at Secunderabad, Amar Singh took 4/33, 5/82, and hit 58 runs with the aid of five sixers and four fours to nearly cause the tourists' second defeat of the tour. Their only reverse had been at Banaras against Maharajkumar Vizianagram's XI. Prime factor of the home team's 14-run victory was Nisar's machinations on the lively matting-wicket: 20/4/60/6 (five clean-bowled), 23/8/57/3.

Two years later Ryder's team of Australians found Nisar in torrential form and lost two of the four unofficial 'tests' to share the series. Amar Singh missed the tests at Calcutta and Lahore, but Nisar crashed through time and again unassisted to record 32 wickets at 13 runs per wicket for the series. On the hard-baked Bombay wicket, except Ryder (104) and Morrisby (67), nobody faced Nisar with any confidence to yield him 6/72 in 29 overs. In the more humid air of Calcutta, Nisar swung the ball about to thoroughly ruin Australia's first innings to a meagre 99, his own spoils being 17.5/5/35/6; India, of course, were bundled out for 48 and thus lost the match. At Lahore, the Indian batsmen backed up Nisar's four wickets in either innings to wrest a 68-run victory. In the low-scoring final test at Madras, with Amar Singh back in harness, India's famed spearhead was turned on at full blast and they shared evenly the first innings wickets (Nisar 5/61, Amar Singh 5/54); in the second outing, Nisar maintained the high pressure to register 16.4/4/36/6, putting the Australians out for 107, leaving India winners by 33 runs. A week earlier, at Secunderabad, they aided and abetted each other in acts of violence (Amar Singh 4/51 and 6/36, Nisar 4/56) for another Moin-ud-dowlah's XI to inflict an innings defeat upon the tourists.

Thus they were in fine trim for the next tussle with England in England in 1936. Amar Singh was available only for the test matches, so some of their twin-engined efficacy was absent in this series. At Lord's, India were sent in to bat and dismissed in less than a day for 147. When England batted, Amar Singh took 4 wickets for 13 runs in his first nine overs to so damage the English resistance that India obtained a lead of 13 runs—Amar Singh finished with 25.1/11/35/6, Nisar with 17/5/36/3. But India fared worse in their second innings and England romped home by nine wickets. No rain fell at Manchester and batsmen dominated a match that ended in a draw. At the Oval, England scored abundantly again, declaring at 471 for 8. The total might have been greater but with the score at 409 for 4, Nisar obtained the third new ball and secured four wickets in the next six overs to finish up with 5/120. For perhaps the only time in his test career Amar Singh was collared, particularly by Walter Hammond (217), and he gave away 102 runs in 39 overs for the wickets of Fagg and Sims.

Back in India in 1937–38, Lord Tennyson brought out an unofficial team of near-test standard to meet India at her pre-War best—an excellence that has perhaps not been reached again. India won two of the five tests, a new star arose in the person of a sixteen-year-old boy from Jamnagar, Vinoo Mankad, but the most remarkable phenomenon of the season was Amar Singh's superlative form. Apart from his 36 wickets against the visitors in various matches, Amar Singh took 24 wickets (at 8.95 per wicket) in the Ranji Trophy and also scored 370 runs – the latter including a hurricane 140 in 100 minutes against Bombay, 5 sixers and 14 fours – to wrest Nawanagar into the national final.

Lord Tennyson's team had a foretaste of the shape of things to come in Amar Singh's 4/69 in the Lahore Test where (and also at Madras) Nisar did not play. The Bombay wicket proved uncooperative, but at Calcutta Nisar was the master with 5/79; Amar Singh remained in the background, with 3/65, and 4/76. At Madras Amar Singh emerged into the limelight again with paralysing spells that fetched him 5/38 in 25 overs and 6/58 in 27 overs to give India an innings victory. Subsequently India lost the needle game at Bombay by 156 runs, but that was in spite of Amar Singh—25.5/9/47/5 and 33/8/95/4. Nisar, with 2/27 and 1/71, was a co-labourer of India's cause in this match, the last time either of them played for India.

In computing their test averages, I find that though Amar Singh's 74 wickets cost him 21.83 runs a piece as compared to Nisar's 68 at 24.83, Nisar's striking-rate was higher: a wicket per 40 balls to Amar Singh's one per 63 balls. Which perhaps reveals the essential difference between them as craftsmen of the same trade.

Nisar ran to bowl like a bull at a gate. After a preliminary pawing of the ground, he charged up in eighteen thundering strides. His immense shoulders heaved like billows, his feet in outsizeboots pounded at the ground harder and harder, his right hand pistoned up and down purposefully, as he approached the bowling crease—not unlike, to change the simile, an express train at a railway crossing. There was no inhibition in his movements, no holding anything back, no husbanding of his forces. From the first ball he strained nerve and tendon and sinew to achieve his sole and single-minded purpose—that of bowling fast.

For this purpose, he strove to get his six feet and sixteen stones to attain the maximum momentum at the instant of delivery. He did not leap to a climax like many of his trade, but depended on a dragging right boot to offer him brakeage behind the crease. His left arm shot out and up straight as a mast, his small head nearly vanished behind bulging biceps, as his right hand came over in a muscle-stretching sweep. As the bowling arm attained its rapid zenith, Nisar was at the peak and also the finest point of his delivery. After that headlong rush to the wicket, he was now a mighty machine of destruction poised beautifully and perilously on the brink of crisis. The entire impetus of his exertions was trasmuted into the propulsive power of that upflung right hand. Then the fingers unloosed the ball and the left foot stamped down and Nisar careered off the pitch in a flurry of flannels and dust.

More gentlemanly than most fast bowlers in his attitude to batsmen, Nisar seldom deemed it necessary to bump the ball to scare an obstinate adversary. Such an act of supererogation would have gone against the grain of this true-believer, who depended on the honest-to-goodness straight fast ball to cause momentary myopia among batsmen. As was said of fast bowlers in days before the swerve, there was little time for the ball to do anything else. With the new ball, of course, Nisar produced the orthodox out-swerve, and the draught caused by the ball sucked a hesitating bat into its swift passage. As variation, he bowled one ball from the return crease diagonally towards the legstump and frequently succeeded in getting batsmen to tickle it to Hindlekar behind the stumps. Like all bowlers of express pace, he found the yorker an effective weapon and used it intelligently. At full throttle, even under India's energy-sapping sun, Nisar could maintain his tearaway pace for six overs at a stretch. Whenever he reclaimed his cap from the umpire, tension visibly slackened all over the field.

Compared to Nisar's gallumphing approach, Amar Singh's was a less audible effort. Physically built like a whip, Amar Singh's bowling was like the cracking of one. His right arm, bent at an angle to his body during the run-up, straightened behind his back during delivery stride, swept up and down with a whiplash movement. A loose wrist tightened only at the moment of releasing the ball, so that Amar Singh was able to introduce that last minute snap which put the fly in the flier. When he withheld that wrist-snap, he bowled a slower ball without the slightest change in action and had batsmen playing strokes before the ball had arrived. Watching his ungainly action from a distance, it was always a matter of wonder whence he derived his efficacy. He moved to the crease in a tangle of arms and legs, his chest pointed squarely at the batsman, his face grimaced with the effort of bringing his arm over, he seemed to lose balance and almost fall over as he bowled the ball. Everything looked wrong about his bowling, except the results.

Careful study from mid-on, however, explained some of the secrets of Amar Singh's success. In addition to the aforesaid wrist-motivation, there was exemplary use of bodyswing that compensated for whatever he lost in unmethodical approach. The two-shoulder delivery made the in-swerve a natural and inevitable consequence, whether the ball was new or old; with the increasing age of the ball, Amar Singh's left toe pointed more and more towards the slips, the left boot was planted more and more wide. For the out-swerve, his forward foot came down in line with the rear foot, his torso swivelled anti-clockwise as his right hand dipped across the body brushing the outside of his left shin as he finished. By exercise of bodyswing, he was able to control the amount of swerve without sacrificing speed, so that he never wasted the new ball by swinging too much or too early.

Lacking the sheer dimensions of his Muslim fellow-destroyer, Amar Singh relied for power on the rope-chord muscles of back and shoulders, rather than on the energy evoked by the product of mass and velocity. He derived little operative benefit from his utterly disorganised run-up which was more of a hurried scramble to somehow traverse the eight or ten yards to the bowling crease and get at the batsman. Once at the firing line, the improvised appearance of his approach diminished. As his left foot punched forward, his whole body leaned back in a great arch from knee to neck, like a tightly strung longbow. Then his arm came over, the arrow was shot, and his body curved forward to balance his delivery in one of the lowest follow-throughs in modern test cricket. The visual impact of Amar Singh's bowling was not pleasant to the connoisseur's eye; its material impact was not any more pleasing to batsmen's footwork. In a world where ends justify the means, the inadequacies of Amar Singh's bowling method were obliterated by the results achieved.

Often while he bowled, Amar Singh kept his shirt sleeves buttoned to the wrist. A rare sight this among pace bowlers, it somehow made his bowling arm sinister, full of malign forces not palpable to sight. In strategy, he had the old ability of Maurice Tate to gouge unsuspected speed off the grass, and he supplemented it with the more recent diabolism of Alec Bedser of being able to cut the ball both ways off the seam. At a lively medium-fast pace, he was able to command blandishments with the ball that much slower bowlers would resort to. Bowling against the wind with the new ball, he mixed his normal tide of inswingers an away-swerve as abrupt as it was late, and worked relentlessly upon the minds of batsmen, softening them up to make sudden inroad easier for the less subtle Nisar. Yet it was with the old ball that his genius came into full play. Changing over to bowl with the wind, he increased perceptibly in speed through the air to present fresh problems to the batsmen. An action-born off-break that struck back as if galvanised turned just enough to bring him the large number of clean-bowled victims. A long-fingered reverse flip off the seam sometimes brought the ball back like a genuine 'leg-cutter', a term made fashionable after his death. By an access of vitality from the wicket not hinted at by his hand, he could cause the fundamental difference between a stroke and a stroke too late. On days with a cross-wind from mid-on, his slower ball developed the barest whisper of an out-swing late in its postponed flight. It was in his wicketless spells, in fact, that Amar Singh appeared to be at his greatest, for defiance only urged him on to give of his very best. When he was among the wickets, it seemed a natural outcome of his endeavours and robbed him of his transcendental stature. Among medium-fast bowlers of modern times, only Tate and Bedser have belonged to the exalted class that Amar Singh made his own.

Nisar began his career as opening batsman of his college, made his way down the batting list, and his highest score in first-class cricket was 32 not out for Southern Punjab against Rajputana in 1939. That same season Amar Singh completed his Ranji Trophy double – 1009 runs and 105 wickets – and thus has claims to consideration on grounds other than as an indefatigable bowler. In spells of savage stroke-play that overtook him in fits and starts, Amar Singh could easily be counted among the most attacking batsmen of modern cricket.

The earliest instance of this was his death-or-glory 51 in the 1932 test at Lord's, made in 40 minutes out of a ninth-wicket partnership of 74 runs, at a time when India were virtually beaten. Against Europeans in the 1934 Quadrangular, he whetted his appetite with a whirlwind 90 before claiming 6/42. This year his 5/78 in the final was replied to by Nisar's 6/69—one of the many instances when these two cavaliers pitted their lances against each other. In Nawanagar's halcyon season in 1936–37, Amar Singh carried the team to triumph with his 28 wickets (at 16.82) and 335 runs (at, 47.85). Against Sind this year he recorded one of his several omnipotent displays—103 and 55, 6/48 and 4/35, the century in the first innings being conjured up in 76 minutes. Next year he was again in tremendous form and it was no fault of his that Hyderabad nosed Nawanagar out in the final by one wicket. Against Sind, he nearly repeated his feat of a hundred runs and ten wickets in the same match (achieved only three times in the Ranji Trophy) when he knocked up a hurricane 86 before being caught off a skier. He had his fill of Bombay bowlers, however, filling the sky with sixers and fours in his tempestuous 140 in less than two hours.

Southern Punjab reached the final for the first time in 1938–39, not a little due to Nisar who took 17 wickets at 11.94 in the tournament, just bettering Amar Singh's 17 wickets at 14.11 this year. Nisar did not appear in the final against Bengal, but he caused an astonishing reverse in the semi-final against Sind. Sind scored 339 to obtain a first-innings lead of 142 runs, before Nisar demolished them for just 23 runs in the second innings to enable Southern Punjab to win the match. Nisar bagged 6 wickets for 17 runs in 42 balls during this bowling blitzkrieg at Patiala; six Sind batsmen scored ducks and there were four extras in their total. In the Hindu–Muslim encounter this year, Nisar surpassed Amar Singh with a spell of 5/20.

The curtain-call season of 1939–40 opened as fruitfully as usual for Amar Singh with a quick 67 against Bombay. When the Nawanagar innings was falling to pieces against Baroda, Amar Singh waded into the fray with his two-handed sword of a bat to hack up 113 not out in 90 minutes. A strangely passive Amar Singh contributed little to the Pentangular final of 1939, ultimately won by Hindus after being 40 runs behind in the first innings, mainly due to a resurgent Nisar who hammered away relentlessly to take 20/3/50/6.

Thus, in late November 1939, the double destroyers appeared in the same match (though on opposite sides) for the last time. On 21 May 1940, following a brief attack of pneumonia, Amar Singh passed away at Jamnagar. In a cricket sense, Mohammed Nisar passed away the same year. Except for one or two subsequent appearances in the Ranji Trophy, Nisar has not played serious cricket again.

[1968]

Magnifico

The advertisements used to insist that Vinoo Mankad's successes on the cricket field have been partially due to his using Brylcream on his score-board-black hair. Whether he did so or not, I have seen him come back to the pavilion after a full day's batting or bowling with not a hair out of place. The pendulum fortunes of a day's cricket left not the least impression on Mankad's hair, where other men generally register the way the wind has blown on their luck. Sometimes Mankad used a cap that bunched up behind his head above his neck like a pair of baggy trousers, but even this never disrupted the polished set of his hair. This apparently permanent hair-do and the never fully buttoned shirtfront were two impressions one most readily gathered about India's most prodigious all-rounder.

Calm must have been the middle name of Mulvantrai Mankad who was born on 12 April 1917. At the batting crease, his was a statuesque calmness while he awaited the ball, gazing up the pitch out of eyes whose lower lids were underlined with *surma*. While bowling, his calm inscrutability made onlookers wonder whether Mankad knew Mankad was bowling or not. Fielding at his favourite post behind the batsman close up on the legside, his legs yawning apart like a pair of dividers, Mankad's calmness amounted almost to indifference as to the state of the game in which he seemed to be participating only casually.

Yet this calm was a carefully cultivated attitude; it was the calm that resulted of absolute control of activity. Nobody who has seen Mankad hunt eagerly up the wicket in search of slow bowling can accuse him of sloth. Nor anyone who has watched him field so accurately to his own bowling so as to dispense with orthodox mid-on and mid-off can complain of any lack of agility on Mankad's part. No, the studied imperturbability of Mankad was part of the economics of his cricket. Knowing full well how much he could contribute to the day's proceedings, he preferred to conserve his stupendous energies until their expenditure became inevitable.

Not the least remarkable instance of this was the Lord's Test of 1952. The Indian team was touring England that year without Mankad in its ranks. High among the list of acts of maladministration of the Cricket Control Board in India (CCBI) stands the blunder by which it was possible that Mankad should be present in England all summer playing in the Lancashire League while his country's team was making the rounds of country-grounds without conspicuous success. After India lost the first test at Leeds, it was freely acknowledged even by Englishmen that with Mankad there to augment the guile of Ghulam Ahmed, there would have been a different story to tell. After frantic negotiations, permission was obtained for Mankad to appear in the three remaining tests. Mankad combed his hair, packed his warbag, and arrived at Lord's two days before the second test.

Before the first hour had passed on the cloudless morning of 19 June, it seemed evident that Mankad had forgotten he was batting in a test match and not in the League. After some cautious sparring at the new ball attack of Bedser and Trueman, Mankad pounced upon legspinner Jenkins, lifting him for six over the sight-screen, sweeping him largely to long leg, then crashing him through the covers with vehemence that hinted at some personal animosity against the Worcester bowler. Veterans of the Members Pavilion shook hoary heads sadly at such brazen indiscretion on the part of an accredited test cricketer. Unconcerned, Mankad reached his fifty with two impudent late-cuts off Watkins and seemed destined for further fantasies. Only a breathtaking catch by Watkins arrested Mankad's unbelievable advance when he was 75—unbelievable because it was so patently absurd that a man could step out of League cricket to take England's test bowlers by the scruff of their necks. Before the match was three hours old, Mankad had achieved enough to justify his much publicised inclusion.

England batted through Friday (20 June) till nearly tea-time on Saturday to compile 537 in reply to India's 235 in the first innings. Mankad came on to bowl when England's total was 34 and immediately had Mantri fumbling an easy chance of stumping Simpson, who went on to make 53 out of the opening stand of 106. By pinning Hutton down to four successive maidens, Mankad raised an ironical cheer when the great Englishman scored his next run. Ultimately Mankad bowled Simpson outright and beat Hutton on several occasions without causing harm. Of course, in view of imminent rain, Hutton was taking chances he would not normally take. With his own score at 115, Hutton drove Mankad in and out of Umrigar's hands at extra-cover. The scoreboard read 264 before India broke through a second time, again via Mankad, when he had Peter May caught by Mantri. Before stumps were drawn, Mankad added Watkins to his collection of scalps in the match and was still justifying his inclusion.

Next morning Evans's buccaneering bat scattered the Indian bowling to bits to enable England to top five hundred. India began their second innings on the usual doleful note – one for 7, two for 59 – but there was no dolour in Mankad. As soon as Roly Jenkins appeard within range, Mankad smote him soaringly over square-leg for his second sixer of the match. This time the pavilion greybeards did not make premature comments, as Hutton opened out his field like a man opening his umbrella against the weather. On the widespread defences Mankad's strokes pelted and showered, almost as if this was a continuation of his first innings effort without any interruption. In just over an hour Mankad had crossed his second fifty of the match, and would surely have achieved his hundred before close had Hazare, temporarily struck scoreless, been able to lend him more of the bowling. On a magic Saturday afternoon, Mankad transformed the Lord's ground into an arena of his private aspiration and personal glory.

Over the weekend the English dictionary emptied itself of superlatives and the English language of its comparatives as critics and commentators wrung from words a description of Mankad's fabulous batting. More, surely, could not be achieved on a cricket field by man. On Monday morning Mankad raised his feat beyond the reach of language as he narrowly failed to attain a separate hundred between breakfast and lunch. An electrified crowd of thirty thousand sat and cheered themselves hoarse as this intrepid Indian did what he liked with the English bowling. When he was bowled for 184 fifteen minutes after the break, it seemed something contrary to nature had taken place.

In spite of Mankad's epic endeavours, England won comfortably by eight wickets. When statistics were compiled at the end of the test, even the onlooker's imagination was staggered. During the game Mankad had batted some six hours to score 259 runs, bowled 97 overs to take 5 wickets, had altogether been on the field for nearly seventeen out of the twenty-five hours of actual play. This match will go down inerasably in history as Mankad's Match. During it he seemed to have discovered the secret of perpetual action. It was but a microcosm of his entire cricket career. Looking back upon his twenty years of test cricket alone, we shall find little evidence of his ever having been idle.

In that prologue of the 1937–38 season he topped both batting as well as bowling averages in the five-game series against Lord Tennyson's team although he did not play in the first test. This season he played in six matches against the visitors and crossed the half-century mark in every match, his highest being 113 not out in the fourth unofficial 'test' at Madras.

The War only interrupted and did not inhibit his predilection for prodigalities. At the end of the 1946 tour of England, he established himself as the best left-arm slow bowler of the time. Along with his 134 wickets, he scored 1122 runs to become only the second visiting cricketer after Learie Constantine in 1928 to achieve this rare 'double' on an England tour. The season following in Australia, he gamely bore the brunt of India's bowling though the quick-footed Australian batsmen mauled him rather badly. He sought whatever compensation he could find by taking two test centuries off Australian bowlers. Back home he captured 17 wickets in the West Indies series but he was obviously still recovering from his Australian wounds. Against the two Commonwealth sides, he produced his best only rarely—91 at Calcutta in 1950; 4/30, 3/75 at Madras in 1951. During this period, in between the Indian winters he was playing League cricket in England, and thus gave himself no rest from the game. With the arrival of the MCC in India in late 1951 Mankad was back again to his true international form. His 34 wickets in this series stands as an Indian record in official tests. If his 38.5/15/55/8 and 30.4/9/53/4 at Madras speak abundantly of his supremacy over the visitors, no less impressive is the proof of his consistency as reflected in the second innings figures of the first test at New Delhi—76 overs, 47 maidens, 59 runs, 4 wickets.

Back in India after the 1952 summer in England, he bewildered Pakistani batsmen into quick and painless surrender at Delhi where he bagged 8/52 and 5/79. When he bowled Waqar Hasan in the third test at Bombay, he signed his name to the quickest 'double' of a thousand runs and a hundred wickets in test history. Touring West Indies next year he played two valuable innings – 96 in the first test, 66 in the fourth – and bowled persistently if without penetration. In his only appearance against the SJOC side, he saved India from possible humiliation at Bombay by batting nearly seven hours for his 154. Entrusted with the captaincy of India on our first tour of Pakistan in 1954–55, Mankad had his leanest test season as batsman, scoring only 51 runs, and took 15 wickets. As a feat of endurance, his 115 overs in the Peshawar Test (61/34/71/1, 54.1/26/64/5) may be noted. Some critics were disturbed at his being persisted with in the India side when the New Zealanders visited India in 1955–56. Mankad silenced them for ever with copious innings of 223 at Bombay and 231 at Madras to take his place besides Don Bradman and Walter Hammond as the only batsmen in the world to have scored two double centuries in a test series. His Madras effort stands supreme among individual test scores by Indian batsmen, while his 413-run first-wicket association with P. Roy wrote his name yet again in the higher altitudes of test batting.

Only in his last full test series – against Australia in 1956 – did he comprehensively fail with both bat and ball. At Bombay, I saw him being caught in the slips off the third ball of the match in trying to cut a rearing outswinger from Lindwall; in the second innings, he steered Lindwall's very first ball through the slips for four. It struck me that Mankad had at last reached the stage when the pursuit of personal convictions came uppermost: which is not the most suitable mental attitude for test cricket.

The dimensions of Mankad's achievements on the cricket field make it very difficult to visualise him in a clear perspective. At best we can draw up in the mind, visions of a pervading glory which one basked in, breathed of, and became one with. But one cannot analyse or describe objectively the superlative skill that made him one of the greatest cricketers of all time. Memory retains, however, indelible impressions of Mankad in action and by stringing together a few such vignettes I shall strive to present a picture.

To see Mankad essay his highly personal version of the late-cut against pace bowling was to experience at the pit of one's stomach the lurch of fear that the jolting of an aeroplane in air-pockets produces in unwary passengers. The stroke was so palpably incorrect, so manifestly feeble to divert the destiny of the speeding ball that one wondered why Mankad had not eschewed it long ago. With the bat-face nearly vertical to the ground, thus nakedly inviting snicks, Mankad advanced the bat conjecturally in the way of the ball, like a child's experimental finger in the spokes of a rotating bicycle-wheel. As the ball connected, he would effect a curious dab at it which appeared to increase the velocity. Mankad's aim seemed to be to rob the ball as little as possible of its original energy and, at the same time, place it beyond the reach of slip-fieldsmen whose nerves were always on edge when Mankad batted for any length of time. Considering the number of times he edged catches behind in playing this shot, any right-minded schoolboy could have advised him to avoid it. To do so would have gone against Mankad's grain, because he plainly enjoyed the hazard of this shot far more than the runs it produced.

Another favourite weapon in the Mankad armoury was the pulled drive which he perfected after the War and which lately became his principal source of revenue. Once his eye was in, he could employ this against any tossed up ball with pulverising effect. Particularly against medium-paced bowling, Mankad made it a point to remind the bowler that mere good length was not enough in big cricket. Without the slightest warning whatsoever, Mankad would choose a perfectly honest delivery and clout it to mid-wicket. By spaced advance of the left leg, he left sufficient room for the unorthodox swing of the bat, down and athwart the direction of the ball. A low right hand enabled the bat to seize the ball and fling it in the air as if with a shovel. The thick-muscled shoulders strained his shirt-seams as he struck the ball like a hammer, carting the ball to the on-side. By the minutest loosening of wrists, he kept it along the ground when necessary, but most often lofted it into the air. The better the length of the ball, the harder he seemed to hit it. Once again it was not a shot out of the copybook, which made its employment so heartbreaking to the bowler.

As he matured as a batsman, Mankad grew to respect the bouncer. His hook, short-armed and with elbows hugging the body, was not the most effective answer to the bumper on the stumps. Whenever he could, he would simply turn around and let the ball spend itself upon his capacious back. When the ball did not climb far, Mankad slugged it to square-leg with a baseball-club swing, hitting the ball from the front of his pads. Most of his strokes had his unmistakable signature on them, clearly distinguished from the correct and the orthodox. Yet at unexpected moments, he would produce a leg-glance as dainty as a lady's purse, or flourish into an off-drive as sculpturesque as that of Hazare himself. The firmly printed left foot and towering follow-through of the bat lent a rhythm that his other strokes lacked. This lack was born of the fact that he seldom played with an upright torso. From the ducked couch of his stance, he moved to play like a tiger emerging from its lair. He ran his singles with body low, stubby legs making ground rapidly with boyish haste. Prior to squaring up to face the bowler, he often plucked at his pads before settling down.

Those who had watched the seventeen-year-old Mankad pillage Lord Tennyson's bowlers in 1937–38 found little of that Mankad in the batsman who sedulously compiled the two encyclopaedic innings against New Zealand in 1955–56. In his green years, Mankad eagerly demonstrated his array of strokes from the first ball, particularly on the off-side. On the strenuous Australian tour, much of the gilt had worn off the brilliant surface of Mankad's batsmanship; the solid gold that remained glittered only occasionally. In the recent tradition of Indian batsmen, Mankad cultivated circumspection until it became second nature. Many of his notable test innings, thus, turned out to be valuable rather than pleasuresome. Lacking the virtuosity of Merchant or the grandeur of Hazare, Mankad's serious moods could be trying in the extreme. All the more so when everybody knew that he was all the time capable of treating the bowling in a cavalier manner but just did not choose to do so. Often in test matches he was not designated his lawful office as opening batsman, the post where he has accomplished all this world-beating. Being shuttled about in the lower middle order of batting possibly injured his attitude towards run-making in test matches.

It is not easy to predict now whether Mankad will be known to posterity as a great opening batsman or as a no less great slow bowler. Certainly there has been no left-arm spinner superior to him since World War II. Mankad the bowler comes more clearly to mind than the batsman, because it is so much simpler to conceive of him as such. The primary recollection will be of his tirelessness. To mention but one proof of this, he played in 31 of India's 33 matches on the 1946 tour of England without going stale or breaking down bodily. The fact that he was a slow bowler, essentially a less taxing profession, explains only part of his superhuman endurance. What it does not explain is his utter dedication to his task, for it is not mere brawn that enables a man to wheel up over after over, day after day, for nearly twenty-five years of big cricket.

The actual process of Mankad's bowling is easy to describe. After walking three steps, he glided his next three strides to the wicket so smoothly as to be practically soundless. Instead of the curving run of many slow left-handers terminating in a body-rotation, Mankad adopted a straight approach for his side-on delivery. Practically without breaking stride, he looped his left arm round, trouser-pocket height, to over his head, in an effortless movement synchronised perfectly with the final thrust of his right leg across the crease. He did not raise the right arm higher than his face, so that he had to bring his right shoulder around more than most bowlers of his type and point it towards the batsman. As the left hand released the ball, the right fell to his side with the fingers curled and the thumb extended. The whole procedure was so fluent that he did not look left-handed at all at first glance.

Watching Mankad bowl his customary thirty overs or so during a day's play could be compared to a spider weaving its web. There was the same single-minded absorption in the immediate task, the same apparent lack of immediate purpose. Almost habitually, as it were, Mankad tossed down consignments of six balls each, without really a care about what was happening at the other end. He seemed no more concerned or ambitious than a machine that has been perfected to bowl at a test match. It was only when he bent back a stump or caught the edge of an unsuspecting bat that one realised that Mankad's bowling could never be mechanical. Like the spider he bided his time warily but unobtrusively casting his net wider and wider to await the arrival of a victim. Once the batsman was caught in the strong coils of Mankad's grace, his despatch was swift and unexpected. Only by batting to Mankad could batsmen sense the hostility that hung in the air from wicket to wicket while Mankad had the ball, though seemingly his chief virtue was persistence. That aura of constancy itself was Mankad's most fatal lure. Batsmen of four continents will bear testimony to the betrayals they have suffered at the hands of this Indian juggler whom Hazlitt would have revelled in portraying.

Though he did not achieve conspicuous success in Australia (neither did Verity, nor Valentine, for that matter) he is internationally reputed to have obtained his firm place among all-time great slow bowlers, not so much through blandishments of break or spin, but through finesse of flight and trajectory. As prime essential of this form of air-attack, Mankad had to bowl a fuller flight than contemporary left-handers like Valentine and Tony Lock, Wardle and Tribe, who relied to a great extent on their ability to spin the ball extensively or deceptively. The very core of Mankad's craft lay in his concern with defeating the batsman before the ball had pitched—sometimes, it seemed even before the ball had been bowled. To rely on the vagaries of the wicket would have been a reflection on the purity of his art. The parabolic journey of a Mankad ball was full of the sort of allurement that destroys more by suggesting dangers than by any direct deadliness. Like a decoy damsel, it drew gallants into perils that do not exist if the temptation is denied.

All this emphasis on Mankad's flight is not to conceal any want in his spinning propensities. Blest with strong fingers which welded so smoothly with his wrist-action, Mankad could turn the ball perhaps even on a surface of pyrex glass. When he first went to England in 1946, to his own exasperation he found he was turning his stock leg-break far too much for real damage. He tried to counteract this by bowling over the wicket – a method not common among first class left-handers – but soon learnt to control the amount of turn according to the current character of the wicket. He never went in for new-fangled things like turning from the off to a right-handed batsman, but did bowl a manifest spinner which did not ultimately turn.

To the essentials of flight and spin Mankad added the third dimension of length. It was not worth going a long way to see Mankad bowl a long hop because he bowled it so seldom. Because of this prime virtue, he could convert himself effortlessly from an offensive bowler to a defensive one. With his usual seven-strong off-side field and the ball glued to an unpunishable patch on the off-stump, Mankad could rein back the rungetting even when he was not getting wickets to achieve those fantasies of economy that Lord Keynes or Shylock would not surpass.

Insatient critics used to accuse Mankad of playing batsmen in by bowling mechanically. How monstrous this allegation was could be best understood by batting against him. Under cover of that harmless-looking constancy, a probing intelligence was at work all the time. Batsmen found themselves being drawn out irresistibly ball by ball before they were stumped, or they were beaten back upon the wickets to be reduced leg-before at the first instant of negligence. Even when he was apparently bowling a negative width outside the off-stump, there was always the danger of his "armer" which dipped just before the bat and sometimes took on the alarming proportions of a genuine inswinger. His quicker ball was superbly concealed in the ball-bearing action of his left shoulder which enabled him to effect a surge of power without any prior hint in his arm movement. His tricks were few in number, but used with his masterly discretion, they appeared to be legion in effect. No Indian bowler to my knowledge ever gave batsmen less of rest and relaxation than Mankad, though he has bowled so much more than all of them.

Having bowled a ball, Mankad did not – like so many bowlers – think that his immediate concern was over. On the off-side particularly, Mankad fielded so adequately to his own bowling that he could dispense with an orthodox mid-off and use him as yet another extra-cover. Caught and bowled opportunities were rarely lost by Mankad because he watched the ball as closely as if he were batting himself. His favourite position in the field was at short square-leg where he has been known to move to catches with an alacrity one would not suspect from his usual deliberate movements on the field. If required in the outfield, he preferred to stand in the covers. Yet I remember him making an astonishing overhead catch on the square-leg boundary at Bombay in 1949 when he arrested a high-altitude hook from Allan Rae long after the hit had seemed destined for six of the best. But he excelled in that round-the-corner position on the legside, scooping up catches with a certainty that suggested prescience.

As batsman, bowler and fieldsman, Australia's Keith Miller, England's Trevor Bailey and Frank Worrell of the West Indies have excelled him in one performance or another. But as the day-in-and-day-out all-round cricketer, Vinoo Mankad stands unsurpassed. Or, to put it another way, he has been by turns the world's best all-rounder and finest left-arm slow bowler, before taking his place among the greatest opening batsmen of all time.

[1968]

V for Victory

While the rest of the world, for the second time in this century, was engaged in destruction on an unprecedented scale, two batsmen in Indian cricket seemed to have devoted themselves single-mindedly to the wrecking of batting records. Both bore identical first names, Vijay, the home-grown version of 'V for Victory'.

In the very first war-time season, Vijay S. Hazare set a new mark in high-altitude runmaking by scoring the first triple-century in Ranji Trophy cricket. He had only recently brought his all-round talent to Maharashtra, and on the then perfect Poona Club wicket Hazare gave initial promise of his insatiable appetites. Chasing Baroda's first innings total of 303, Hazare surpassed it off his own bat remaining undefeated with 316. It may surprise Hazare's latter-day critics to learn that this Bradmanesque effort occupied him little over a day—387 minutes to be exact. Of course, the feat would not have materialised without the red-faced assistance of Norse Nagarwala, who missed his own century by two runs but helped Hazare put on 245 runs for the ninth wicket. Even with the news of Panzer divisions sweeping across the fair fields of France, Hazare's history-making did not go unnoticed. That year his Ranji Trophy aggregate was 619 runs in five innings; next year, with a century each against Gujarat, WISCA and Madras, he totalled 565 runs in six innings. The might of Maharashtra's hitting this year can be gauged from the fact that during the same season Professor Deodhar collected 508 runs and S. W. Sohoni, then at the peak of his productive batting, aggregated 655 inclusive of three centuries and a double century.

In nearby Bombay, Vijay Madhavji Merchant was as yet marshalling his stupendous powers. His first Ranji Trophy hundred had occurred in 1935 when in successive matches of his first full season for Bombay, he scored 94 vs Maharashtra, 101 vs WISCA, and 120 vs NICA in the final. An automatic choice for the 1936 India team to England, Merchant collected 1745 runs in 40 innings at an average of 51.32 to be acknowledged as the soundest of the visiting batsmen. Thereafter, until 1940, he did little that was sensational and many must have wondered if Merchant had passed his prime, like a river placidly on its way to the ocean.

In answer, just turned thirty during the 1941–42 season, Merchant burst his banks and fairly overflowed. He signalled his large designs with an unbeaten 170 against Nawanagar. Then, between 19 and 23 December, he scored 243 not out against Muslims, 221 against Parsis, and 153 not out against Sind. In eight innings of the two concurrent tournaments Merchant compiled 932 runs and put every other Indian batsman of the present and the past in the shade. All these runs were made with that unrelaxing concentration and technique that had come to be associated with his name even before this. His extended effort against Muslims, incidentally, bettered the previous highest individual score in the Pentangular—Lala Amarnath's 241 against the Rest in 1937.

It was in the 1943–44 season that the giants really got to grips, and the limitless possibilities of careful batting on good wickets made fearfully evident. At 3.30 p.m. on 1 December, Hazare nudged a ball from Saeed Ahmed to leg to beat Merchant's two-year-old record. When he was caught and bowled for 248, he had helped the Rest attain a total that gave them the necessary first innings lead over Muslims and earn the right to meet Hindus in the final. Three days later, at 4 p.m., Merchant square-cut Bhalerao for two runs to complete an innings of 250, at which point he declared the Hindus' innings closed at 581 for 5. Through nearly seven hours of batting, Merchant received some support from young Hemu Adhikari who scored 186 and made their third-wicket partnership worth 345 runs in as many minutes. The Rest followed on after having been spun out for 133 by C. S. Nayudu and Sarwate. After four second-innings wickets had fallen for 20 runs, Hazare entered and was almost immediately dropped by Sohoni off Banerjee. By virtue of this lapse was born perhaps the most remarkable innings to be played in India in first-class cricket.

At the end of the third day of the game, 26 December, the Rest had scored 189 for 5 of which Hazare's share was 125 not out. In spite of the helplessness of the situation, Hazare seemed to set himself tasks and achieved his first hundred in three hours. Batting with him was his younger brother, Vikram, who made exactly ten runs in two hours and continued in the same vein when the match was resumed next morning. Twenty-five thousand people watched Hazare reach his second hundred in 317 minutes, and shook the stadium with their applause when Hazare surpassed Merchant's three-day-old record in the afternoon. By flawless judgment, Hazare kept his partners away from the varied Hindus' bowling (Banerjee, Sohoni, C. S., Sarwate and Mankad) and reached the third hundred for the second time in his career. At 5 p.m., the unbelievable happened: Hazare was out, caught and bowled by C. S. Nayudu. He had batted six and a half hours for his 309 while his ten team-mates scored 59 and the extras contributed 19 runs to the Rest total of 387. For supreme courage and determination, apart from the necessary skill, this innings of Hazare in the 1943 Pentangular final can never fade from memory.

A week later the argument was resumed during the Bombay–Baroda match, though on a much lower tempo. Merchant's 141 for Bombay provoked a retort of merely 101 from Hazare, and there the matter seemed to rest. But on the last day of 1943, in Bombay's match against Maharashtra, Merchant arrived Galahad-like at 359 not out on a mission that had begun nine hours back on the previous morning. To the end of his career Hazare never parried that final thrust. At the time, Merchant was taking no risks. He began the 1944–45 season with 221 not out against Parsis. Hazare took a century in either innings off the Maharashtra bowlers. Merchant celebrated yet another New Year with 217 against WISCA. Both failed, curiously enough, when Bombay met Baroda in the zonal final. But Merchant embellished the national final versus Holkar with an innings of 278 that kept him at the wicket for eight hours under the March sun. Thereby he completed 3000 runs in Ranji Trophy cricket, his season's accumulation in the tournament being 607 runs in seven innings. At the other crease, however, a new destroyer had arrived: Rusi Modi battered all opposition to wrest the richest plunder ever, a thousand run aggregate for the Ranji Trophy season, and thus overshadow both Merchant and Hazare for the time being.

Comparison of only figures cannot tell the quality of batsmanship of India's two greatest rungetters. To see Merchant playing forward was an experience not easily forgotten. Like Uday Shankar in another artistic medium, Merchant too could make the onlooker wonder at sheer anatomical poise and harmony. From start to finish, the whole stroke was one complete fluid motion, like water pouring down a given channel, effortless and entire. A dapper man of average height, Merchant appeared extremely lightfooted in all his movements at the crease. In forward strokes, his foot would advance like a sensitive antenna, seeking secrets of the course of the ball. His bat, seldom raised higher than waist-level in the backlift, would descend in the plane parallel to his body, down beside his left pad and out before it, meeting the ball with a sure, heartening sound. In following through, his elbows were stretched and classically clear of his body, bearing the bat towards the end of a perfect pendulum. Unselfconsciously elegant, Merchant would pause the barest moment at the end of his stroke before returning to guard, the very picture of unstriving perfection.

Though he batted lower down for Bombay or for Hindus, in the eyes of the nation Merchant will always figure as an opening batsman. Against the new ball, no one in India played the ball later. Contrary to the traditional practice of opening batsmen, Merchant preferred to judge the quality of each delivery while moving out on the front foot. This predilection for forward play was possibly the outcome of his being brought up, in the cricket sense, on the shirtfront wickets of Bombay where even the underpitched ball seldom climbs higher than the bat's shoulders. Yet so elastic was his technique that on English wickets, where the normal run of forward players are soon in trouble, the unperturbed Merchant scored 1745 runs in 1936 and 2385 runs (average 74.53) in 1946. Particularly on the latter tour, during a fairly wet summer, Merchant's model consistency secured him a place among great batsmen of all time. The confident thrust of the front foot gave to his play a symmetry that has been sadly wanting in modern masters.

For all his favour of the front foot, Merchant's repertoire of strokes did not exclude the time-honoured gestures of opening batsmen—the cut and the glance. After Professor Deodhar, nobody in India has equalled the certainty and swiftness of Merchant's late-cutting. He could leave the stroke till so late that sometimes he seemed to snatch the ball out of the wicketkeeper's clutches. His right foot slid across, his body arched over, as his bat stroked the ball down and through the slips, wristwork imparting a speed to the ball that was not perceptible till one watched it racing down to third man. So consummately well did he play this shot that I do not recall his ever being caught behind in attempting a late-cut. His glances to leg were so delicate that sometimes they were practically soundless. When there was a choice, he preferred to divert the ball from the front of his advanced left pad. Again wristwork controlled the final direction of the ball and ensured that it stayed down. At the moment of impact, a plumb-line through his head would drop upon the toes of his left boot. The great Alec Bedser may have found an answer to the post-war Bradman in his devouring array of short-leg fieldsmen, but Merchant experienced little difficulty in guiding Bedser's intricate in-swing through the cordon. In seven innings against Bedser in 1946, Merchant was dismissed only once by the Surrey bowler while his scores included 53, 78, 128.

During his maiden test series in 1932–33, Merchant batted in the middle order against a variety of bowlers (Clarke, Nichols, Marriott, Townsend, Verity) with a serene competence that bespoke many successful hours in the sun. He developed that enviable quality of being able to bat endlessly without ever boring the bystander. The formal outlines of his batting had their frills, all unmistakably his own. When the flighted ball called for advance greater than his customary forward movement, Merchant went yards down the wicket on deft half steps to drive or smother. He pulled the short ball with studied concern for the bowler's feelings, as it were. He drove straight meticulously if not powerfully, and his square-cut rang out again and again like a bugle on the parade ground. Even his abstention from a stroke was worth watching, the bat checked and drawn clear of the passage of the ball and raised overhead as his body rose on tip-toe.

Against quicker bowling he was at his most fluent and felicitous best. Essentially a genteel striker of the ball, pace bowling put at his masterly disposal that extraneous energy inherent in the situation with which to fashion those cuts and glides. He could dispose of the bouncing ball with a hook as swift as it was certain, but he avoided the shot unless pressed. It was in his nature to exert little and achieve much, and this economy of effort enabled him to bat through a full day and more without visible signs of strain. Merchant in possession at the Brabourne Stadium was like the British rule in India—'just', decisive, and interminable. It is a pity he never went to Australia where he would obviously have thrived. Also, he could have put his skill to the final test by ordeal of fire—the new-ball diabolisms of Lindwall and Miller. It was left to Vijay Hazare (and also Mankad, occasionally) to speak there on behalf of Indian batsmanship.

Hazare, of course, has always revelled in out-Merchanting Merchant. Throughout the 1946 tour of England, Merchant consistently outscored Hazare, but a week after Merchant obtained an unbeaten 242 against Lancashire, Hazare scrupulously compiled 244 not out against Yorkshire, which remains even now the highest score made by an Indian batsman outside India. Thereafter, due to Merchant's abstentions, Hazare had to carve out his records in a sort of vacuum. I wonder if he enjoyed himself as much.

Hazare's technique of batting seemed to depend solely upon two vastly simple and comprehensive judgments—this ball could be hit, that ball could not be. On these pillars the great edifices of Hazare's innings have securely rested. There was no middle way with Hazare as there was to the Buddha. All great batsmen have their prods and pushes, intermediary gestures between the large flourishes, to keep the scorers alert and the scoreboard moving. Not so with Hazare. He eschewed the potboilers not out of any philosophic scorn but because they did not fit into his simple scheme of things. The ball that could be hit he endeavoured to despatch for the maximum; the ball that could not be hit he dropped dead or dying at his feet. Add to this the number of balls he left alone, and the mystery, is clear why Hazare took so long, over the making of his runs.

A common criticism against Hazare has been that he was a slow rungetter, that he was – an estimate that bears the authority of Bradman himself – a matchsaving batsman rather than a matchwinning one. While admitting the truth of this, I would call it a description of Hazare and not a condemnation of him. Ever since he took up the lost Pentangular cause of the Rest upon his insatiable bat, Hazare never had a chance to change his role; at the height of his test career, when his superiors in style fell by the wayside while he had to stand steadfast, there was no other role for him to play. It was no fatal flaw of character but the sheer force of circumstance that made him the dour, unspectacular batsman of many large and memorable innings. As scorer of 6312 Ranji Trophy runs (highest aggregate, average 69.36) and 12 test hundreds (largest number for India), I do not think Hazare has ever regretted having batted the way he felt fit.

Standing at the crease to receive the bowling, Hazare was a picture of discomfort, even of reluctance. He dug his chin into his chest, his shoulders sloped despondently, his knees were crooked and crowded each other. His arms pressed into his body, plainly denying him freedom of movement. Under the shade of his hat or cap – he never batted bare-headed – his face wore a distinctly resigned expression, like that of a man who has tried but failed to evade some onerous duty. I do not think there has been another batsman of his calibre in the world who looked more unimpressive at first sight.

The impression was likely to continue even for the first hour of an innings by Hazare, during which he fended at the bowling from a suspicious, antiseptic distance. He scarcely raised his bat as with small shuffles he moved into position to let the ball spend itself against the bat. A lot of bat-handle could be seen between his hands as he played defensively back. When a more ample flight drew him out, he stretched the utmost extent of his left foot far enough to play the ball well behind the out-thrust boot, his body so low that he could well stop the ball on his chest if he missed with the bat. This lunge of negation practically spread him flat on the wicket and he had to thrust himself upright again with the aid of his bat, like a tent being erected. It did not seem possible that with such clumsy footwork he would ever be able to hit the ball, much less hit it hard.

Then, almost before you realised it, he would hit a couple of superlative off-drives, whip a square-cut past bewildered fieldsmen, and pull a ball voraciously to mid-wicket. You sat up and began to take notice. For the next half hour, Hazare would keep playing the ball back to the bowler, till you were disgusted with him again.

This curious tempo of Hazare's batting baffled and annoyed and angered many people who had not the patience or privilege of watching Hazare bat for a long time. Unlike batsmen who command more graces, Hazare could not convey to the spectator the essentials of his craft rightaway. Only by watching him carefully and for a length of time was it apparent that Hazare was a perfectionist in his own way, that he chose to know rather than to guess. Like a piece of precise long-range artillery, he moved inch by inch into position before firing the next accurate salvo. Consequently, there was never any beginning or end to an innings by Hazare. Whether his score was two or twenty or two hundred, he was assessing the bowling with the same exacting concern that characterised his every moment at the crease. It was thus that he bored and stifled the common onlooker while saving matches and winning some during the post-war period of India's test-cricket infancy.

Unlike Merchant, Hazare really let himself go when he decided to hit. His bat seemed fairly to explode when he struck the ball square of the wicket on either side. One had only to watch the helplessness of off-side fielders to realise the fierce power of his cover-hitting. In square-cutting, Hazare smashed the ball into the ground with such force that the ball often bounded over the heads of close fielders on its way to the boundary. Often Hazare gave himself more leeway for this shot by moving his right foot back outside the leg-stump, particularly against legbreak bowlers. When the ball did not rise enough from the ground to warrant the orthodox cut, Hazare leaned back on a bent right knee to slash the ball through the covers. Although he hit this ball off-balance, he lost nothing in power, denoting great strength of wrist and forearm.

In fact, Hazare's number of cross-batted shots equalled his more conservative methods, and no orthodox field could be set for him once his eye was in. From that Simhagarh of his clamped back foot, he could force the ball on either side of the wicket. The same legbreak, which he normally cut behind point, he could, hitting totally against the spin and text-books, send rocketing past the left hand of mid-wicket. He played the pull-shot with great relish, whirling round with the force of his own stroke to turn full circle before going for the run. His hook, stabbed down from no matter what height the ball had climbed, dropped the ball on the ground seldom more than ten yards from him, so that fast bowlers soon tired of bumping the ball at him.

For all the ruthless efficiency of his square-of-the-wicket strokes, one had not seen the complete Hazare portrait unless one had seen him drive. In an innings of 175 not out against the First Commonwealth side at Calcutta, I saw him drive nineteen boundaries in a great arc between mid-off and mid-on, and the full Hazare regalia of batsmanship was spread before my eyes. Habitually a heavy-footed man, Hazare brought his left foot out with the exaggerated but exact care of an elephant walking on treacherous soil, as he fastened upon the driveable ball. Down went his head and up went the bat behind him, as he seemed to smell the position of the ball, his whole bodyweight shifting almost visibly from foot to foot, while his bat descended in a pulverising curve. As the ball sped from his bat in a blur of red, one noticed that the right hand did not dominate this shot as it did the others. A copy-book left elbow kept the bat in the classical groove and his right toe was almost moved but not quite from its moorings behind the crease. He never raised the ball in driving, and thus had to place the hit along precise bisections between possible fieldsmen. On-driving with complete control, he added a last-minute rotation of the wrists to guide the ball towards the normally untenanted wide mid-on region. The easy rhythm of his drive concealed its power from the onlooker, but the ball went scorching through the grass to cause a sudden and delighted scramble among spectators squatting on the boundary. In essaying that stroke of modern disuse, the cover-drive, he got his left leg so well across that the ball was nearly hid from the umpire's view as the bat connected. The pile-driver punch of the hit brought him low, his right knee brushing the ground as his bat flared into the sky over his left shoulder. Should ever a sculpture be made of Hazare, it should be in this the most glorious of his batting postures, in playing the cover-drive.

When his innings was over, Merchant returned to the field to take up safe posts at mid-on or third man where he chased the ball diligently and accepted the rare catches that came his way. Hazare's work was only half done after he had unstrapped his pads. Besides scoring the largest number of runs in the Ranji Trophy, Hazare's 291 wickets in the tournament are second only to C. S. Nayudu's bag of 295. Medium-paced with an exaggerated square-armed delivery, Hazare was required to open India's bowling in twelve tests at home and abroad. With that curious arm-action he could not but have bowled outswingers, which was excellent foil to the inward bent of Amarnath and Phadkar who opened with him. Hazare's real value, however, lay with the old ball which he brought back from the off at an indomitable length; he also bowled a genuine spun legbreak at that same pace, but could not control it enough to use it regularly. Before cares of captaincy removed him to pensive stations near the bowler, he used to hold slip catches with that unemotional ease that pervaded his every action on the cricket field.

After all has been said and done about the record-wrecking propensities of the two Vijays of Indian cricket, it remains to note how surprisingly seldom they have batted together for India. In the sixteen tests they were both in the team, Merchant was dismissed before Hazare entered in twenty innings; three times either one or the other did not bat; once Hazare returned without scoring in the presence of Merchant. This leaves only five occasions in fourteen years on which they were associated in the middle. Which is all the more extraordinary when we recall that Hazare's customary lease began only two wickets down after Merchant. One can only marvel at the great good fortune of India's international opponents that they have nearly never been caught between these two rungetting grindstones.

Besides, there were a number of voluntary withdrawals on Merchant's part, which left Hazare alone to undertake statistical upsets. By scoring a century in each innings at Adelaide in 1948, Hazare became the only Indian to have done so in a test match and only the fourth batsman in the world to achieve this in a test against Australia. Against the West Indies in India the following season, he was the first Indian batsman to hit two centuries in an official test series. At his bombastic best in 1949–50, Hazare aggregated 677 runs (average 96.42) in the First Commonwealth series besides scoring 609 runs (average 120.18) in the Ranji Trophy including a pair of hundreds in the final against Holkar. This astronomical magnitude has never been approached by an Indian batsman. Against the Second Commonwealth side, Hazare reeled off a century in each of the first three tests, scored 75 and 80 in the fourth, to attain another sumptuous aggregate of 634 runs. He began the next home series against the MCC in the grand manner with a large hundred in each of the first two tests before a bouncer from Ridgway caromed off his bat onto the side of his face at Bombay. I trace Hazare's downward career in test cricket from that wayward ball: though he continued to bat impressively on occasion in three more test series thereafter, he ceased to stagger the imagination and befuddle the statistician.

Hazare thus possesses many of the Indian batting records that Merchant could not protect as his own. On the global level, Hazare's 577-run stand with Gul Mohammed for Baroda against Holkar in 1946 continues to challenge fourth-wicket batsmen of all cricketing lands.

To bring our story to a close, the earliest Merchant–Hazare association was at the Oval in 1946 when Merchant was well on the way to his second test hundred in England; Hazare stayed about half an hour to score 11 while 20 runs were added. Four years later they were party to a second-innings recovery at Bombay against Livingstone's side, putting on 91 staid runs for the fourth wicket in two hours. Against Ames's team the following season, Merchant played in all the tests to total 407 runs; at Madras and at Kanpur they had a third-wicket partnership of 49 and 30. Even mere laws of causality should have ordained more opulent joint service from them for their country. Only on the last occasion they played together did the much-awaited phenomenon materialise.

This was in the opening match of the 1951–52 series against England at New Delhi. England were retired on the first day for 203 and India began her reply on the second morning by losing one wicket by lunch for 56 runs. Soon after lunch, Umrigar attempted a run that wasn't there, and India was 64 for 2. Thus when Hazare came in, walking his familiar unhurried head-down walk to the wicket, Merchant had already been in occupation for nearly three hours with thirty runs to his personal account.

The next wicket did not fall until after lunch on the third day and at long last a Merchant–Hazare test-partnership had accrued to the tune of 211 runs. But how they betrayed expectation! One would anticipate that once having set their sights, India's two greatest bowler-killers would decimate this mediocre bowling beyond recognition. On the cushion-paced wicket, Statham's fangs were drawn before the ball was old, while Tattersall was able to turn only in millimetres. While the visiting fieldsmen turned various shades of scarlet under the afternoon sun, these two plodded home like two of Grey's farmers, having increased the total to a weary 186 by draw of stumps on the second day. Slowed down footwork kept Merchant from taking complete charge of things as he would have even five years back; the elegance was still there, but the tensile strength had departed. As for Hazare, perhaps more preoccupied with Merchant's presence than with the bowling, he indulged in slow self-petrification. Like a man huddling against the cold, Hazare shrank from making runs until the observer's eyesight cramped, and was barely forty when play closed. Merchant duly arrived at his hundred, as if by prolonged previous appointment, in four-and-three-quarter hours. Off bowling that had succeeded in barely getting one wicket the whole day, the two masters scored 33 runs in the ninety minutes, after tea; in the last 25 minutes, literally one run was scored. Several spectators had to be woken up when the game ended for the day and many others swore they would not return when play was resumed.

Next morning the dreariness did not depart. By lunch another 88 runs were made more or less incidentally. The cricket hereabouts was like an invincible fortress being besieged by ineffective but obstinate invaders. Hazare's fifty came up, then 200 of the innings. In a spurt of delicate cutting off pace bowlers, Merchant overhauled India's previous highest individual test score—Hazare's 145 against Australia. In the third over after lunch Merchant played Statham on to his wicket and passed from the scene, for good. In raising the individual innings record to 154, Merchant had batted seven-and-a-half hours and hit twenty fours.

Hazare endured. True to tradition, three hours later he overhauled Merchant's recent record and was still there at day's end, unbeaten with 164. He had been at the wicket eight-and-a-half hours and barely remembered to hit fifteen fours.

Merchant has not played for India again; Hazare put away his test bat two years later after leading two tours to England and to the West Indies without ruining more records. His last gesture of defiance was at Leeds in 1952. India lost three wickets for 42 in the first innings before Hazare (89) and Manjrekar (133) put on a partnership of 222 runs. As if to test him further, India lost three wickets without a run on the board when Hazare came to bat in the second innings; intrepidly as ever, he scored 56 out of a 105-run fifth-wicket stand with Phadkar.

[1968]

Behind the Stumps and Before

Indians have achieved world-class in every aspect of cricket except in wicketkeeping. Why this should be so is a matter which defies explanation much more than that other mystery of Indian cricket—our inability to produce fast bowlers. Wicketkeeping ought to be an occupation which matches the Indian temperament. It is a slow and patient business, a waiting and watching game, which stretches time out of shape and demands attention to the trivial and respect to the ordinary. A nation bred on ten thousand verses of the Mahabharata, one lakh reiterations of the gayatri mantra, and countless commentaries on the Bhagavad Gita should take to wicketkeeping as easily as bird to air. Alternately, a people who have for ages produced such marvels of ivorycarving and miniature painting and silver filigree work should be able to transfer their mastery of the minute to the task of keeping wickets. Somehow this has not happened and, in spite of the raptures of Sir Neville Cardus over Farokh Engineer, let us admit that we have never had a wicketkeeper worthy of being ranked with the finest of our batsmen and bowlers and fieldsmen.

In saying this I am not forgetting the numerous occasions on which a breathtaking catch or a split-second stumping has been achieved by Kirmani and his predecessors. But like the single swallow which does not make a summer, a catch here or a stumping there does not make a noteworthy wicketkeeper. The Evanses and the Don Tallons of the world are remembered because of their exalted standards of sustained performance season after season, series after series. Even the very best make mistakes, but excellence in wicketkeeping consists of reducing mistakes to a human minimum. Thereby wicketkeepers gain the confidence of bowlers and captains and influence the course of cricket matches.

One reason for this relative underdevelopment of the art and craft of wicketkeeping in India is that it did not achieve full cabinet-rank, as it were, until fairly recently in our test cricket. Appointments were made so casually that as many as six persons officiated in four years at our first eleven international appearances (7 official and 4 unofficial). Perhaps the wicketkeeper was the last to be chosen for the team in those days, and the first to be dropped when the next team was selected. Can many cricket-followers today recognise these names – Abdul Aziz, S. V. T. Chari, M. O. Srinivasan, T. V. Parthasarathi, K. Srinivasan – as belonging to wicketkeepers who have all a ppeared in a 'test' for India? The turn-over of wicketkeepers has been rather large in our test-cricketer production because our selectors have taken a long time to realise that a wicketkeeper occupies a focal position in the field. Changing this focus too frequently invariably results in loss of sight of objectives.

Then, of course, the incidence of wrongly motivated – when not merely bad – selection has been remarkably high where national wicketkeepers are concerned, especially for tours abroad. Neither D. D. Hindlekar nor R. B. Nimbalkar appeared in any of the three 'tests' against the Australian Services in 1945–46, yet it was they who went with our 1946 team to England. An even more startling choice was that of J. K. Irani as first keeper for our maiden tour of Australia in 1947–48. How M. K. Mantri and P. Sen came to be preferred over younger and no less competent specialists for the 1952 tour of England is anybody's guess. In 1953, E. S. Maka was exhumed from an undistinguished past to accompany the Indian team on its first tour of the West Indies. Among more recent cases of manipulation was that of sending R. Jeejeebhoy abroad when his export quality could hardly be taken for granted.

Finally, wicketkeeping for India has been hindered as a specialisation because we have somehow always expected our 'keepers to pull their weight as batsmen as well. Most state sides give unashamed preference to the wicketkeeper/batsman because success in the Ranji Trophy generally means out-batting the opposition. In such circumstances, the extra batsman in the shape of a wicketkeeper is a bonus few selectors are able to ignore. Even the national committee has fallen to this temptation time and again. Although Hindlekar and Meheromji were members of the

1936 touring team, Dilawar Hussain was often called in to deputise—even to the extent of playing the third test. R. B. Nimbalkar's inclusion for the 1946 team to England was surely based on expectations of what he would do in front of the stumps rather than behind them. A similar expectation sent Mantri to England in 1952 and to Pakistan in 1954–55. The dilemma posed by Kunderan and Engineer was never because they rivalled each other with the big gloves but because they were far more likely to do something unexpected with the bat. If Kunderan had been advised by authority to cultivate his batting or Engineer been warned to concentrate on wicketkeeping, the Indian team would have derived greater value from these two vivacious cricketers.

The low productivity of wicketkeeping in India is betrayed even by Ranji Trophy figures, which generally register some inflation. No wicketkeeper has yet taken ten wickets in a match. Mantri came close to it on his debut for Maharashtra in 1941 when he caught four and stumped five NICA batsmen. P. G. Joshi (Maharashtra vs Gujarat in 1959) and K. S. Inderjit (Saurashtra vs Maharashtra in 1965) have equalled this figure in 50 years of the tournament. As for total number of wickets during a Ranji Trophy season, twenty victims were not exceeded until 1945–46 when R. B. Nimbalkar stumped ten and caught eleven for Baroda (mostly off C. S. Nayudu) and thereby underlined his claim for a berth to England. This record has steadily risen with the introduction of the league-cum-knock-out format, and now stands at 31—achieved by Bombay's C. S. Pandit in 1983–84. Consequently, the feat of participating in a hundred Ranji Trophy dismissals – which had seemed quite unlikely in the old days – has now been achieved by 16 wicketkeepers.

Clearly, such relatively opulent acquisition was possible for the wicketkeepers named above because many of them belonged to teams which reached the Ranji Trophy final in these years. That is, they played in the maximum number of Ranji Trophy matches possible in a season. This reveals another aspect of Indian wicketkeeping in higher echelons of the profession. Unless one is lucky enough to be keeping wickets for one of the major sides, one has no chance of making the national team. Unlike the batsman or the bowler who can get into the headlines by virtue of single performances, the wicketkeeper has to be seen in match after match before he can hope to make an impression.

In a country where competitive domestic cricket is so scattered and communications still so ragged, the national selectors simply cannot watch all the promising candidates in action all the time. Understandably, they fall back on short-cuts. While the Ranji Trophy tournament was in its formative years, the Pentangular matches used to provide the vital data. The essential choice was then confined to two or three representatives of respective communities—the Hindus' Hindlekar, the Muslims' Dilawar Hussain, the Parsis' Meheromji.[1] In an early gesture of the secular state-to-be, all three played by turns for India in 1936. Thereafter, the penultimate rounds of the Ranji Trophy have sorted out the grain from the chaff. Between 1946 and 1961, Rajendranath's was the only instance of a wicketkeeper being granted national honour without his belonging to one of the 'big eight' (the usual quarter-finalists) state teams. Since 1961, additional guidance is derived from the Duleep Trophy tournament. As with the Pentangular, the Duleep Trophy teams perform a kind of preliminary selection (or rejection), narrowing the field down to four or five contenders who have been chosen to represent their respective zones. For the home stretch before the team is announced, the contenders have often to depend upon the way patronage has been shared and disseminated by the selectors. At this point, wicketkeeping skill and potentiality are set aside while other considerations emerge—or so it has seemed in several cases.

Twenty-five men have so far (mid-1986) been nominated to keep India's wickets and twenty have actually done so in test matches.[2] Of these twenty – by an older reckoning – four were Parsis, three Muslims and the remaining thirteen Hindus. In Meheromji and Engineer, the Parsi community has supplied two of the most handsome cricketers ever to don India blazers. Among the Hindu candidates, Maharashtrians predominate with eight.[3] Sociologists may some day determine what the co-

---

1 Neither the Europeans nor the Rest ever produced a wicketkeeper for India.

2 B. E. Kapadia on the 1932 tour of England, R. B. Nimbalkar on the 1946 tour of England, R. Jeejeebhoy on the 1971 tour of West Indies, S. Khanna on the 1979 tour of England and C. S. Pandit on the 1986 tour of England.

3 Nine counting the non-combatant Nimbalkar.

relation can be. The others are one each from Mysore and Hyderabad, one Sindhi, one Bengali, one Saurashtrian, two Punjabis and five South Indians—three from Karnataka and one each from Andhra and Tamil Nadu. If we take the Vindhyas as the dividing line, more wicketkeeping talent lies to the south of it than to the north. More specifically, the old Bombay Presidency region has produced thirteen of our twenty test wicketkeepers—which is about the proportion that would be of test cricketers in general.

The earliest of these western India monopolists was D. D. Hindlekar whose test career began in June 1936 and closed in August 1946. He was not our first wicketkeeper but he was the first regular functionary and necessary component of an India XI. Before him, probationers came and went. Chronologically J. G. Navle was the first—both against Arthur Gilligan's MCC team at Bombay in 1926 and against England at Lord's in 1932, it was Navle who kept wickets as well as opened the batting. In the latter game, he inscribed his name in the opponents' score-card when he caught by D. R. Jardine .off C. K. Nayudu. Navle also presided when India played her first official test at home – against England at Bombay in December 1933 – but was displaced by Dilawar Hussain, five years younger, for the other two tests of the series. Dilawar immediately drew attention upon himself at Calcutta by getting hit on the head by a bumper from Nichols. He returned later to the crease to top score for his side in both innings with dour knocks of 59 and 57. England had only seven runs to make for a win, but lost two wickets in doing so—the second to Dilawar who stumped B. H. Valentine with a flourish off Naoomal, thus recording the first such dismissal by an Indian wicketkeeper.

Two wicketkeeping feats during 1934–35 – D. D. Hindlekar (Bombay) pouching six catches against WISCA, K. R. Meheromji (WISCA) catching five and stumping one against Sind – brought these two 'keepers to the forefront during the following season. Hindlekar entered the Hindus team but could not make the All-India eleven in any of the four 'tests' against Ryder's team for which a different wicketkeeper was used for each occasion. Meheromji appeared at the Lahore 'Test' and impressed just enough to be included among the sixteen who were selected to tour England in 1936.

Hindlekar was the other alternative. A third candidate, Dilawar Hussain, had proceeded separately to England and made himself available when the tour-programme began. The result of such surplus was that none of the three really settled down to his job. That they appeared in a test each was a fair index of the difficulty of choosing among them, none giving adequate evidence of form. Hindlekar's tour record (16 matches: 26 c, 13 st) was better than Meheromji's (7 matches: 14 c, 1 st) or Dilawar Hussain's (8 matches: 13 c, 4 st) but Dilawar stole the show in the third test. He did not concede a single bye during England's long innings of 471 for 8 declared, and took three good catches. He also impeded English bowlers long enough to score 35 and 54—to fulfil the expectation of selectors who obviously valued his obstacular batting more than his rather haphazard wicket-keeping. But it was really Hindlekar who gave clearest evidence of an international wicketkeeper in the making. Calm and unhurried – except when opportunity winked – consistent and unpretentious, Hindlekar had won sufficient confidence by 1937 to be retained for an entire series of five 'tests' against Tennyson's team and would most certainly have been nominated for a similar spell had the 1939–40 series against England materialised.

The unofficial series in 1945 against the Australian Services team was used to try out candidates aspiring for a place on the 1946 tour of England. While the main batsmen and bowlers practically selected themselves – and most of them were already established before 1939 – the field was most open to wicket-keepers.[4] None of the three who appeared in the 'tests' – M. O. Srinivasan at Bombay, T. V. Parthasarathi at Calcutta, E. S. Maka at Madras; by coincidence they all batted no. 11 – gave much proof of class, manifest or potential. A fourth candidate, 23-year-old Imtiaz Ahmed of Lahore, was unjustifiably overlooked. Playing for North Zone in the visitors' first match of the tour, Imtiaz (138 not out) helped Abdul Hafeez (173) rescue the home team after six wickets had fallen for 106; their seventh-wicket partnership realised 268 runs in 266 minutes. In this game Imtiaz kept wickets competently enough for Lindsay Hassett to

[4] As many as three were in the Indian Universities XI which played the Australians at Poona—Imtiaz, Mantri and Rajendranath. The last named actually kept wickets.

mark him out – in a post-tour analysis – as one of India's young hopefuls.[5] The pressures of Indian history would soon carry Imtiaz – along with Abdul Hafeez Kardar and Fazal Mahmood – across the border, where all three played with such distinction for Pakistan. But the overlooking of Imtiaz was typical of flabby selection-policy which ultimately decided to send 37-year-old Hindlekar and 29-year-old R. B. Nimbalkar to England in 1946.

This selection was unwise because it failed to look ahead into the future. In a match or two in 1946, both Hindlekar and Nimbalkar were the equal of any challenger to be found in India then. But the taxing schedule of an England tour was bound to tell on the physical capacities of two nearly middle-aged men. More important, their experience of a foreign tour was no investment for Indian cricket since they were obviously approaching the end of their careers. Our selectors had to grope in the dark all over again during 1946–47 when they had to find two new wicketkeepers to send to Australia. As for the England tour, Nimbalkar fractured two fingers in the fifth game and took no further part in the on-field proceedings until the last three matches.

Hindlekar fought off fatigue and bouts of lumbago throughout the tour, being compelled to appear in as many as 23 games—on three occasions, Gul Mohammed had to stand in for him. Three catches in the tests were Hindlekar's only rewards, the third being a special prize when he caught Hutton off Amarnath for only two in the second innings at Manchester. It was also at Manchester that Hindlekar stoutly defended his wicket for the last half-hour (along with Sohoni) and denied victory to England.

For the team to Australia, selectors made practically blind choices in J. K. Irani and P. Sen. Irani had first played for Sind in 1937 but not as wicketkeeper; by 1946, his highest score in the Ranji Trophy was 46. He began keeping wickets for Sind in 1942 to fill a gap in the team, but had done nothing in this role to merit consideration for the national side. In fact, he probably had not appeared in twenty first-class matches before he was playing for India in Australia and included for the first test at

5 Other wicketkeepers in action against the Australians were K. V. Bhandarkar (Princes' XI), R. R. Chandorkar (W. Zone), S. Sanjiva Rao (S. Zone).

Brisbane. A neat legside catch off Amarnath to dismiss Bill Brown and a stumping off Mankad to get rid of Lindwall came Irani's way, and earned him a reappearance ten days later in the second test. But every time P. Sen appeared in the other matches he displayed far greater ebullience and better understanding of our two main bowlers, Amarnath and Mankad. Sen was given his chance in the third test, took it with a broad smile and broader gloves, and thereafter shut Irani out of the picture altogether. Practically unknown in big cricket before this tour, Irani faded back into oblivion when the team returned to India.

Sen's trip to Australia had not been very much more warranted than Irani's. But at least he had been playing Ranji Trophy cricket regularly since 1943 when he was eighteen. This year he scored a century against Holkar and Bengal reached the final, so he had a growing reputation behind him when the selectors assembled in 1947 and decided to replace the two 'keepers who had gone to England. Once launched into test cricket, Sen made eight successive appearances for India—something no Indian wicketkeeper had been able to do before. Also, a happy disposition wedded to an unending store of energy made him an invaluable person on the field during these tests when the Indian team had to spend long hours in the sun chasing interminable runs made by Australian and West Indies batsmen. Radiating good cheer to those near him in close positions, Sen also transmitted fellow-feeling to those fielding in the deep, making a lot of ground to take bad throws. Sen may have originally earned selection as Bengal's sole candidate for the Indian team, but within a year he was very much a full-fledged national representative. Not forgetting the durable 'Darfu' Hindlekar, 'Khokon' Sen was our first modern test 'keeper who would do duty in three continents for five different series in four years.

Perhaps in order to teach Sen proper humility, our selectors did not use him at all in the ten 'tests' between 1949 and 1951 against the Commonwealth sides. Another explanation could be that these unofficial contests were being used as trial ground for new contestants, such as M. K. Mantri, P. G. Joshi and N. Rajendranath. Two of them graduated to official standing in the first two tests of 1951–52. For the third, possibly in deference to the Calcutta crowd, Sen was recalled. He lost no time in registering his presence when he took the catches which dismissed Spooner

(71) and Watkins (68), topscorers for England in the first innings; in the second, he stumped opening batsman Robertson almost as soon as Mankad came on, and later held on to Graveney's snick off Divecha. Reappointed for the fifth test at Madras, Sen outdid himself as well as his predecessors by a stumping spree which fetched him five victims, all of whom had been lured to their demise by Mankad. Sen also handled the more awkward angle of Ghulam Ahmed's spin competently, leaving no doubt in selectors' minds about who was best qualified in 1952 to keep India's wickets on the forthcoming England tour.

The other wicketkeeper provided for this team was Madhav Krishnaji Mantri, four years older than Sen and with a much bigger bank-balance of Ranji Trophy runs to his credit as well as a wicketkeeping record for this tournament of helping to dismiss nine batsmen in a match, which he achieved at his maiden appearance, Bombay vs NICA in 1941. Next season he appeared for Maharashtra, for whom he was qualified by birth, Nasik being his town of origin. Then he moved back into the Bombay side in 1943 and bided his time patiently. To Bombay's fifth title in fifteen years, Mantri contributed three centuries in succession—117 vs Bengal, 116 vs Madras and 200 vs Maharashtra. His 'keeping, like his batting, was dogged and down-to-earth, seldom spectacular but generally reliable. Mantri's perseverance was recognised in 1949–50 when he played in the first four 'tests' against Livingston's side. He opened our batting in the first two games and scored 54 in the second innings at Delhi. Dropped to no. 9 in the other two games, he registered improvement in his other function. His tally of 9 wickets (8 c, 1 st) for the series would remain the highest for some time. Mantri was set aside for the 1950–51 'tests' but recalled for the Bombay Test of 1951–52 against England—more to make an opening pair with P. Roy, Merchant having just announced his last retirement, than to strengthen the wicketkeeping. Mantri obliged with a modest 39 out of the first-wicket stand of 75 in the first innings.

This must have been the main consideration which earned Mantri a place in our 1952 tour of England. With Mankad not available for the tour programme, Roy was the only opening batsman who selected himself. D. K. Gaekwad was tentatively put forward as another candidate and Mantri must have been part of the same wishful thinking. How he came to play two tests of this tour – and not as opening batsman, in preference to Sen – is of course beyond any historian's purview. Mantri had a good match in the second test at Lord's – where he claimed four batsmen and allowed only eight byes in England's long innings of 537 – but he should not have been in action at all. Cricket logic prevailed for the other two tests in which Sen was restored, though this did not affect the outcome of these matches.

One more chapter remains to be added to the Mantri story. Enough younger and better wicketkeepers were available during 1952–54 to disqualify him for further consideration—permanently, one would have thought. But Mantri wore better than one expected. The sixteen Indians chosen to tour Pakistan in 1954–55 included Mantri. He played in the first test at Dacca, batted at no. 3 (scored 0 and 2), but did not keep wickets. He was not required for the remaining tests. Presumably he had been included as reserve 'keeper. Or it may have been the reserve opening batsman argument which had worked in his favour once more. The honest but limited worth of Mantri earned him a place in eight matches for India (three official) and two tours abroad.[6] But he must have been the cricketer most envied by younger Indian wicketkeepers of the time.

Sen disappeared from the test scene more or less concurrently. Two games against Pakistan in 1952 – in the first and the fifth tests – proved not only that he continued to be in great form but that our selectors were dithering as usual. They even called him out of near-retirement to officiate at the third 'test' of the SJOC series at Calcutta. Was he on trial, as other 'keepers were in these games? We shall never know. This was the only unofficial appearance which Sen made. In 13 tests, he took 19 catches and made 11 stumpings to set a figure which successors could aim at lowering. Also, he made the Indian test wicketkeeper an active participator in the proceedings, rather than the passive picker-up of crumbs he had been for so long. As long as Sen was on the field, he did not let anybody forget he was there.

Between them, Sen and Mantri succeeded, however unwittingly, in keeping Padmakar Govind Joshi out of the running for much longer than the Pune wicketkeeper deserved. As long as they were around, Joshi could look forward to nothing better

---

6 Mantri's record is 6 c, 1 st in 3 'tests' and 12 c, 3 st in 4 'tests'.

than an occasional exposure to test cricket. Even afterwards, in spite of two tours abroad with the India team, Joshi never kept in all the matches of a series. Being suspended on the tenterhooks of selection throughout his long international career – longer than that of any other contemporary Indian wicketkeeper – gave him little opportunity to settle down and do his best. Always he had to strive unduly for effect and results, and not surprisingly he made mistakes through trying to do too much. Anybody who watched the first day's play of the first test against England at Delhi in November 1951 will remember a flawless day of wicket-keeping. Not only did Joshi take two catches practically off the bat and execute two stumpings with eye-defying speed, the smooth and certain ease with which he gathered Mankad and Shinde bespoke the kind of instinct which reveals the truly top-class wicket-keeper. Yet four days later, from his first fumble with a difficult stumping chance he was unable to do anything right as Lowson and Carr, then Carr and Watkins managed to see England through to a draw. Each of them was allowed at least one escape by Joshi, whose triumphant first appearance in test cricket was much tarnished by the time the match finished. He reappeared in the fourth test at Kanpur, but failed ultimately to claim a place in the 1952 side to England.

Nana Joshi was a distinct departure from the Hindlekar–Sen–Mantri line in that he was a more conscious stylist. Trim in figure, unlike the other three who looked stubby when padded up, Joshi gave the impression of sartorial elegance because of his well-cared-for equipment. He moved quickly in whatever he did on the field, including the walking across between overs which in his case was a smart trot. When he dropped the ball in gathering, he retrieved it so quickly that sometimes watchers failed to notice the error. His was a craft which balanced itself on the knife-edge of speed and perfection. Its achievements were marvellous but its failures frequent. Nevertheless, he lasted in the India team longer than all other fellow-craftsmen, though not continuously.

Though born in Baroda, Joshi made his Ranji Trophy debut for Maharashtra against Baroda in 1946. Within the space of three seasons he was making a bid for the highest circles. During 1949–50, he scored an unbeaten century for the M. P. Governor's XI against the touring Commonwealth side, and earned an invitation to the fifth 'test' at Madras. The bowlers – Phadkar,

Hazare, Chowdhury, Nayudu and Mankad – were all unfamiliar to him, but he had no trouble taking them and helped in the dismissal of six batsmen (4 c, 2 st). Australian pace-bowler Fred Freer bowled him for a duck in his only turn at the bat; in revenge, Joshi stumped Freer off Mankad in both innings.

Two more 'test' appearances against the Second Commonwealth team in 1950–51 saw Joshi perform a shade better than another new aspirant, Rajendranath, who was unexpectedly called up from the underdeveloped Bihar team to serve India in the other three 'tests' this season. Rajendranath's histrionics never equalled his actual performance, but he had the necessary qualities – technique, speed and confidence – which could have, with greater domestic opportunities, been developed to meet regular test standards. Joshi was well placed for permanent appointment when the setbacks of the 1951–52 series knocked him out of the running for the time being. Sen won his place back by actual performance; but with the future in view, the second wicketkeeper's place for the 1952 tour should definitely have been awarded to Joshi since he obviously had more years of cricket ahead of him than Mantri.

Both Joshi (at Kanpur) and Rajendranath (at Bombay) were on retrial in the 1952 tests against Pakistan. Now it was Rajendranath's turn to suffer while Joshi was at long last recognised as our best bet behind the stumps and sent off to the West Indies. Rajendranath kept impressively, particularly in relation to Subhas Gupte, but he was not even considered for the second place. This was given to E. S. Maka, whose inclusion in the fourth test against Pakistan had been widely criticised. Maka, it will be recalled, had appeared in a 'test' against the Australian Services in 1945 and dropped out of consideration thereafter. Now just turned thirty and with continuous non-achievement behind him, he was suddenly found fit not merely to keep in a test match but also to accompany the national team on a foreign tour. Maka's lucky star shone as far as Port of Spain, where he was included for the third test. He sat in the pavilion throughout the first day while India batted; when his turn came on the second morning, he received a ball from Lester King on the back of his left hand and took no further part in the game. Manjrekar deputised and stumped Walcott off Gupte, besides taking two catches, to make up for his batting failure in both innings. With both Maka and Joshi out of action for the final test, Manjrekar had to keep wickets again.

Joshi began the 1953 series against West Indies confidently and collected six scalps in the first two tests—four of them stumpings off Gupte, whom he appeared to read most accurately. Being excluded from the third test may have damaged his self-confidence, because he seemed noticeably off-colour in the fourth test and for the first time in his eight appearances for India he failed to take a wicket. Worse was to follow after he returned home and the SJOC came to India for the 'test' of 1953–54. Joshi's services were not called upon until the final game at Lucknow—even P. Sen was remembered before Joshi was. Of two new wicketkeepers tried out in these matches, N. S. Tamhane emerged quickly to the forefront and took the India gloves away from Joshi for the time being.

When Joshi was not deemed fit to act as alternate wicketkeeper on our 1954–55 tour of Pakistan, he must have considered his test career as closed. India played three successive series without him and were halfway through a fourth, when the panic reshuffles made during the 1958–59 series against West Indies gave Joshi an unexpected opportunity. Recalled after a gap of sixteen tests to the India side, Joshi kept wickets with due care at Madras, cutting out all the frills from his manner which used to lead him into error. He also gained some extra merit by batting at no. 3 after the first wicket (A. K. Sen Gupta) had fallen at 11 and holding his own against the pace bowlers until the total reached 60. Though he was not used for the final test, he was among the sixteen selected to tour England in 1959.

India batted and bowled erratically throughout this tour, but at least the wicketkeeping was consistently good. Joshi and Tamhane ran neck-to-neck for a place in the test eleven, and Joshi won by a narrow margin. He officiated in the first two tests and again in the fourth, collecting seven wickets altogether through catches. In personal satisfaction, he must have felt amply compensated for the injustice that was done to him seven years earlier. For the second time in his career, he reached the status of the nation's leading wicketkeeper. In the first test against Pakistan in 1960–61, it was Joshi who was invited before other 'keepers were tried. In the match against Pakistan at Delhi – on what was to be his last appearance for India – he partnered Desai in a merry ninth-wicket stand of 149 runs, his own share being 52 not out. One more catch or stumping would have enabled him to equal P. Sen's total bag of 30 in official tests,[7] but Joshi's average was better. Had it not been for unmerited gaps in his test career between 1953 and 1959, Joshi would surely have set records in Indian wicketkeeping.

If Sen and Mantri had frustrated the earlier half of Joshi's cricketing life, in the latter half it was Tamhane who blocked his way. Naren Tamhane's rapid rise up the national ladder must have been marvelled at and envied by brother 'keepers. His first big match was for the Combined Universities side against MCC in 1951. Next season he got into the Bombay University side. The following year he made his Ranji Trophy debut with a bang—aiding and abetting the dismissal of as many as seven Baroda batsmen. The noise was heard by our selectors who pushed him into the second 'test' at Bombay against SJOC, to keep wickets as well as open the batting. The latter gained him a duck; but he took two catches in his other function and left an overall impression which paved his way into the India side which toured Pakistan in 1954–55. In the astonishing time of three years, Tamhane graduated from university cricket to full test standing.

Part of Tamhane's meteoric rise may be explained by his belonging to a champion team like Bombay, which gained him ample exposure to discerning eyes. But getting into the Bombay team is never easy – as Chandrakant Patankar was to learn soon – and Tamhane had to develop a reputation early for reliability. In this he should be placed in the Hindlekar tradition. He never attempted the impossible but seldom missed the possible opportunity. It is as difficult to remember a spectacular episode concerning Tamhane's wicketkeeping in test matches as it is to recall an instance when he missed a simple catch or muffed an easy stumping chance. Joshi's finesse often made one aware of Tamhane's lack of sophistication. But in the long run Tamhane gave better service, equalling Sen's record of 30 wickets in a stretch of sixteen tests between 1955 and 1959, interrupted by one absence through injury when Patankar substituted for him in the fourth test against New Zealand in 1955–56.

---

[7] Thirteen wickets in unofficial 'tests' gave Joshi a career-aggregate of 42.

Patankar, of course, made the mistake of reaching big cricket at the same time as Tamhane and had to remain second choice even for the Bombay team. Any chance of his developing as an alternate test wicketkeeper was ruined by Nana Joshi's comeback in 1959. Patankar had played for Bombay CA against the First Commonwealth in 1949 but did not enter Bombay's Ranji Trophy team until 1953–54, in which season he also captained the Combined Universities XI against SJOC. But thereafter, no further opening offered itself apart from that one test against New Zealand at Calcutta. Here he took the first two catches which got rid of the opening batsmen, later made another catch and a stumping—but somehow never got beyond this to form a test career.

Playing regularly for Bombay gave Tamhane the additional advantage of handling Subhas Gupte, India's main wicket-taker of the 1950s, more often than any other wicketkeeper in the country. In his first test series, however, Tamhane proved that he was equally capable of taking other Indian bowlers and claimed 19 Pakistani batsmen altogether (of which 8 were in collaboration with Gupte) to set a record for Indian test 'keepers. Tamhane also scored his test highest in this series—54 not out at Bahawalpur, helping Ramchand (53) rescue India after seven wickets had fallen for 107.

The Pakistan tour consolidated Tamhane's place so firmly that it would probably have gone unchallenged for longer than it did, had it not been for the unexpected rejuvenation of Joshi during the 1958–59 series against the West Indies. Tamhane had reached 40 wickets at the end of this series and, but for Joshi's intervention, would have reached the fifty mark. Five years older than Tamhane, Joshi seemed the younger man during the 1959 tour of England because of his lively manner behind the wickets. Their rivalry continued until 1961, when both appeared in their last matches for India. Tamhane's final tally was 47 (32c, 15st) in 21 tests[8] which gave him a slightly lower wicket-per-test factor than Sen.

The places vacated by Joshi and Tamhane were quickly taken by a wholly new breed of wicketkeepers whose first love was for batting – and this consisted of hitting the new ball as hard and as

[8] In 2 unofficial 'tests' he took 9 wickets.

often as possible – but who cultivated a second love for wicketkeeping because this combination assured a passport to exalted circles of Indian cricket. The combination was not new – Dilawar Hussain had shown the way long ago – but the presentation was very different and the effect wholly novel. Nobody who has seen Kunderan hook or Engineer drive, Kunderan snatch at a snick, or Engineer scatter the wickets in stumping, will disagree that these were cricketers whom it was well worth paying to see.

Budhisagar Kunderan arrived on the scene earlier. Born in Mangalore but schooled in Bombay, Kunderan not merely represented the Bombay State school team in cricket but also won the 100 metres sprint at the State Junior Athletics one year. He was not yet twenty when CCI invited him to play for them against the touring West Indies team of 1958–59. Kunderan took part in the dismissal of five batsmen and had a close look at Jack Holt (103 not out) and Gary Sobers (93). Next year he got a job with the Indian Railways, mainly on his sports background, and celebrated his new wage-earning status with a razzle-dazzle 205 for Railways against Jammu & Kashmir. The feat of scoring a double century on first appearance in the Ranji Trophy had not been repeated since G. E. B. Abell scored 210 for Northern India against the Army in 1934–35. That he also took 20 wickets this year for the Railways should not be forgotten when we feel surprised that Kunderan should have been selected to play for India during his first full season in first-class cricket. Three tests against Australia in 1959–60 fetched him four wickets, but what endeared him to Indian hearts was the run-a-minute 71 he knocked off Australian bowlers at Madras, where he was required to open the batting. Not all the strokes he made were to be found in any book, but there was no denying the venturesome spirit in which he made them.

Having made the gamble, our selectors were more cautious with Kunderan against Pakistan in 1960–61, holding him back for the first three tests. But in the Board President's XI vs Pakistan match at Bangalore preceding the fourth test, he chalked up five dismissals and forced his way back to the India eleven. He did not open the batting but took four catches at the Madras Test to ensure being retained. When the 1961–62 series against England began, Kunderan was an automatic choice for the first test at Bombay. He took five wickets here, but surrendered his place for the remaining tests to Engineer not so much because Engineer was ostensibly the better 'keeper but because another specialist had to be tried out with the forthcoming West Indies tour in view.

Farokh Engineer, a year older than Kunderan, took two years longer to make the test grade. But once having made it, he dogged the other's bootsteps until he emerged in the clear as the country's number one wicketkeeper. In the process, the man who suffered most was Indrajitsinh[9] who had started earlier than the other two but was squeezed out of the race, apart from the short 1964 series against Australia.

Engineer, like Kunderan, made his first-class debut in 1958–59 when he kept wickets for Combined Universities against the West Indies. Also like Kunderan, Engineer made his first Ranji Trophy appearance in 1959–60, for Bombay against Saurashtra. Next year he had a poor match in the first tournament game for Bombay against Gujarat – he was bowled for nought by, of all people, Nari Contractor while only one of Gujarat's twenty wickets fell because of him – and he was replaced by Tamhane for the next two matches. Recalled for the semi-final against Delhi, Engineer scored a duck but caught 7 Delhi batsmen to equal a Ranji Trophy record[10] But this was too late in the season to lead to better things. He had not been considered for the West Zone eleven against Pakistan. Joshi represented the Zone, scored 85 and claimed five wickets, and found a way to the first test team.

When Engineer did get his chance at last – and it came to him without warning because Kunderan had not faltered until then – in the second test against England in 1961–62, he clutched it so firmly that he remained in possession for the rest of the series and continued his lease for the first three tests against the West Indies in 1962. At this stage, there was not much to choose between them as wicketkeepers. Both were as liable to silly mistakes as they were capable of patches of utter brilliance. So the seemingly sounder appearance of Engineer's batting, especially his knack of getting unexpected runs low in the order, weighed in his favour. An eighth wicket stand of 101 with Nadkarni (Engineer 65) against England, another of 94 for the same wicket with the

---

[9] This is how the name is given in the latest *Indian Cricket*. When he was in active service, he used to be called Indrajit.

[10] M. J. Limaye had taken 7 catches for Baroda against the Services in 1957–58.

same partner (Engineer 53), were arguments which kept Kunderan out of business until the last two matches of the 1962 series. In these he made 11 runs and took 5 catches.

During the home season of 1962–63, Kunderan played only one match for the Railways (scored 24, stumped 4) before the team was withdrawn from the tournament (as was the Services team) on account of the outbreak of hostilities with China. Engineer had a full season for Bombay, during which he scored 337 runs (with 162 against Bengal as highest score) and claimed 13 wickets (10 c, 3 st). On the two occasions they were pitted against each other (West Zone vs North Zone in the Duleep Trophy, Bombay vs Rest of India in the Irani Trophy) Engineer opened Bombay's batting a couple of times with fair success partnering S. G. Adhikari in stands of 269 against Bengal, 146 against Rest of India and also scored 96 at number three against Maharashtra (158 for the second wicket with Adhikari), thus further spoiling Kunderan's chances of a return on recovery of batting form.

But Kunderan returned, precisely in those terms, when the 1964 series against England began at Madras. He was not in the original eleven but came in as a late replacement for Engineer who was slated to open the batting as well. Pataudi won the toss and elected to bat, giving Kunderan immediate opportunity to prove himself. This he proceeded to do in no uncertain manner by batting through the whole day, forming associations of 85 for the first wicket with Vijay Mehra (17), 143 for the second wicket with Dilip Sardesai (65), and was unbeaten with 170 at the end, having hit 28 fours. Next morning, he overhauled Mankad's record score against England (184 at Lord's in 1952) but fell short by eight runs of a double century. Such batting did not exhaust his resources because he claimed six wickets as well (4 c, 2 st) and insured his presence in the remaining tests. Kunderan completed the series in a blaze of batting glory (525 runs in 10 innings, with another three-digit knock of 100 in the fourth test at Delhi) but let his wicketkeeping slide somewhat. The impetuosity which characterised his batting and made it so thrilling to watch also imbued his 'keeping, giving it a snatch-or-muff air when observed over the duration of a whole series.

A third candidate now entered the contest after having cooled his gloves on the sidelines for a long time. Indrajit made his Ranji Trophy debut at the age of seventeen for Saurashtra in 1954–55, but it was as a Delhi University cricketer from 1957–58 to 1960–61 that he came into prominence. In the latter season he scored four zeros for Delhi as opening bat but collected 23 victims (13 c, 10 st), setting a Ranji Trophy record in the semi-final against Bombay when he claimed 6 wickets in an innings. He also appeared for Combined Universities and North Zone against Pakistan, but did nothing of note. The following season he returned to his home state team, Saurashtra and was lucky to be selected for West Zone's first match in the Duleep Trophy against Central Zone. He made two stumpings and scored a fine 67 as opening batsman, sharing a third wicket stand of 165 with Chandu Borde (116) after Contractor and Sardesai had gone cheaply. But Engineer was preferred over him in the final. Some compensation awaited Indrajit when he was included in the West Zone XI which played MCC at Ahmedabad, and later he toured Australia with the CCI team.

Indrajit was thus faced with the task of out-batting Kunderan and out-keeping Engineer if he was to have any future. When the other two toured West Indies in 1969 and Kunderan monopolised the 1964 tests against England, Indrajit may well have thought of giving up the struggle. Yet, as a result of one of those selection brainwaves which so often happen in Indian cricket, neither Kunderan nor Engineer but Indrajit played in the tests against Australia at the end of 1964. He failed as opening bat at Madras, but stumped Simpson off Durrani when the Australian skipper had just got going, and also took three catches. At Bombay, he drew first blood again by catching Lawry off Durrani, added two more victims to his bag, and played a vital supporting role to Borde in the last half-hour of the match which gave India her second victory over Australia. The same eleven players were retained for the third test at Calcutta, and Indrajit claimed one more wicket here to complete a moderately successful series.

If Indrajit had visions of continuing to serve India, these were quickly shattered. Thereafter he appeared in one 'test' against Ceylon, made the 1967–68 trip to Australia and New Zealand without playing a test, and substituted for Engineer in the Nagpur Test against New Zealand in 1969. His three successive appearances against Australia in 1964 were thus a freak, attributable to the powerful fancy of some selector. But it cannot be denied that he was on par with Engineer as a wicketkeeper and in overall performance above Kunderan, though he had little of their surplus utility as a batsman. Habitually spruce in equipment and neat in movement, he reminded one occasionally of Joshi. For a time Indrajit grew a beard—India's only test 'keeper to have done so.[11]

The Engineer–Kunderan contest resumed in the 1965 series against New Zealand, with Engineer returning to his post after a break of ten tests. He quickly asserted his batsmanship with a hard-driving 90 at no. 9 in the Madras Test (creating an eighth-wicket record partnership of 143 with Nadkarni). Kunderan was used in the Calcutta Test, but only as opening batsman. Engineer came in one down and briefly these two batted together. In the second innings Engineer opened with Jaisimha and struck 45 thrilling runs to overshadow Kunderan, who was not selected again for this series. Kunderan's turn came in the 1966–67 tests against West Indies where he was nominated for the first test. Whereas Pataudi and Borde countered the West Indies bowlers with patience and technique in the first innings, in the second, Kunderan battered the opposition for 79 with fifteen fours. He led another assault at Calcutta, where he opened, but was cut off at 39 by a Hall yorker. His wicketkeeping, however, again developed patches of inadequacy and he was replaced for the Madras Test by Engineer—in spite of the smashing century Kunderan scored for South Zone against the tourists at Bangalore. Engineer, of course, hit West Indies for 109 at Chepauk and forced all critics of his selection to eat their hats.

Hereafter, Engineer was unquestionably our number one wicketkeeper and had an unprecedented run of fourteen successive appearances. In spite of the double strain placed on him in having to open the batting as well, his performance behind the stumps improved and fell into a steady rhythm. Kunderan accompanied him to England in 1967, but was not used as a wicketkeeper in the tests—he appeared in two as batsman, opened the bowling in one of these, and revealed himself as a fleet-footed fieldsman in the deep in both games. Indrajit was chosen to understudy Engineer on our southern tour of 1967–68. Engineer exceeded Sen's aggregate of 30 wickets on this trip, capturing 10 each in both four-test series against Australia and

[11] Except for Kirmani who occasionally disguised himself.

New Zealand. When Australia returned this visit in 1969–70, Engineer surpassed Tamhane's more recent record of 47 and for the first time an Indian wicketkeeper filled a bag of fifty victims and more in test cricket.

Engineer was recruited by Lancashire in 1969 to play county cricket for them. He returned home in time to appear in seven out of the eight tests of 1969–70. Indrajit deputised for Engineer against New Zealand in the Hyderabad Test and this was a clear hint to Kunderan that he was not wanted any longer. He publicly announced his dissatisfaction with Indian selectors and his decision to migrate to England. Engineer was played a worse trick by our selectors on the eve of the West Indies tour when they ruled him out of consideration for not having played enough domestic cricket in 1970–71. The path seemed to have been cleared again for Indrajit, but the selection committee thoroughly outguessed everybody by nominating P. Krishnamurthy (Hyderabad) and R. Jeejeebhoy (Bengal) for the West Indies tour.

This decision was quite out of keeping with the judgement and foresight displayed by this committee, chaired by Vijay Merchant, when it selected among others Dilip Sardesai, Salim Durrani and M. L. Jaisimha.[12] On earlier occasions, one or the other wicketkeeper has been a whimsical choice – J. K. Irani to Australia in 1947, E. S. Maka to the West Indies in 1953, M. K. Mantri to Pakistan in 1955 – but now a double fault was committed. Neither Krishnamurthy nor Jeejeebhoy was in anybody's picture in 1971 where test wicketkeepers are concerned. Looking back on the Duleep Trophy matches of the 1965–70 period, one could pick out Shiraz Dharsey of Railways or Daljit Singh of Bihar, both of whom had runs to their credit as well as experience as opening batsmen. Bombay had recently promoted diminutive Sharad Hazare while Maharashtra's emergence as West Zone champions was not a little due to Hemant Kanitkar who must have spent nearly as much time in front of the stumps as behind them. As against this, Jeejeebhoy, a Bengal regular from about 1965, had appeared neither in any Irani Trophy

[12] None of these three was an obvious choice, but they all contributed to India's success on this tour—Sardesai by the number of runs he scored in the test matches; Durrani by taking two vital wickets in the second test; Jaisimha by his counselling to Wadekar.

match nor in the Duleep Trophy tournament when he was selected to tour the West Indies. Krishnamurthy narrowly missed the same lack of distinction when he found a niche in the South Zone team in late December 1970 as replacement for Budhi Kunderan who had been sole occupant since 1965.[13] Krishnamurthy, who had made his debut for Hyderabad in 1967–68, won out finally because he attempted very little, thus failed even less. He appeared in five tests in the West Indies (7 c, 1 st) and in three unofficial matches against Sri Lanka to remain the most unremarked upon wicketkeeper to have stood behind for India. As for Jeejeebhoy, he returned home without having played any test match and soon faded out of Bengal cricket as well. His inclusion on that tour can only be understood as a token of eastern India being represented in the national combination.

However, saner counsel prevailed when the Indian team was due to visit England in 1971 and Engineer was invited back, by courtesy of Lancashire authorities, to play for the tourists in test matches. For the other games, however, the team carried two wicketkeepers, P. Krishnamurthy and S. M. H. Kirmani (Mysore), which made it nearly as overstaffed in this department as the 1936 team to England. Krishnamurthy never appeared again in an official test match but he played both matches against Sri Lanka in 1974 and one more against the same opponent in 1975. His best performance was in the second 'test' of the 1974 tour at Colombo, where he pouched four catches in the first innings and three in the second – all off Salgaonkar or Madanlal – to consolidate India's win. With Krishnamurthy's amazing selection luck re-asserted itself when, though passed over for the 1974 tour of England, he was taken to New Zealand and the West Indies in 1976. However, he made no test appearance on this tour, hence his actual test career foreclosed in April 1971 at Port

[13] An additional distinction claimed by Krishnamurthy was that he kept wickets for South Zone even though P. K. Belliappa (formerly of Mysore, then of Tamil Nadu) was also in the team that year. Belliappa, a proficient batsman, may have been a higher contender as wicketkeeper because we find that during 1967–70, when the Australians played South Zone at Bangalore, it was Belliappa and not Kunderan (or Krishnamurthy) who was assigned this job.

of Spain where he caught D. Lewis (72) off Bedi, stumped D. A. J. Holford (44) off Venkatraghavan, and hit his highest score of 20 which enabled him to add 39 runs for the eighth wicket with Venkatraghavan.

Reprieved in 1971 for the England series, Engineer managed to stretch his test career by another four years which contained two more series with England. His English experience served India critically in the Oval Test of 1971 when it was Engineer's counter-attack in the first innings (his 59 was the top score, just exceeding Sardesai's 54) which raised the total from 125 (for five wickets down) to 222 and gave India a fighting chance. Quite appropriately, in the second innings he was at the middle (28 n.o.) when Abid Ali made the winning hit. For a couple of seasons around this time Engineers's wicketkeeping was rated highly enough for him to play two matches for the Rest of the World against England in 1970 and retain his place in the Rest side for the 1971–72 series in Australia.[14] Back home in time for the 1972–73 series with England, his wicketkeeping began showing signs of fatigue but he batted so consistently (405 runs in 10 innings) that he could have kept his place as a batsman alone. Certainly it was this factor which weighed in his favour during the 1974 series in England. After Gavaskar's 101, and 58 at Manchester, it was Engineer's 86 (131 for the first wicket with Gavaskar) at Lords and 64 not out at Birmingham which gave some body to India's feeble resistance. He was still capable of unexpected and critical action behind the stumps – for example, he caught Vivian Richards (2) and stumped Clive Lloyd (7) both off Prasanna, at Madras to hasten the second West Indian defeat of the 1974–75 series – but, nearly thirty-seven years old now, he was obviously approaching the end of his test career. This happened, marked by two catches and two ducks, in the final test of the series at Bombay.

Both in the span of his test career (1961 to 1975) and in the number of appearances (46 altogether), Engineer retired as our most durable wicketkeeper until then. He saw India through thirteen test series and toured England, Australia, New Zealand and

[14] He appeared twice against England; Deryck Murray (West Indies) replaced him in the other three matches. In Australia he played four times, with Bob Taylor (England) taking over in the last match.

the West Indies with the India team. Between the Madras Tests of 1967 and 1970, he had a run of nineteen tests with just one break, then an uninterrupted sequence of sixteen onwards from the Lord's Test of 1971. Along with claiming 82 victims (66 catches and 16 stumpings; strike rate of 1.78 per test) he scored 2611 runs (average 31.08; two centuries and one more in an unofficial test). Thus, how much of his durability was insured by his batting prowess can be debated. That he could bat aggressively as an opener was an additional bonus for a team which was often short of confident opening batsmen. There was no question, however, that for several years he touched the world's highest class as a wicketkeeper. In this job too, he exuded the kind of aggression and confidence which brought psychological pressure upon batsmen, especially when they had to contend with India's famous spin-bowlers. And there must have been instances when the histrionics of Engineer appealing for a catch behind overwhelmed umpires into giving a decision in his favour. When the Calcutta crowd gave vocal support to an appeal by Engineer, the noise was surely heard in other Indian test centres as well…

[1972]

Ten Feet Tall

Standing ten feet tall – that is, if they were to stand on each others' shoulders – Sunil Gavaskar and Gundappa Vishwanath[1] have flown high the flag of Indian batsmanship wherever test cricket is played in the world. The first time they did this jointly was in March 1971 on the Bourda Oval of Georgetown, Guyana. In a fourth-wicket partnership that was as strokeful as it was archetypical – two little men defying men much bigger and stronger than themselves – they announced a new era in contemporary Indian batting. Sharing nothing but their year of birth (1949) and a penchant for holding sharp slip catches, they differed vastly in the way they dealt with the bowling. Whenever they batted together in a test match – which, alas, was not often enough – the study in contrast they presented tugged inexorably at every cricket-writer's fingers.

Not yet twenty-one when he played for India against Australia at Kanpur in November 1969, Vishwanath looked about twelve years old—as slight in build as he was short in stature; no long hair yet nor overgrowth above or under his mouth; and still goggle-eyed in wonder that he had been admitted into such exalted company. Predictably, it seemed, Alan Connolly hustled him out for a duck within five balls. Gavaskar, on the other hand, never looked out of place, no matter where or when. That air of sturdy self-sufficiency that most Maharashtrians like to assume in public marked him out even in the early days. Padded, gloved and capped, he presented a somewhat square shape that went well with the neat geometry of his batting. Adequacy was always

---

[1] For some reason the *Indian Cricket* annual changed the spelling of the latter's name from Vishwanath to Viswanath to Visvanath. I have kept to the original, from which the popular form 'Vishy' derives.

the philosophy of Gavaskar's craft. He was not dismissed without scoring until his seventh test match; in his first he scored 65 and 67 not out—the latter effort concluding with the winning hit of India's first ever victory over West Indies.

The difference in their origins and cricket upbringing may explain the essential difference between them as cricketers. Belonging to a family where his grandfather as well as father were enthusiastic club cricketers, Gavaskar may be said to have been born under the sign of bat and ball. He used the Bombay boy's advantage of shinning up the readymade ladder of interschool matches in the Giles Shield and Harris Shield towards the Cooch Behar Trophy tournament, then onto inter-university contests and entry into the Ranji Trophy team. Denied such advantages by circumstance, Vishwanath still appeared in the Ranji Trophy tournament three years earlier and played for his country fifteen months before Gavaskar did.

Vishwanath was born (12 December 1949) in the small town of Bhadravati in Karnataka. His family's move to Bangalore when he was five years old brought him within reach of what would become a test cricket arena ten years later. Neither the Vishwesarapuram Middle School nor the Fort High School, which he attended, afforded him much cricket. This he sought and found mainly with the Spartan Sports Club in the third division of the Mysore cricket league. Mysore had been Ranji Trophy runners-up in 1942, again in 1960, and national championship ambitions could not have been wholly absent in the minds of Bangalore cricketers and administrators by the time Vishwanath was making his mark in junior cricket. Somebody was watching and at least one critic, K. N. Prabhu of *The Times of India,* had spotted him—and assured us several times in print that beneath the apparently carefree charm of this boy's strokeplay was a foundation of technique that was fit to be tested by higher stretches of Indian cricket. Good scores in the southern inter-association matches for the P. Ramachandra Rao Memorial Trophy led to Vishwanath's being summoned to play for Mysore against Andhra at Guntur in November 1967. Mysore had already lost to Madras and yielded first innings lead to Hyderabad, and thus could afford to experiment with the next season in view.

By that month and year, Gavaskar (born 10 July 1949 at Bombay) had made his debut for Bombay in the Irani Trophy but had not yet played in the Ranji. Even with as many as six players away in Australia for the latter part of the 1967–68 season, Bombay did not require Gavaskar (Sudhir Naik and Ashok Mankad were preferred as opening batsmen) and he remained among the reserves for the next season as well. That 'reserved' status had already come his way in 1966–67 when he was Bombay's twelfth man for one match; but was left out of even the fourteen in other matches.

Yet Gavaskar's tremendous reputation as a schoolboy cricketer would have walked him into any other Ranji Trophy team in the land. Selected for Bombay Schools as early as 1963–64 (when he was fourteen years old), he was dropped during the season because of indifferent fielding. He won his place back the following year by noticeably improved showing in this department and really exceeded all expectations in the Cooch Behar matches of 1965–66. With scores of 246 vs Central Zone (record opening stand of 421 with Anwar Qureshi), 222 vs East Zone and 85 in the final against North Zone, he was awarded the J. C. Mukherjee Trophy for the 'Best Schoolboy Cricketer of the Year'. He reeled off another string of good scores (116; 55; 35; 57) in 'tests' against the visiting London Schoolboys team of 1966; his aggregate of 309 in six innings (2 not outs; average 77.25) would have grown further had he not stood down from the final 'test' because of his own school-final examinations. Once more in his early career Gavaskar would have to allow academic requirements to take precedence over runmaking opportunities. No such dilemma ever inhibited Vishwanath; he did matriculate in some year not generally known, but his college studies were fairly indeterminate.

Thus unencumbered, Vishwanath fended delicately at the limited Andhra bowling at Guntur (of their five bowlers, only legspinner Mahendra Kumar was of any account), then mastered it, finally toyed with it to accumulate 230 runs in 340 minutes, aided by 33 fours and one five. This feat broke two records. One, the highest individual score for Mysore, V. Subrahmanyam's 213 against Madras only the previous season; the other and more notable, G. E. B. Abell's double century score on Ranji Trophy debut, 210 for Northern India against the Army at Lahore in

December 1934.[2] The most striking element of Vishwanath's large innings was not the stroke-play, which was eye-catching enough, but his seemingly unpremeditated resolve to make the most of an unexpected opportunity.

Opportunities were rare for Vishwanath because he figured in neither the Cooch Behar nor the Rohinton Baria Trophy tournaments. Gavaskar on the other hand went straight from one to the other and scored 81 against Calcutta University in the semi-final of 1966–67. Bombay lost in the final that year to Osmania; Gavaskar batted at number three (scored 19 and 27), since the opening berths were occupied by Sudhir Naik and Ramesh Nagdev. The Vizzy Trophy matches that followed at Nagpur saw two more future contenders for these top posts in action—Chetan Chauhan of Poona, for West Zone; K. Jayantilal of Osmania, for South Zone. Naik's 98 in the Vizzy final was pipped by Gavaskar's 111, while Chauhan got 88 and 63; all three were surpassed, by Jayantilal's patient 218 which nearly won the day for South Zone. Next year Gavaskar could not appear in the inter-varsity matches because of his studies, but in 1968–69 he lowered Jayantilal's record in the Vizzy Trophy by hitting 247 not out against South Zone. Less avariciously he got only 113 not out against North Zone in the following match. He did not make it yet to the senior West Zone team for the Duleep Trophy, though Vishwanath did for South Zone—but batted no higher than number seven. From this position, his 76 not out against West Zone could not grow into what may have been a century on his Duleep Trophy debut.

Neither appeared in the Irani Trophy match of 1969–70 at Poona, the season which saw first New Zealand, then Australia, visit India. Selected for the Combined Universities team which played the New Zealanders just before the first test, Gavaskar scored only 25 and 10. With two tests already over, Vishwanath made better use of the opportunity provided by the Board President's XI match at Indore against the visitors. Batting serenely for five hours – specially secure against pace bowlers Collinge and Taylor – he made 68 before being run out. Eight other batsmen in the home side did not even reach double figures.

---

[2] Abell, a Cambridge Blue and later private secretary to the Viceroy, also kept wickets brilliantly in this match to hold four catches and make two stumpings.

Only Chandu Borde (63) stood firm to put on 99 runs for the fourth wicket with Vishwanath. Vishwanath was duly called up for the third test at Hyderabad, but was left out of the playing eleven which nearly lost the match. When his turn came against Australia at Kanpur, he lasted only five balls in the first innings but nearly six hours in the second—and used the latter duration to score a century on test debut. Again he showed that in a difficult situation, he could steel himself at short notice and undergo any strain. One hundred of his 137 runs at Kanpur came in fours, a remarkable proportion considering the time and place.

Vishwanath blossomed against the Australians—20 and 44 not out at Delhi, where he shared the unfinished fourth-wicket stand of 120 with Wadekar and hit the winning run. He made 54 and 5 at the first appearance on the Eden Gardens wicket; 6 and 59 at Madras, the latter being part of a 102-run third-wicket partnership again with Wadekar—Gavaskar, however, was not selected for West Zone against the Australians, Nagdev being preferred as opening partner to Dilip Sardesai. Bombay also did not need him for their Ranji Trophy matches within the zone but called on him for the semi-final against Mysore at Bombay. Going out to open the batting with Ashok Mankad, he asked to be allowed to take first strike and was out leg-before off the fifth ball of the innings from Rajappa. He remembers being booed off the field, some spectators shouting that he had been included only because his uncle (M. K. Mantri) was in the selection committee. He nearly achieved a pair in this match, being dropped at leg-slip off the fifth ball of the second innings. Reprieved, he played out time quietly depositing the first 27 runs in his Ranji Trophy account. On the other side Vishwanath, batting for the first time at Bombay, missed his hundred by just five runs in the second innings. This silky display that lasted just under three hours was watched closely by Gavaskar from the slips, where the latter took three good catches and probably retained his place in the side mainly on this account.

In the final against Rajasthan, also at Bombay, Gavaskar made handsome amends—114 of an opening stand of 279 with Ashok Mankad (171). This improved upon the 273-run record set by Nazar Mohammad (Mudassar Nazar's father) and Jagdish Lal (Arun Lal's father) way back in 1941 for Northern India against NWFP. Dropped at 11 and again at 66, he reached 99 with a streaky shot through the slips off Salim Durrani. Gavaskar thus demonstrated that these occasional lapses did not disrupt the concentration, which carried him through 255 minutes of batting as solid as any seen at Brabourne Stadium. An informal group photograph of the champions shows Wadekar holding the trophy aloft, Gavaskar squats below—obviously the baby of the side.

Given his previous experience so far with selectors, Gavaskar could not afford to relax during 1970–71. On tour in Sri Lanka as vice-captain of the Indian Universities team, he hit an unbeaten 203 in the second 'test' against Sri Lanka Universities, with Jayantilal partnering him in an opening sortie worth 174 runs. Captaining Bombay in the Rohinton Baria matches held that year in Pune, he fairly devoured the bowling in the Western Zone with successive scores of 226, 99, 327, 124. That triple-decker against South Gujarat broke Wadekar's twelve-year-old inter-varsity record of 324 (for Bombay against Delhi). In the Ranji Trophy programme he missed Bombay's first match against Baroda, being away in Sri Lanka. He apparently found a place in Bombay's eleven against Gujarat in the next match only when an indisposed Wadekar had to drop out. He did not waste the opportunity, getting 104 good runs for himself and putting on 166 for the first wicket with Ashok Mankad. Following this up with 176 against Maharashtra (opening stand of 227 with Sudhir Naik), he left no doubt about which way he was headed. When the Indian team to tour West Indies was announced in early January 1971, Gavaskar's name was among the sixteen.

Those who marvel anew when they look up the cold figures of Gavaskar's stupendous maiden series in test cricket – 774 runs in eight innings, average 154.80; two centuries in successive tests, followed by a century and a double century in the same test – may not always remember that he missed the first match of the series or that his second innings of the sequence remained unfinished at 67. Otherwise he would surely have pushed that large aggregate towards even more extraordinary dimensions. The portrait of the youngster as mature batsman, which Gavaskar drew on ground after ground in the West Indies that season, remained true of him throughout his career. That metronomically accurate move back or forward in defence did not change, except occasionally when an unexpected spurt of express pace hurried him or an unruly bound of the ball made him drop his right hand in apprehension. Otherwise, hands and forearms kept the bat within an unvarying groove in line with the ball's approach. Normally there would be no attempt to force the pace, no violent exertion in pursuit of runs, but a calm conviction that runs would come by themselves so long as he stayed there. As he stayed the slightly overpitched ball would be methodically driven back to the more distant boundaries behind the bowler, the slightly short ball on or outside the off-stump dismissed with a square-cut as clinical as it was decisive. It was easy to separate the theory and practice of batsmanship when Gavaskar brought bat to ball. Nothing short of a comprehensive, theory could have sustained such plentitude of practice for so long. But like all theories that are ultimately superseded, even on that extensively productive series of 1971, some flaw in application sometimes drew the outer edge of Gavaskar's bat into the away-going ball of some pace. At that height it should perhaps be more aptly termed as an Achilles' elbow rather than heel. That occasional flaw apart, Gavaskar had shown in his very first series that he had come fully formed in body and mind to guard the portals of India's test innings for years to come.[3]

Vishwanath took a little longer to reassure that he would permanently occupy the post three places below Gavaskar in the batting order. All centurions on test-debut for India had disappointed for nearly forty years – Lala Amarnath, Deepak Shodhan, A. G. Kripal Singh, Hanumant Singh and Abbas Ali Baig in official tests; Pamanmal Panjabi and Chandu Gadkari in unofficial – and Vishwanath's first test series could not be taken on faith. Like Gavaskar he missed the early matches of the West Indies tour, including the first test at Kingston. Gavaskar then tuned up with knocks of 82 and 32 not out against the Leeward Islands and 125 and 63 against Trinidad. Vishwanath's first outing was in the

---

[3] Early detractors of Gavaskar used to insist that he had been phenomenally lucky in his first series inasmuch as he offered many catches that were dropped. In actual fact he was dropped only three times—at 12 off Holder in the first innings of the second test (when he scored 65), at 6 off Shillingford and again at 94 off Noreiga both in the first innings of the third test (when he scored 116). The far more noteworthy fact than Gavaskar giving these catches was that each time it was Gary Sobers who dropped them.

later match. His wrenched knee not quite operative yet, he failed in both innings (1 and 16) and did not even qualify for the second test. Moderate gains in the following match against Guyana (25 and 44) brought him back into the eleven for the third test. Though a third-wicket stand of 112 between him and Gavaskar ensued, Viswanath was plainly struggling. Gavaskar went on to his first test hundred while Vishwanath reached only fifty. At the end of the series Vishwanath totalled only 135 runs in five innings. And we had to bide our time and await further proof of his worth. Though Gavaskar fared badly – even without comparing his recent dizzy deeds in the West Indies – in three tests of 1971 in England, he was included in the Rest of the World team (along with Farokh Engineer and Bishen Singh Bedi from India, Intikhab Alam and Zaheer Abbas from Pakistan) which played five full-length 'internationals' and other matches in Australia in 1971–72. In view of the fact that each would soon be regarded as the top batsman of his country, it is interesting to note that neither Zaheer Abbas nor Gavaskar impressed very much on their first trip to Australia. Zaheer did somewhat better in the international matches, totalling 261 in nine innings, which included knocks of 51, 86 and 73. Gavaskar just crossed two hundred in eight trips, with a top score of 68 not out. This was the only time he crossed fifty in that series against Dennis Lillee (who got him out four times; Zaheer once), Graham Mackenzie (both once each), Bob Massie (Gavaskar once; Zaheer twice), Kerry O'Keefe (Gavaskar once; Zaheer twice), and Terry Jenner (both once each). At the Melbourne 'Test' they switched roles and Zaheer opened the batting while Gavaskar went in at number five. Had Gavaskar stuck it out longer in the second innings, he would have seen some parts of Sobers' great 254 at close quarters. The other memorable experience he brought back from Australia was his meeting with Sir Donald Bradman.

Back home, therefore, skeptics – especially in northern and eastern India – waited not only for Vishwanath but now also for Gavaskar to prove themselves finally. Vishwanath provided conclusive evidence at home in 1974–75 (when the West Indies were here) and Gavaskar abroad in 1975–76 (when India toured New Zealand and the West Indies) that their early successes were not false dawns. Neither had been notably productive in test matches against England either in 1971 or in 1974, and British critics were characteristically patronising in their praise. Under tremendous pressure to produce his 1971 Caribbean form in England later that year, Gavaskar totalled only 144 (average 24) in six test innings, crossing fifty only twice. Vishwanath's tally was fractionally superior, 128 at 25.60, but his 68 in the first innings at Lord's was a timely prop while his 33 in three hours in the second innings at the Oval inched India towards victory. Vishwanath had very much outshone Gavaskar in the first half of the tour programme, suggesting that his subtle and varied art was more effective in dealing with the vagaries of English wickets than Gavaskar's more candid craft. In one spell between 30 June and 17 July, Vishwanath recorded 100 not out vs Robins' XI, 0 and 115 not out vs Kent, 90 vs Warwick, 52 and 5 vs Glamorgan, 122 vs Hampshire—his most purple patch ever on tour with India. He did not however reach one thousand runs (aggregating 938 at 40.78) on this trip. Gavaskar did (1141 at 43.88) with large innings in the last two matches—194 vs Worcester, 128 vs Pearce's XI, the latter struck quite unusually for him in 155 minutes with 10 fours and 4 sixes. Their 1974 trip to England must have disappointed them greatly. Gavaskar didn't notch a hundred until the seventh match (104 vs Lancashire), Vishwanath not until the ninth (103 vs Northants). Neither was able to stave off the three–nil drubbing inflicted by England. Their best efforts were at Manchester, where Gavaskar (101 and 58) finally hit a century at last after a gap of 16 test innings and 35 restive months. Vishwanath (40 and 50) partnered him in a fourth-wicket stand of 73 in the first innings, and his series total of 200 (average 33.32) was comparable in meagreness to Gavaskar's 217 (average 36.15). In between, the 1972–73 home series with England failed to show up these two as the batting mainstays they had promised to become. Two of the first three tests were won by India without any help from Gavaskar (12 and 8; 18 and 2; 20 and 0 not out) and little from Vishwanath (27 and 3; 3 and 34; 37 and 0). They did help to draw the last two tests (Gavaskar 69 at Kanpur; 67 at Bombay) and secure the series. Of the two, Vishwanath performed distinctly better. When India, trailing by 40 runs in the first innings, were 39 for four on the last day at Kanpur, Vishwanath quelled all panic with a calm and unbeaten 75. Given a little more time, he could easily have broken the jinx of not reaching three figures again in a test match after having done so at his first appearance—on this same ground, three years ago. His 113 at Bombay settled this matter and raised his series total (365) well above Gavaskar's (284).

However, the years between 1970 and 1974 witnessed the entrenchment of their high potential in domestic cricket. Gavaskar marked his debut in the Duleep Trophy with 101 vs East Zone at Jamshedpur. His relish of eastern India bowling was made even more manifest that season in Ranji Trophy matches during innings of 282 (in seven hours) vs Bihar and 157 (in over six hours) vs Bengal, which gave him a tally of 495 (average 123.75). Vishwanath hit his first Irani Trophy hundred in 1971–72, a matchwinning second-innings effort which enabled the Rest of India to defeat Bombay. His Ranji Trophy matches of 1973–74 fetched 584 runs (average 53.09), including 140 vs Tamil Nadu and 162 vs Bombay. The latter occasion saw Bombay losing a match in this tournament after fifteen years. Karnataka went on to defeat Rajasthan for their first championship, at third try, despite Vishwanath falling for 15 and 0. At this point in their careers – and on their 1974 performance in England – it was still not clear who would serve Indian cricket better and longer. Gavaskar was plainly the kind of batsman who dug deep and took roots whenever he could, while Vishwanath just as obviously preferred to wave and flutter on the boughs.

The Bangalore boy forged ahead during 1974–75, the season which brought the West Indies (minus Sobers or Kanhai, Hall or Griffith, but plus Fredericks and Viv Richards, Boyce, Julien and Roberts) under Clive Lloyd to India. The Irani Trophy match this year at Ahmedabad found the little but-not-yet masters on opposite sides as usual. After Karnataka had scored 359 (Vishwanath 52), Gavaskar carried his bat (156 not out in 408 minutes) through the Rest of India first innings of 307. The likely outcome now secure, Vishwanath indulged himself in a double century (200 not out in 345 minutes; 29 fours and 2 sixes) out of Karnataka's second innings total of 314 for two declared. The West Indians began their programme with a match against West Zone at Pune. Gavaskar scrutinised the visitors' bowling during an opening stand of 144 in 142 minutes with Sudhir Naik (whose 65 and 68 not out in this game would bring him back into the test eleven). Gavaskar had struck 11 fours and 2 sixes in his 81 when he was run out—a mode of dismissal rare for him. One match later West Indies were in Hyderabad to play South Zone, who posted 313 for five on the first day and declared. The fireworks came from Jayaprakash (50) and Brijesh Patel (106 not out) but the altar was laid by Vishwanath's five-hour-long innings of 114, part of which went into the fifth-wicket stand of 210 runs with Patel.

Thus Vishwanath was in good trim for the test series, in which Gavaskar had to miss three matches because of a finger injury and India were two down by the time the third test began. From this point onwards Vishwanath, seemed to be batting at his end as well as at Gavaskar's, while India won at Calcutta, then levelled the series at Madras. Vishwanath concentrated on taming Andy Roberts (who collected 32 wickets at 18.28 from this series) and outwitting Lance Gibbs (24 wickets at 21.62). Trimming no frills from his batting but applying just that much more discrimination than usual, Vishwanath scored 52 (in 199 minutes) and 139 (in 376 minutes) at Calcutta, 97 not out (228 minutes) and 46 (253 minutes) at Madras, 95 (283 minutes) and 17 at Bombay. The finest of these essays was his first innings effort at Madras where India were two down for 21 when Vishwanath entered, then six down for 76, before he found a foothold. Even Chandrasekhar was inspired to stay in for half an hour while the last wicket added 21 runs and the total reached 190, leaving Vishwanath undefeated with 97.

Gavaskar announced his return to the side in the final test at Bombay with a reassuring 86 (15 fours), which Vishwanath topped with his 95 though with three chances. Vishwanath's series aggregate of 568 (average 63.11), far more than double the next highest (Engineer 222, Gaekwad 220), bore testimony to the lonely eminence he had achieved this season. The pocket-size performers opposed each other again at the end of the season in the Ranji Trophy final. Bombay won, but Vishwanath (144 and 70) again outscored Gavaskar (96 not out) who, however, had once again injured his damaged finger.

The finger healed and Gavaskar restored the balance in 1975–76. The Sri Lankan bowlers bore the brunt of Gavaskar's reclamation of sovereignty. He (203) and Vishwanath (117) plundered their bowling at Hyderabad in a second-wicket assault of 215 runs in 177 minutes, their longest ever association in an international contest. Typically, Vishwanath relented after he had crossed his hundred (with one six and 15 fours) but Gavaskar did not until he had reached a double century. The same form and run-hunger fetched Gavaskar three successive Ranji Trophy hundreds this season – 112 vs Gujarat, 190 vs Maharashtra, 171 vs Saurashtra – before the Indian team departed for the double tour of New Zealand and the West Indies. Standing in for Bedi as captain in the first test at Auckland, Gavaskar celebrated with 116 (this test century coming after a gap of eighteen months) and also by winning the match. India drew the second test at Christchurch with Vishwanath (83 and 79) struggling alone against the odds of bad weather and the spirited bowling of Collinge and Dayle Hadlee. Both failed at Wellington, where New Zealand won by an innings when India collapsed for 81 to the other Hadlee, Richard (seven for 23 in 8.3 overs).

Returning to the Caribbean four years after his famous debut there, Gavaskar did not repeat those prodigal feats but reserved his best for Port of Spain. After Bedi had put the West Indies in and disposed of them for 241 (Bedi five for 82), Gavaskar set about building up a position of strength from which the opposition could be harassed. Early departures at the other end notwithstanding, he stayed 480 minutes for his 156 (only 13 fours) and it was not until the fifth wicket – 204 with Brijesh Patel (115 not out) – that he found somebody to stay in with him. Declaring at 402 for five, India chased West Indies (215 for eight) throughout the final day and partly wrote off the humiliation of the innings defeat suffered in the first test at Bridgetown. Whoever rescheduled the third test at Port of Spain had not taken into account Gavaskar's pronounced partiality for that wicket, which other Indian batsmen found equally partisan on the present occasion. Shortly after tea on the fourth day Clive Lloyd declared his second innings with a lead of 402 runs. This was methodically whittled down by Gavaskar (69 for the first wicket with Gaekwad, 108 for the second wicket with Mohinder Amarnath) while he scored 102. Mohinder took over the job in his 85, adding 159 for the third wicket with Vishwanath, and Vishwanath (112), then 56 for the fourth wicket with Patel. To add to the drama, first Vishwanath and then Mohinder ran themselves out with the mandatory overs in progress. Happily, Brijesh Patel was still in the mood and hit off the remaining runs to bring India home by six wickets. For only the second time in test cricket history, a side batting last had scored more than 400 runs and won. The West Indies selectors took serious measures to prevent a similar thing happening again. Holding and Daniel as well as Julien and Holder were turned on full blast in the final test at Kingston and three Indian batsmen retired hurt on the second day. On the first day, India had yielded only Gavaskar's wicket (for 66) while collecting 178 runs—much of it deposited during the opening stand of 138 between him and Gaekwad.

Gavaskar (with 266 runs in the New Zealand series and 390 in the West Indies) returned home with more test runs on the twin tour than Vishwanath (197 and 253), and thus resumed his lead over the latter. Adversaries again in the Duleep Trophy during 1976–77, Vishwanath (14 and 53) had no reply – except catching Gavaskar off Chandrasekhar – to Gavaskar's marathon 228, for which he batted eight and a half hours. Perhaps he was getting his eye in for the whole season, which would contain a two-series home programme. At the same deliberate pace, Gavaskar batted four and a half hours for 119 (with 29 fours) in the first test at Bombay against New Zealand. It was his first test century on home soil, slow but solid, giving us the full portrait of what we would see and grow to expect in so many test matches at home. In contrast, Vishwanath surprised with the ease and speed of his 103 against New Zealand at Kanpur, played almost by touch in indifferent light. It occupied him 150 minutes, during which 163 runs were added for the third wicket although his partner was the plodding Gaekwad. Another felicitous knock of 87 at Madras promised that Vishwanath was well set for a glad season. His 324 runs (at 64.80) off the New Zealand bowlers were generally of a higher order than Gavaskar's 259 (at 43.17). But the Mysore charmer completely mislaid his touch in the five tests that followed against Tony Greig's team. Except for that 79 not out in the fourth test at Bangalore – which India won after having lost the first three running – Vishwanath batted so poorly that he collected only 96 runs from nine other innings. Gavaskar, too, performed well below expectation, his series aggregate of 394 getting a belated boost with the century he scored in the final test at Bombay. Over these 108 runs – his tenth test hundred but only the second at home – he spent more than a day, proving more to himself than to others that even in reduced circumstances he had qualified to become India's batting vanguard as well as mainstay.

Vishwanath challenged the latter distinction in Australia, which he toured for the first time in 1977–78. Gavaskar had been there with the World XI in 1971–72. Now playing his first series for India against Australia, he reeled off a century in each of the first three tests. Each, curiously, came in the second innings following first innings failures—3 and 113; 4 and 127; 0 and 118. Vishwanath took longer to warm up, then punctuated the last with knocks of 59 and 54, 79, 89 and 73. At the end of the series, without having got to a hundred in any innings, he posted an aggregate (473 at 52.55) which was slightly better than Gavaskar's (450 at 50.00). In the second innings at Melbourne they batted briefly together, putting on 98 runs in under two hours—a display of modern Indian batting at its most cultivated. This season Gavaskar skipped the Ranji Trophy programme altogether, but Vishwanath returned home from Australia with appetite still unsated. Appearing only in the knock-out stage matches, he went from 82 vs Bihar to 118 and 8 vs Delhi to 247 vs Uttar Pradesh in the final at Mohan Nagar, raising his hoard in the tournament to 3320 runs (while Gavaskar remained at 2880, but at a superior average).

The balance swung back in Gavaskar's favour during the test matches of 1978–79 when India toured Pakistan, followed by the West Indians' tour of India. Neither his 97 (and Chetan Chauhan's 93; their opening stand of 192) at Lahore, nor his brace of hundreds at Karachi (111 and 137) could save these matches for India. But they raised his series total to 447 (at 89.40). Vishwanath totalled nearly two hundred less (249 at 49.80), despite a leisurely 145 in six hours at Faisalabad; two of these hours were spent in Gavaskar's company in a third-wicket stand of 101. Against West Indies on home wickets Gavaskar came close to repeating what he had done to them on their wickets in 1971. First a long-winded 205 with 2 sixes and 29 fours in the opening contest of the six-test series at Bombay. It occupied all but twenty minutes of seven hours, delighted the adoring home crowd, and gave ominous promise of what was to come. He seemed set for another century in the second innings and got to 73 in a different mode—brisk and opportunistic, with the opening stand of 153 (Chauhan 84) coming in even time.

Out off the first ball (c Shivnaraine b Clarke) in the second test at Bangalore, the third time in succession Clarke had got him,

Gavaskar must have spent the rest of the match (India did not bat again) in planning how he would make up at Calcutta. He rather overdid such making up, scoring for the third time a century in either innings of a test match (107 and 182 not out). But for a second innings declaration that became necessary, Gavaskar could easily have reached two hundred and an even more remarkable feat (century and double century in the same test) for an unprecedented second time. What he achieved instead was an unfinished record second-wicket partnership (for India against any country) of 344 with Dilip Vengsarkar (157 not out, his first century in tests). Meanwhile Vishwanath, who had compensated for Gavaskar's blob at Bangalore with 70 of his own, repeated such compensation at Madras where Gavaskar was dismissed for 4 and 1 (in the second innings again by Clarke). India were 11 for two in reply to West Indies' 228 when Vishwanath entered; when he left, last out at 255, he had got to 124 and put India in the lead. Whether or not inspired, the timely repair wrought by him may have contributed to India winning this match—the only one of six to be decided. Gavaskar, with one more hundred – 120 at Delhi – finished with a series-average of 91.50 for 732 runs. Vishwanath, too, carved one more stylish century – his eighth in tests, 179 at Kanpur – and totalled 497 (at 71.00) for the series. He would have to remain content, it seemed, as second fiddle hereafter.

When India went to England in 1979 – for the Prudential Cup matches, to be followed by a four-test series – it was Venkatraghavan and not Gavaskar who led the side, with Vishwanath as deputy leader. Apparently India's greatest run-getter in tests was being reprimanded for having considered a Kerry Packer offer. He could not very well be left out altogether, but it was an unhappy side which lost all its Prudential Cup matches (including the one with Sri Lanka) and drew four country fixtures prior to the first test at Edgbaston. Here England amassed 633 for five declared (David Gower 200 not out, Geoff Boycott 155) and India went down by an innings, despite Gavaskar's 61 and 68, Vishwanath's 78 and 51. In the second test at Lord's, India were bundled out for 96 (Gavaskar topscoring with 42) in the first innings but saved the match when Vishwanath engineered a second-innings recovery by placing his 113 alongside Vengsarkar's 103 in a second-wicket stand of 210. Rain robbed two and a half days' play at Leeds and both sides batted only once. Gavaskar had just enough time (242 minutes, actually) to score 78 after India had lost three wickets for 12. The Oval Test saw India struggle to 202 in reply to England's 305 in the first innings. Part of the struggle was borne, as usual, by Vishwanath who came in at two down for 9 and scored 62. Mike Brearley's second innings declaration left India 438 runs behind and 445 minutes (plus 20 mandatory overs) of batting ahead. Even when Gavaskar and Chauhan (80) staged a record (India vs England) opening of 213 runs, nothing more remarkable seemed in the offing. But when Gavaskar and Vengsarkar (52) put on 153 for the second wicket, India seemed poised for an incredible feat that was less than one hundred runs away. Gavaskar had put behind his personal hundred long ago (in 242 minutes) and was moving irresistibly towards the most significant double century of his career so far. At this point (366 for two) there occurred what will always be regarded as a tactical error. Instead of Vishwanath coming in at his customary place – and perhaps accompanying Gavaskar on their most memorable journey together in the middle – in came Kapil Dev, obviously with instructions to hasten the end. After a couple of ambitious swishes, Kapil was caught in the deep without scoring and this seemed to throw India's drive to victory out of gear. Gavaskar reached 221 (389 minutes, 23 fours) before surrendering his wicket at 389. Now Vishwanath entered and immediately drove Hendrick to the cover boundary, as if to promise that he would easily complete what Gavaskar had begun. But Vishwanath was given out to a doubtful decision and all hopes vanished again. At the end India fell short of a win by eight runs—which Gavaskar, alone, had made conceivable.

That innings finally convinced English spectators that Gavaskar was equal to his reputation. It completed his thousand runs on the tour and 542 (at 77.43) in the tests—the latter figure outstripped Vishwanath's 341 (at 48.71) by about the number of runs Gavaskar had scored in that outbreak at the Oval. Far from being content to play second fiddle, against the Australian visitors of 1979–80, Vishwanath (518 runs at 74.00) bettered Gavaskar's returns (425 at 53.12). He capped Gavaskar's two centuries (115 at Delhi; 123 at Bombay) with his own 161 not out at Bangalore and 131 at Delhi (where he and Gavaskar put on a 159-run third-wicket stand). A third hundred from Vishwanath almost materialised at Calcutta, where he made his only mistake when he was 96. He stayed on par with Gavaskar for the first three tests against the Pakistanis who arrived in India even as the Australians were about to depart. From the fourth test at Kanpur onwards, however, Gavaskar soared (337 out of his final total of 529) while Vishwanath sank (61 out of his final 228). The latter produced not a single large effort like Gavaskar's 166 in 593 minutes at Madras, where India won their second match of the series. The Golden Jubilee Test with England at Bombay on 15–19 February 1980 saw Gavaskar yield his sceptre to Vishwanath on the plea that he (Gavaskar) would not be available for the forthcoming tour of the West Indies (which was eventually deferred). During this match Vishwanath exercised his new-found authority in an unusual manner by recalling Bob Taylor after he had been given out, caught behind, by the umpire.

Future historians may point out that during 1978–80, India twice faced Australia and once each West Indies and England while these countries had refused to call upon their 'World Series' players, hence the copious runs scored by Gavaskar and Viswanath in these tests were made under sub-normal conditions. This point was brought up again when Gavaskar was about to surpass Bradman's record of 29 test centuries. The answer to such thinking should have been provided[4] by the runs Gavaskar as well as Vishwanath earned off the Packerite bowlers of Pakistan in 1978 and 1979. Yet the fact remains that both were woefully short of runs when India went to Australia in 1980–81 and had to contend with Dennis Lillee and other 'World Series' bowlers. Vishwanath, who mustered 213 runs (at 35.50) in three tests, was known to have had lean patches earlier. But Gavaskar's 118 runs (at 19.66) from six innings – with which he finished sixth in the averages, below even Kirmani – was as inconceivable as it was unprecedented. His frustration with himself boiled over on the fourth day of the third test at Melbourne, and nearly caused a situation without parallel in test cricket history.

This match began with India, put into bat by Greg Chappell, challenging Vishwanath to repair early damages (22 for two, then

[4] Another kind answer was given by the foreign commentator (was it Richie Benaud?) who pointed out that Gavaskar never batted against Indian bowling in test matches—as Bradman or Weekes did and hit four centuries in five tests.

99 for five). With nearly a dozen successive failures trailing him Vishwanath remembered who he was and took root for about four and a half hours for his 114 (11 fours) – which, incidentally, was his first ever test century in Australia – and nudged his side's total along to 237. Australia replied with 419, gaining a lead which seemed formidable until Gavaskar and Chauhan crossed 150 for the first wicket in the second innings. Gavaskar in particular (his earlier efforts in the series had terminated at 0, 10, 23, 5, 10) was beginning to promise some large design when he, (on 70) was declared out leg-before-wicket to Lillee. He was sure he had played the ball and, in a hitherto unheard of form of protest in a test match, he asked Chauhan to walk off the field with him. Luckily for India, the team manager intervened before Chauhan actually left the field and the crisis was averted. Gavaskar apologised later for this incident which, in fact, lost its punch the very next day when Kapil Dev (five for 28 in 16.4 overs) shot Australia out for 83 and won India the match.

Gavaskar (aggregate 126) and Vishwanath (64) fared even more poorly in the five test innings they had in New Zealand, and run-famine persisted with the latter in the early part of the 1981–82 season at home. Gavaskar reassured himself (50 and 102 not out vs the Rest in the Irani Trophy match; 164 not out vs Central Zone in the Duleep Trophy tournament), thus seemed ready and willing to take on England for the sequence of nine tests with them that had been scheduled, six of these at home. Once the first test was won at Bombay, it was clearly in India's interest to play safe in the remaining matches – but it produced a very dull series. Vishwanath joined the holding-on operation a little late but contributed 466 runs (at 58.25) to its success and Gavaskar gave 500 (at 62.50). Both played their temporally longest test innings – Gavaskar (172) for 708 minutes in the second test at Bangalore; Vishwanath (222) for 638 minutes in the fifth test at Madras, including a third-wicket stand of 316 with Yashpal Sharma. Vishwanath had given notice earlier of runs in the making. Facing England's total of 476 for nine declared in the third test at Delhi, India two wickets for 41 and Vishwanath entered sniffing battle; when Gavaskar (46) left at 89, the battle was truly joined. Vishwanath's 114 provided the base of resistance on which India rallied to reach 487. The series won – his second as India's captain – Gavaskar went on a spree in the Ranji Trophy semi-final against Bengal. Bombay overtook Bengal's first innings total (252) without losing a wicket, the opening stand erected by Gavaskar and Ghulam Parkar (156) mounting to 421 (which surpassed the 405 put on by Chetan Chauhan and Madhu Gupte for Maharashtra against Vidarbha in 1972, but falling short of the 451 put on by Roger Binny and Sanjay Desai for Karnataka against Kerala). Gavaskar batted on remorselessly for about eight hours to score 340, his first triple century (and only the sixth altogether) in the tournament. His Ranji Trophy aggregate of 4381 (in 77 innings) strode ahead of Vishwanath's 4180 (in 92 innings) and would remain so hereafter.

What was denied to Gavaskar in 1979 – captaincy of the Indian team touring England – was awarded to him in 1982. He celebrated it in the very first county fixture, against Warwickshire at Birmingham, by hitting 4 sixes and 20 fours in his second innings knock of 172. But England remained on top in all three tests and won the first one convincingly. This was at Lord's, where Gavaskar (48 and 24) had the unusual experience of getting out twice on the same day. He fell for 2 at Manchester in India's only innings there and could not bat at all at the Oval after getting his leg in the way of an Ian Botham off-drive. Vice-captain Vishwanath fared somewhat better after failing in the first test (1 and 3). When India were robbed of three wickets for 25 in the second test, Vishwanath (54) showed night-watchman Kirmani (58) how to bolt the door. In the third test Vishwanath gave two light-fingered exhibitions (56 and 75 not out) that restored our faith in him.

That faith, alas, was rudely betrayed a few months later in Pakistan when Vishwanath was reduced to no more than 134 runs from as many as eight trips to the crease. Gavaskar survived more on will-power than on willow-prowess (434 in ten innings), but there was almost no respite for his brother-in-law. The countdown for Vishwanath probably began in Madras at Sri Lanka's official induction into test cricket in September 1982. Here he surrendered his wicket rather carelessly to D. S. de Silva for 9, then to Asanatha de Mel for 2. As opposed to such leniency, Gavaskar taught Sri Lankan bowlers several lessons in his long 155 during which he put on 156 runs for the first wicket with Arun Lal (63) and 173 for the second with Vengsarkar (90). On tour in Pakistan, from the moment Vishwanath flirted with Imran

Khan outside the off-stump at Lahore (to be nabbed by Wasim Bari for 1), he was a doomed man. Flags should have been at half-mast for Vishwanath as the second test at Karachi concluded. Even granting Imran's deadly scythe of an in-swing, only something resembling thrombosis could have caused Vishwanath to freeze in padding up, bat upraised, to a ball that hurtled in and bowled him horribly. He tried, in the third test, to regain credibility and reached a dogged 53 before he was beaten and bowled by a Mudassar Nazar floater. But he surrendered tamely to Imran again (for the third time) at Hyderabad, this time with his leg in front before he had scored. It seemed increasingly clear that his bat and feet and eyes were no longer in reliable conjunction. He did not need to bat in the fifth test; at his only try in the sixth, Mudassar diddled him out again, now for 10. Those who watched this sad episode were the last to have seen Vishwanath batting in a test match.[5]

The statistical outline of his career reminds us that he had played 91 test matches from 155 innings of which he garnered 6080 runs (average 41.93). This included 14 centuries (highest 222, his only double century) and 36 innings of over fifty (including three that crossed ninety); he also held 62 catches. In the Ranji Trophy tournament, where he lingered for a few more seasons, his aggregate stands at 5653 runs from 136 innings (average 47.04), with 15 centuries (two of them doubles; highest 247). These are impressive enough, especially the close correspondence between his test record and his domestic performance. But even more opulent figures would not tell us how he used to fill our eyes with pleasure whenever he stayed at the crease for any length of time. Bearing the name that he does, many times over a span of fifteen years he was truly lord of bowlers threatening his *vishwa*.

[1983]

---

[5] For the rest of Gavaskar's career, see the chapter, "Running Over" in my *Matched Winners*, New Delhi: Orient Longman, 1996.

An Abbasid Monarch

Images of royalty come naturally to mind as one watches him make runs. On television from Pakistan, however, with viewing interfered with by cigarette-manufacturing sponsors, one is likely to think of him as a king-size batsman—think even of his batting as fitted with a filter, so smoothly does he draw on his strokes. But years from now, when his reign has passed into history, cricket historians will surely speak of him as an Abbasid monarch who founded not a line of kings but a dynasty of regal innings.

Zaheer Abbas's name is pronounced with due reverence these days by Indian cricket-followers, but I wonder how well he was known to this country until test cricket between India and Pakistan was resumed in 1978. On me at least the name had made little impression until I saw a cricket book on one hundred all-time cricket greats, consisting of full-page illustrations arranged in alphabetical order of names of those selected. The hundredth name was that of Zaheer Abbas. For a moment I thought he had been selected because his name fitted the final letter of the alphabet. But then I recalled, lurking somewhere behind exalted memories of what the India team had achieved in England in 1971, the splash made earlier the same year in the same country by Zaheer Abbas with his 274 for Pakistan at Edgbaston—in what was his first test against England and only his second against any national team.

I also remembered then that he was selected for the Rest of the World team to tour Australia in 1971–72. Our own champion, Sunil Gavaskar, was also in that team, but neither performed particularly well on their first outing down under. Zaheer did somewhat better, totalling 261 runs in 9 trips to the crease, which included innings of 51, 86 and 73. Gavaskar just topped two hundred in eight trips, with a top score of 68 not out, the only time he crossed fifty that season against Lillee (who got his wicket four times; Zaheer's once), Mackenzie (both once each), Massie (once Gavaskar; twice Zaheer), O'Keefe (once Gavaskar; twice Zaheer), and Jenner (both once each). At Melbourne they switched roles and Zaheer opened the batting while Gavaskar went in at number five—thus probably saw from close quarters a bit of Sobers' 254 there.

Both India and Pakistan visited England in 1974, and again a comparative study of productivity against the same bowlers would put Zaheer (48 and 19; 1 and 1; 240 and 15) ahead of Gavaskar (101 and 58; 49 and 5; 0 and 4). By then or soon after, Zaheer Abbas was an established English county batsman with Gloucestershire. And since then, he has broken or set so many batting records there that only Walter Hammond's feats for this county remain comparable. Pakistan did not visit England in 1979 when India did, so Gavaskar's best ever series in the motherland of cricket (61 and 68; 42 and 59; 13 and 221) – in the final flourish of which he nearly carved a fantastic victory off his own bat – went unmatched by Zaheer. However, to Gloucester's seven-wicket win over the touring team, Zaheer contributed 59 and 53 not out, as against Gavaskar's 116 and 30.

The comparison is neither necessary nor fair—not necessary because they are both great in their own rights, not fair because they are such different batsmen. The point that has to be made, however, is that while Gavaskar has had only one wholly bad series for ten years at home or abroad, Zahir failed against the West Indies at home (1974–75; 71 runs in 4 innings and 1980; 57 in 5 innings), against New Zealand at home (1976; 60 in 5 innings), against Australia away (1978; 117 in 4 innings), against Australia at home (1980; 45 in 3 innings). The further point is that he seems to reserve his best to be employed against England in England, and does the same against India in Pakistan. In fact, in home series, he has scored prolifically only off Indian bowlers.

Like most monarchs on this subcontinent, Zaheer Abbas has been erratic in his dispensations. But in purely cricket terms, there is some unresolved riddle in his career or capabilities, which experts who have seen him play elsewhere may one day like to solve. Common cricket-watchers like me, who have seen him on television from Pakistan and in real life on our own wickets, find it difficult to match and make a whole of these experiences. Within a year of that commanding performance of his when Indo-Pak test cricket was resumed at Faisalabad (179 and 96; 235 not out and 34 not out; 42; 583 runs in 5 innings; average 194.33), he crossed fifty only four times at sixteen attempts on his 1979–80 tour of India, and hundred only once. He trotted so leanly in the tests – 40 and 31 not out; 3 and 50; 2 and 11; 5; 0 and 15 – that he declared himself unfit for the final test at Calcutta. And now two years later, he has already taken a thousand runs off our bowlers in two months, mainly in the form of six centuries, of which again three were in successive test innings. What explains this blowing hot and cold, this plunging trough and crest?

If there is some weakness in Zaheer's batting, Bishen Bedi and his cohorts never discovered it in 1978, nor have Kapil Dev and his co-labourers found it so far on the present tour. Yet in between, on our own wickets, every other Indian bowler, appeared to know about it. Not once in fourteen dismissals (out of sixteen innings) was he declared out leg-before-wicket; caught eight times, bowled four times, once each stumped and caught and bowled were the various means of subduing him. In eight test innings, Kapil Dev got him five times (twice bowled), Roger Binny twice (once bowled) and Dilip Doshi once (stumped). Outside the tests, left-handers of various pace and direction (Suresh Shastri, Dhiraj Parsana, Vasudeva) got him out five times.

No pattern emerges from such analysis. Does Kapil have his number? Or are left-arm spinners more likely to dismiss him? Neither conclusion can be drawn from the way he has been batting on the current tour of Pakistan by India. He seems to have resumed at Lahore in November 1982 where he had left off on the same ground in October 1978. As seen on television, the only perceptible difference is that he used to be less productive then against bowling aimed at his leg-stump. That inhibition is gone now, so much so that four test innings have already produced 612 runs, whereas in the earlier series five had produced 583.

Born in July 1947, he could easily have been in a cricket team conjured up by Salman Rushdie, and played for rather than against India. On whichever side of the border one sits as a spectator, it is difficult not to enjoy watching him at the batting crease. With what minimum fuss he gets down to the job, a soundless single or two before an effortless crack for four announcing that he is with it now. A tall man, he stoops a little on guard, glasses glinting as if with energy of their own to get the bowler into the correct focus. But as he moves to address the ball, with a lovely lurch of back that brings him upright, his bat seems to know what it will do to the ball. So seldom do bowlers (at least, those from India) compel him to change his mind that Zaheer appears to have read the ball before it has been bowled. Very little strain or effort is attached to whatever he does out there, which explains why we respond so readily and gladly to his batsmanship. He makes it look all so easy and simple that we could all aspire to bat like him. That must also be the essence of kingship—even while remaining superior, a king makes you want to be like him.

More likely than not, the formal inauguration of an innings by Zaheer Abbas will have been a stroke played off the forward foot and with a shot through the covers. That generic term for a fielding territory ought to get reversed while Zaheer is batting, so invariably and with such frequency does he *un*cover this region and lay it bare with shots ranging widely from backward point to wayward mid-off. The utter clarity of his off-side strokes shines like a beacon, showing up the ball bowled at him—not necessarily a bad ball, because he is quite capable of scoring off good balls as well.

Third man and fine-leg may as well enjoy a breather because he doesn't go in much for delicate late-cuts or tender leg-glances. But next over these two fieldsmen will be on the hop if they have the misfortune to get posted to mid-on and mid-off respectively, and Zaheer has crossed over. Even that most exacting of shots, the on-drive, he hits without any air of difficulty, much to the despair of left-arm spinners who hope to keep him quiet by bowling at his leg-stump. Lately he has added a sweep to his weaponry, and it fetches revenue off deliveries he may not have scored from four years ago.

Whether he scores twenty or two hundred, there is never any suggestion of unscheduled haste or undue force while he is in the middle. Such impulses find no place in the balance and sanity of his batting, bearing as it does an old-fashioned courtliness which must disarm bowlers even as he reaches his next hundred. In running between wickets he shambles, unwilling perhaps to hurry in view of the hours ahead of him. Meanwhile runs come to him as if by prerogative, in accordance with some mundane right of kings of the crease.

Like all kings, again – who are but human – he does falter now and then, lose a battle or two, retreat altogether until the next campaign. We saw this happen – and many of us were secretly disappointed – on Pakistan's last tour of India. More recently we saw what happened on the first afternoon of the fifth test at Lahore. The first ball he faced he drove with swift certainty to the long-on boundary. This was a ball from Maninder Singh, who had just deceived a well-set Javed Miandad and prised him out. Young Maninder has, in fact, been the only Indian bowler in the current series to raise a ruffle or two sometimes on Zaheer's clear brow. But here the fledgling spinner was quickly put in his place, as was Kapil after the tea-break when he swung one away and not too short of length—to be cracked past cover-point for four.

A typical and magnificent shot this, which we could reconstruct thanks to the television replay. First, his right foot came back a little; then his left foot went out and across; his body bowed a little from the waist, left shoulder coming round; then his bat, very little off the vertical or straight, struck the ball just after it had passed the front pad about knee-height but still a foot or two away. A less self-confident batsman would probably have played back and essayed a square-cut with a horizontal bat, or perhaps not played a shot at all.

Was it royal overconfidence, then, that made Zaheer repeat the stroke off Kapil's next delivery? This was closer to the stumps and may have swung away a trifle. Another batsman would have been contented to defend. But Zaheer drove again, snicked, and turned away from Kirmani's triumphant toss of the snared catch. That micro-second of misjudgement tumbled Zaheer from his throne, changed his scepter back into a bat, the palace to which he was returning into a cricket pavilion.

[1983]

Imran's Ten: The Mystery

The autobiography of Imran Khan will be published in England in November. Will he have revealed there the secret of what he bowled at our batsmen last season, especially at Karachi and at Hyderabad (Sind)? It couldn't have been a mere cricket ball that he hurled with such telling effect. There was a rumour a couple of months ago that the former Pakistani cricketer (now an opposition-minded lawyer), Aftab Gul, had a couple of SAM missiles parked in his backyard. Did Imran also import a miniaturised heat or sweat seeking weapon that can be concealed within a cricket ball and programmed to hit the stumps unstoppably?

What we saw of those two spells of devastation was on television. We did not have the batsmen there to resist the onslaught. Nor did we have a John Arlott to explain at the time what was happening, nor a Neville Cardus to empurple in prose ever after on what had happened. Thanks to television, each of those ten wickets Imran got he took twice over again in slow motion, and each showing was more mystifying than the one before. Perhaps some creature from outer space took possession of the communications satellite and directed malign beams at Gavaskar and company, causing them to lose sight of the ball and to forget how to use the bat.

Yet, on that Christmas day afternoon of 1982 at Karachi, Imran in his opening spell had induced only care and not myopia or paralysis in our batsmen. Even the fresher Arun Lal saw him well and played him squarely—in fact, somewhat better than Gavaskar did. Then, with Vengsarkar in and putting his best foot forward, Imran would probably have given up and away to another bowler in his second spell had he not, with the last ball of his tenth over of the day, crashed through Gavaskar's defence. Four overs later he had bagged four more wickets with practically the same delivery, which will remain some sort of bowler's F-16 until somebody can tell us all about it. It is unlikely Imran can or will.

A failure of batting nerve among our batsmen has been the usual explanation. That is too simple and comprehensive an explanation to be trusted—at least, for the first debacle. If anything, the opposite may be true—namely, our batsmen got carried away by their confidence in somehow muddling through and did not bother to adjust to the given situation. Take the case of Sandeep Patil. His failure here was in what has generally led to his success—namely, a headlong cavalry charge against the visible artillery. This is how he had conquered Dennis Lillee at Adelaide and Bob Willis at Old Trafford, and there is no reason why it should not have worked here too. So up and away! A few millimetres nearer to the pitch of the ball and Patil would have punched Imran through mid-off for four and thereby broken the spell. Patil's failure then was in his having essayed his natural riposte, whereas the situation demanded an unnatural (to him) parry.

Kapil Dev too must be charged for being himself at a time requiring him to be somebody else—perhaps Vengsarkar, or even Ravi Shastri. More so when the ploy of sending Kirmani ahead of him had misfired and it was the last over of the day. Despite Imran's only too recent exhibition of marksmanship, this delivery of his to Kapil was quite clear of the stumps. Instead of letting it pass harmlessly, Kapil had no business to chop at and drag it on. Yet has he not got away with such indiscretions times without number, including those against Imran himself? Kapil paid here the penalty of not giving due regard to the man and the moment.

On thinking back it would seem that Mohinder Amarnath was the only one who did the right thing under the circumstances, inasmuch as he stuck out his left leg and hoped for the best. Batsmen at all levels of cricket do this whenever in doubt. And doubt Mohinder did create in our minds (though not in the umpire's) about whether the ball, if unobstructed, would have hit the stumps or not. Given the magnitude of Imran's inward bent at the time, it would not have been unduly charitable on the umpire's part if he had reprieved the batsman. Mohinder cannot be blamed for failing where his betters had fallen.

And who better than Gavaskar himself? At no stage of the series did he assume his familiar Reserve Bank of India role, though he tried very hard. It was strange enough at Lahore that, on 82 after five hours of dogged and at times desperate resistance, he should misjudge Sarfraz Nawaz and snick him behind the wicket. Here at Karachi it was quite incomprehensible how, with India needing him to bat through that day and the next – if possible, on the final day also – he should graft his way to 42, only to allow his defence to be violated. I recall that though his backfoot had come across, he had not played back fully. Normally his right foot goes farther back in defence and fortifies his bat, letting no chink remain. I guess that on this occasion, by letting his bat remain in the clear, he was intending either to force the ball into the covers or, if it came in even more, to deflect it to the on-side. Neither intention took into account the unprecedented breakback Imran was extracting from the pitch. In the event the ball drilled through bat and pad, with the inner-edge contact ensuring that the ball went into the stumps.

And so to Vishwanath. A long time (at least since Kanpur 1969) Shaiva like me has not yet recovered from having had to watch the downfall. There is no greater humiliation for a batsman in cricket than being bowled by a ball he has allowed to pass. To the onlooker, shouldering of arms by a batsman may seem just a frill to batting. Actually it is a contumacious act, declaring 'I am here to stay', telling the bowler 'You will have to do better than that'. What Vishwanath did here was utterly out of tune. Throughout that over he had fended frantically at Imran, survived a fairly close leg-before appeal, middled the ball only once. To the last delivery he shuffled across, humped over where he thought his off-stump was, and did not even present his bat in repulse or its semblance. Freely therefore the ball hurried on to castle him behind his back.

The debate has continued. Was it pace or cut or both or neither but some element yet to be named in cricket parlance that destroyed Indian batting that afternoon? The incontrovertible fact remained that in a matter of 25 deliveries, from which three runs were scored, Imran Khan returned five Indian batsmen not just to the pavilion but into a realm of self-doubt—where they remained even when the scene shifted to Hyderabad (Sind).

This time Imran's deed seemed far less inexplicable in terms of the success snatched and, consequently, made the batting look far more inconsequential. At Karachi he was visibly striving for a breakthrough. Once he achieved it, he simply marched through the breach he had made. But at Hyderabad he did not even have to try. As soon as he approached, the beleaguered garrison rushed out and committed 'jauhar' of the male kind not to be found in Tod's annals.

That day Hanif Mohammed, speaking as expert commentator, quite rightly rated Imran's 5 for 3 in 25 deliveries in the third test higher than his 5 for 8 in 19 deliveries in the fourth. At seaside Karachi, a dyke of defiance was slowly built up for over two hours by Gavaskar, and Vengsarkar had looked secure if unhappy. There Imran had had to overcome the spirit as well as substance of that growing fightback. Here at Hyderabad our batsmen capitulated almost before they were challenged, beaten neither in the air nor off the wicket but at the back of their own minds even before Imran bowled.

This parlous state of mind was betrayed by the way Gavaskar scooped back an easy catch off Abdul Qadir so close to the lunch interval. Normally, long before any scheduled break in play, Gavaskar downs shutters firmly. Yet here he sought chancy business. That his timing had not set itself – as it generally does – was apparent an over or two earlier when, in stabbing down a ball from Sarfraz, he was nearly taken at short-leg by Haroon Rashid. And now Gavaskar's bat was so out of control of his will that, in driving Qadir for an easy run or two, he raised a caught-and-bowled hazard. Qadir dropped the ball, after having grabbed it, probably out of sheer incredulity.

Two dollops of good luck should have presaged that our greatest run-devourer in history would now make a large feast off that rich smorgasbord of a pitch—on which, as we saw on the previous day, not more than one or two balls beat the bat. What those two pre-lunch bells actually tolled was the knell to come. Returning to the attack after a break, Imran bowled at little over half-pace what appeared to me nothing more ambitious than an arm-loosener. Predetermined to negate, Gavaskar retreated but not far enough and allowed his bat-edge to be sucked into what would otherwise have been harmless passage of the ball several off-stumps away from the one which matters. Experts observed later that Gavaskar was deceived by an in-slanted delivery which swung out after pitching. The only out-swing I discerned, even after several replays in slow motion, was the deviation in the ball's direction caused by contact with bat-edge.

Imran's pace picked up within another ball or two to near full with Vishwanath to fire at. Gavaskar could scarcely have unstrapped his various items of protection when Vishy was trudging back to the dressing room. Again experts on the spot explained differently, but I thought he was beaten by a ball which came through more quickly than he had bargained for. Fully intending to play a shot on the shuffle and from the crease as he has often done, tucking pace bowlers away to mid-wicket or square-leg, this time he missed the ball altogether and was nabbed in front. It was said that the delivery was Imran's rare leg-cutter. But that may have been a dole of mollification held out for those of us who watched dumbfounded many hundred miles away from where it was all happening.

Short men both, Gavaskar and Vishwanth must have felt smaller and smaller as the afternoon wore on and first Mohinder Amarnath, then Balwinder Sandhu, not only held Pakistani bowlers at bay but also kept the scoreboard ticking over. They did this without any panic or much aid from fortune, but simply by willingness to buckle down to the task in hand. Neither Vishwanth nor Vengsarkar gave any evidence of such willingness. The latter, though relieved by Mohinder of one-down duties, drove hopefully as if he were Sandeep Patil. The delivery may indeed have swung out a little as the commentators saw it. But what top-order test batsman has ever swung his bat in this manner at such a time and place. If Wasim Bari were asked this question that evening, he would have given several names, all Indian.

Not much can be said for or about Imran's fourth and fifth victims of this spell. Three successive days of unsuccessful bowling had robbed Kapil Dev so completely of heart that he seemed to flinch from Imran. Certainly he brought his bat down after the ball had passed. As for Syed Kirmani, he was distinctly unlucky – not that we expected him to save this traumatic day – in that his bat-pad defence was so close-knit that one of the best balls bowled by Imran that afternoon, which might have buzzed past the leg-stump after beating the bat, hit Kirmani's backleg and went into the stumps.

All these, happily, are memories of what has been and, Insha Allah, will never again be. But with Imran Khan having cried off from Pakistan's tour of India, we have been denied the opportunity of uncovering the mystery. Meanwhile, the havoc he wrought less than a year ago has blighted Gavaskar's future and terminated Vishwanath's test career, possibly that of Vengsarkar as well.

[1983]

Part II: Memories

One Magic Afternoon

On a Sunday afternoon many years ago in Poona, I strolled towards a motley crowd ringed round a cricket field, and saw over their heads that a match was in progress. A tall, dark-visaged bowler tossed up a teaser to a batsman in a sola topi whose bat, clutched perpendicularly in ungloved hands, stunted the intention of the ball even as it descended. Soon a bye-run resulted, the batsmen crossed each other leisurely, a dog ran into the field, and the umpire indicated that the over had ended.

On this pleasant and commonplace afternoon, there was apparently nothing remarkable about the batsman or the bowler, nothing remarkable about the ground, and a more casual follower of the game than I would have strolled on to discover other things to engage his eye and mind on a holiday afternoon. But I have been brought up to believe that whenever and wherever twenty-two yards of levelled turf are hemmed in by three erect stumps at either end and surrounded by thirteen cricketers and two umpires, there is no telling what might happen in that dedicated domain. So I spread out a handkerchief at a convenient spot, settled myself on it as comfortably as possible, and gave myself up to the pleasure of anticipation.

The sola-hatted batsman now occupied the other crease. His knees or elbows did not seem to bend easily, giving his movements the appearance of those of a marionette. But this did not prevent him from essaying effective strokes, a fastfooted slash behind point, a lofted pull over mid-wicket's head. Shuffling across his wicket he deflected a ball to fine-leg more by accident, it seemed, than by deliberation. From that distance I could not see his face clearly but imagined lean, seamed cheeks, eyes narrow and creased at the outer corners with long hours of watching in the sun, a stern mouth bespeaking character on the field as well as off it. Prodding the ball to square-leg the batsman set off for a single, and watching that figure trot the length of the pitch so confidently, my mind ran on farther than my eyes, beyond the opposite wicket and fielders and spectators towards events long ago....

Immediately, however, there was enough to occupy my sight, for the tall bowler was about to begin a new over. As he realigned his on-side field, there was no dispute about whose was the most commanding presence on this ground or would be, or has been, on any ground. An eye-catching six feet of him in white clothes, a dark-blue cap atop his dark face, there was enough majesty implicit in his gestures to suggest he could move the destinies of a match as easily as he moved fielders into position. He bowled. In three purposeful strides he reached the bowling crease, his left arm rose classically straight, his right arm looped up in an unbroken sweep to release the ball, till then rather lost in a huge palm, at the highest point of delivery. It was a perfectly harmless ball, pitched outside the off-stump and going through straight. But the tense post-delivery posture of the bowler, straddling the pitch on long legs, betrayed a prerogative that expects a wicket from every ball he bowled. I noted the leased aggression of that athletic frame, and regretted that I had not arrived at the match early enough to watch this person bat, for surely in batting would his entire life and character be revealed.

The mind need not entertain any such regrets, for the mind is not bound by time and place and transport facilities. I stretched out my legs, leaned back against a bank of grass, and was transformed in a moment to a spectator on the mid-off boundary at the Bombay Gymkhana ground...nearly fifty years ago.

The first official MCC team was touring India then and their fifth match (and the fifth in Bombay) was a two-day fixture against Hindus. With no result, obviously forthcoming on a cushion-paced wicket, the MCC batsmen decided to enjoy themselves. Sandham and Tate ran up quick fifties each, but G. F. Earle really set his seal upon the first day's play with an exhibition of controlled but irresistible hitting that no Indian batsman could be expected to equal. The Somerset amateur flailed more sixes (11) than fours (9) in this innings of 128, being particularly severe on L. Ramji who gave away 105 runs in 22 overs. When Hindus started batting and lost their opening pair for twenty runs, it was evident that the match would peter out into a tame draw.

But sensation took shape next day in the form of a dark whip-like man from Nagpur who sprang to retributive action without much preamble. While his colleagues came and went, this batsman reached his first fifty in even time with streamlined drives and powerful pulls. His next fifty he achieved in a fine frenzy lasting thirty minutes, having repeatedly endangered – besides limbs and lives of fieldsmen and spectators – rooftops and roads outside the ground. In a last demoniac burst he wrenched his score to 150 in another twenty-two minutes, the major strikes of this incredible innings being 13 sixes and 11 fours, before a juggling catch in the deep finally removed him. I was, alas, not yet born then, but I can content myself with imagining the savage skill and avenging delight with which this batsman tore up the English bowling and hung it in tatters on the boundary ropes. In those early days of non-violence, this display must have come as a rude reminder to the authorities of India's latent power to hit back.

The other story that I recalled, as I lolled on the grass with the sun leaning down upon the horizon, is not another tale of sound and fury, but one of more profound significance. This happened in the same season, when the MCC met a so-called 'All-India' team, consisting of players drawn from all over the country, in a three-day match at Bombay. Captained by K. M. Mistry, the home team dismissed the MCC for 362 runs and began their reply with a sizeable opening partnership between J. G. Navle and Wazir Ali. Thereafter a rot set in and it did not seem that the Indian team would reach the three-hundred mark, until the 52-year-old skipper came in at the fall of the seventh wicket and stemmed the collapse. In his work of rehabilitation the veteran left-hander found an able supporter in a Poona professor, whose off-side bias grew more and more assured as the minutes went by. The Colonel departed after the MCC score was crossed, having claimed a handsome half-century himself—three more runs than the number of years in his age. But the cricket-playing academician from Erandawana remained to publish a veritable compendium of batsmanship. Late-cutting and off-driving with superb timing, the first century-maker in India–England matches of any description batted over four hours for his 148 runs, to announce to the world that Indian cricket had 'arrived'. The batting exhibition described earlier could be explained away as a passing phenomenon, like a cloud-burst. Here was a historical product, in which the seeds of continued application and successful assimilation had borne fruit, the first fruit of the crop yet to come.

At this stage of my nostalgia, a yelp from the assembly near me brought me back to earth, and I was just in time to see mid-off picking the ball up dolefully from the ground and deduced he had dropped a catch. My tall bowler was the sufferer. His next essay was an unabashed full toss. The batsman, perhaps not yet recovered from his recent lapse, tried to play it back with a straight bat. I did not see the passage of the ball, till the bowler shot up an immensely long arm and plucked a catch out of space. In the blink of an eye the match had come to life again.

But the life was not destined to be long. Only one more wicket remained, some twenty runs still separated the sides, and my batsman of the sola topi was making a last-ditch effort. He leaped to drive a ball past the bowler, struck a venomous late-cut down to third man, then jumped out again but fatally early, and the match was over.

As the crowds converged upon the pavilion gates where the players were coming in, the tall bowler stepped aside for the batsman to precede him—a gesture that was formal yet wholly apt. I wandered away, happy in the thought that I could now tell my own children and their children that I had seen D. B. Deodhar and C. K. Nayudu in action on a cricket field.

[1970]

Bombay Burning

[The happenings at Brabourne Stadium on the late afternoon of 8 November 1969 were so unprecedented and out of character for the setting and its natural occupants that at this distance in time it is difficult to believe that they happened at all. But I was an eye-witness and cannot obliterate them from my memory. I wrote this piece that evening, hoping to convey the sensations of sick shame and fearful apprehension that I felt at the time.]

How one wishes that the smoke billowing up from the Brabourne Stadium at five-o'clock today was not real but only symbolic of the devastation of India's hopes and aspirations at the outset of a test series against Australia. The smoke, alas, was only too real and my personal despondency at the way this match has turned out was drowned in the despair which others must share with me over the behaviour of a test match crowd supposedly the most experienced and knowledgeable in India. When a chair was tossed at the incoming Australians at the end of play from one of the upper decks of the CCI pavilion, the last twist of the knife must have been felt in the ribs of genuine cricket lovers all over the country. Brabourne now enters that infamous list – along with Sabina Park (Kingston), Queen's Park Oval (Port of Spain), Eden Gardens (Calcutta) – of famous cricket grounds of the world where test matches have spawned riots.

There has been nothing riotous on the last three days, either on the field or off it, except perhaps in the first half hour of this game when Engineer and Sardesai plundered 30 runs off the first two overs each of the opening bowlers McKenzie and Connolly. Then India declined to 42 for three, were partially resuscitated by a fourth-wicket stand of 146 runs between Ashok Mankad and the younger Pataudi, and finally fell for 278 just after lunch on the second day. Australia's rejoinder, featured by

Stackpole's century and good knocks from Redpath and Walters, foreclosed at 345 today. The obvious course for India was to bat slowly and carefully for time rather than for runs, towards a draw. Any such prospect had passed well beyond the realm of probability when probability itself was torn inside out and made unrecognisable.

The mightiest tree on earth has grown from a tiny seed. Such was the incalculable relationship between Venkatraghavan's dismissal and the strenuous attempt to disband the game and/or burn down the Brabourne Stadium this evening. The inexorable progress of the disturbances reminded one of Greek tragedy. By the time Venkatraghavan did or didn't snick Connolly to Taber behind the stumps, the main battle was already over and only the formal surrender remained. Yet the morning had not shown such a day. The Australian tail dragged for 45 minutes while competent catches by Surti, Solkar and Bedi were made to restrict the Australian lead to 74 runs. When Australia bowled again, neither Engineer nor Sardesai employed any rhetoric, and for half an hour all seemed to be well. Sardesai was reported to have strained a thigh muscle, but did not seem at unease against the pace bowlers. Engineer tested his luck by swinging at and missing McKenzie, then decided to conduct himself more soberly.

The growing shape of India's reply was stunted as soon as Gleeson came on from the pavilion end in place of Connolly. Bill Lawry had obviously read the wicket much better than we could from our seats. Before we had finished discussing whether the ball would be too shiny for Gleeson to spin, he had deceived Sardesai into playing for an off-break while the ball turned the other way to graze the bat on its way into Taber's gloves. Ashok Mankad promised recovery if not retribution. He had not been particularly disturbed by Gleeson's freak spin in the first innings, and now cut him behind cover for four with a scything action. But within minutes of the lunch-break Mankad was beaten twice over, in the air as well as off the pitch, by a legbreak which knocked back the off-stump.

After lunch Borde bent bat and pad to the essential task of keeping Gleeson out of his stumps while Engineer resumed his studied and unfamiliar role of caution. Mallett had taken over at the other end to make it a double spin-attack, registering Lawry's expectations of this fourth-day wicket which was taking considerable spin but not yet quickly. Mallett pitched an off-break short and Engineer pulled him with relish to bring some health back into the sickly body of India's second innings. Borde drove both Mallett and Gleeson in front of the wicket firmly but not forcefully, perhaps cowed by the state of the match as well as of his own test career. Engineer brought up his side's fifty by prodding Gleeson into the covers off the backfoot and we breathed easy in the hope that India was now on the way to recovery, possibly to a draw.

At this critical phase of the afternoon's proceedings Engineer suffered that spasm of bravado which intermittently affects him while batting. Without provocation or precise purpose, he flung his bat at a flighted ball from Mallett and lofted it straight to McKenzie at deep mid-off. Engineer's well-known reputation for indiscretion will not easily explain away this particular lapse. He had been in the longest so far this innings, had seen off the pace bowlers and was in no trouble against the spinners, yet chose to succumb to an impulse. With him went, as we were to realise in the next fifteen minutes, the match for India. One run later, a spiteful off-break (or googly) from Gleeson popped off the upper half of Pataudi's bat into Stackpole's safe hands at short-leg. And four more runs were added before Borde, stretching forward to another Gleeson off-break, seemed to play the ball on to his left knee and deflect it to the other short-leg, Redpath.

If the super-patriots among the multitude thronging various parts of the stadium had gone home at this point, resigning themselves to the obvious outcome of this match, the rest of us would have been spared the black shame of today's last hour. But they had paid for all five days, had every right to sit through till the end, and were now tantalised by the way the left-handed sixth-wicket pair of Wadekar and Surti ignored the magic being attributed by popular opinion to John Gleeson's bent middle-finger. Both Wadekar and Surti are at present in the zone of doubtfuls as far as the rest of the series is concerned, and by holding up the landslide for nearly forty minutes they strove to vacate this zone. Wadekar was rooted to his crease, from where he slashed Mallett behind point with some of his old confidence. Surti had to receive more of Gleeson and let nothing delude him, moving down the pitch when necessary to stifle any unexpected deviation of the ball. India cleared the first innings deficit at last and Lawry replaced Gleeson with Connolly with perhaps no other intention than the modest one of admitting that his spinners were making no headway. And Connolly exceeded his charge by promptly taking two wickets in three overs—those of Surti and Abid Ali, both l-b-w to balls which seemed to beat them in pace off the wicket.

Venkatraghavan was with Wadekar at the tea-break. Afterwards, they raised the hundred of the innings, and we all recalled Venkatraghavan's brave knock of 30 on this same ground three years back against Hall and Griffith in full cry. At about 4.10 p.m., Venkatraghavan played forward to Connolly and missed, there was a muted appeal from somebody, and a few seconds later the umpire indicated that in his opinion the batsman had touched the ball, hence was out caught behind. Venkatraghavan was plainly amazed, stood his ground briefly before walking back, looked back over his shoulder half-way to the pavilion, then disappeared from the sight of a confounded crowd.

The events hereafter are as painful to relate as they are to recall. First a cacophony of booing against the Australians, then a shower of hard soft-drink bottles on the eastern sector of the field, then several bonfires of litter-paper, finally a massing of human bodies against the wire-net fencing—all in and from the East Stands which generally seats the most vociferous as well as most energetic of Bombay's cricket-watchers. The police now took a hand, streaming into the disaffected areas to hurl the bottles back at the hurlers and dislodge those trying to break down the fence. The counter-action worked for a while, but the East Stand hosts reformed and began piling up chairs in the block adjoining the scoreboard to start a much larger conflagration. Soon the temptation spread to the North Stands where awnings near the sight-screen were set on fire, then one of the club-stands enlarged the growing circle of arson by igniting a wooden bench.

All this while, marvellously, play went on although not many could have been watching the game. This is what ultimately saved the day—that the fieldsmen did not panic and seek refuge in the pavilion, and the batsmen chose to defend India's hopeless cause rather than use the disturbance as a pretext for not continuing. Either side would have been justified in refusing to continue but that would surely have handed the initiative over to the mob. At 4.35 p.m., the official scorer ran into the ground to inform the umpire that operators had abandoned the scoreboard and in any case it was practically impossible to see the game from the scoring box. Later in the evening the two captains agreed to honour the score recorded by the All India Radio (AIR) scorer—thus allowing AIR to regain some of the prestige lost on account of the charge that the crowd had been incited to fury by provocative comments about Venkatraghavan's dismissal by an AIR commentator.

What truly astonished and depressed me was that the reaction of the riotous crowds elsewhere was more or less concurred with by the CCI guests and complimentary ticket-holders all around me. Their incredible reasoning seemed to run as follows:

1. Umpire Shambhu Pan had made a mistake in giving Venkatraghavan out.
2. It was a grievous mistake because Venkatraghavan was batting well and may have saved India.
3. If the umpire could not or would not, the Australian skipper should have withdrawn the appeal and called Venkatraghavan back.
4. Since Bill Lawry did not call back Venkatraghavan, he was being 'unsporting'—even unfair, because he kept on playing in conditions which were difficult for Indian batsmen.
5. In view of these implications, it is not surprising that the crowd should try to set fire to the stadium and force the game to be abandoned.

Luckily for those interested in cricket, the components of the stadium, of Lawry and his men, of Wadekar and Prasanna, and of Umpires Pan and Gopalkrishna, are made of stern stuff. Play ended as on schedule but the police took the precaution of cordoning off the passage into the pavilion from the ground. I went home bemoaning much more than the test defeat. Violence, disruption of order, and destruction of property, are increasingly becoming characteristic features of national life with us. Is the day nearer when no large public occasion will be possible in India?

[1976]

Father and Sons

For organised cricket – both in terms of playing and of being taught to play – I had to wait until I was ten years old and was admitted to the newly established St Xavier's High School, Patna in 1940. In fact, within a few years St Xavier's became a cricket centre not only for those of us who attended this school but for anybody who played cricket in Patna. This may seem strange when it is recalled that the school belonged to a Jesuit mission and was staffed in the early days mainly by American clergy. A half-hour of baseball (really, softball) after classes every day was compulsory for all, but it was cricket which founded and sustained this school's prowess at sport.

The encouragement given to cricket at this so-called 'missionary' school run by American Fathers may not have been an accident, after all. It must have been difficult enough to start a 'foreign' school in the last decade of the British Raj in Patna. The only 'missionary' school in Patna until that time was St Michael's (at Kurji, a few miles upstream along the Ganga from Patna), whose enrolment consisted almost entirely of Eurasians (or Anglo-Indians, by popular classification) who, on passing out of school, went directly into services like the police or the railways which gave them preferential employment. No Patna-bred 'Indian' boy ever sought admission there. St Michael's excelled in hockey but did not play cricket. By fostering cricket, St Xavier's clearly distinguished itself from St Michael's and from whatever else it represented to Patna citizenry. Also, through one of those curious contradictions of a colonial past, St Xavier's must have naturalised itself to Patna society more easily on account of cricket.

No speculation needs to be made about who was specifically responsible for planting cricket in St Xavier's. Who else could it be but Father Kevin N. Cleary, S. J.? He came to Patna from Darjeeling, his Irish origins quite submerged by many years of preaching Christianity, teaching English and coaching cricket in India. Father Cleary died in February 1994, and in the 1940s – when he was passing through the thirties of his life himself – he was the kind of cricketer who, while bowling or batting or fielding, dominated any match in which he played. Above all, because he could so easily demonstrate in action whatever he explained in theory, he inspired emulation as well as devotion.

That he was not American and thus did not share the background and enthusiasms of his other brother clergy at St Xavier's did not seem to hinder whatever developmental plans he had for cricket in the school. One handicap even he could not overcome was that the otherwise excellent location of the school – adjoining the great oval lung of the city, the Maidan – denied it the privilege of possessing its own playgrounds. Such land as was leased from the government had been utilised for the school's buildings, with a few open spaces in between and around. Other than the handball courts at the back and the swimming pool on one side, all games were and still are played outside the school on the Maidan. This is public property, and the maintenance even of shaved and levelled patches of earth on which the matting is laid remains a perpetual problem. For a match or for nets, every item of equipment has to be lugged out before and lugged in after. Only truly Christian malis could have done this week after week, season after season. Yet, during the four years I spent at St Xavier's, the facilities grew from one match-wicket on which we also practised, to separate match and practice wickets for the school team, as well as four to six other pitches on which boys at various levels of competence could play their favourite game. Cricket was never compulsory, but on a Saturday afternoon during the winter there could easily be a hundred boys dotting the western segment of the Maidan in various stages of cricket aspiration. Considering that the pitches were rudimentary, injuries were remarkably few. Even if the pitches got some attention, the outfield never did—and anybody who learnt to field well on such a surface acquired a psychological advantage that lasted him the rest of his cricketing life. Apart from the hazards of the sudden bounces of a rolling ball, a strong hit could send the unobstructed ball seemingly into the next district. You not only needed quick-grasping hands but also long-suffering legs to be able to field successfully in the deep. Less doughty souls like I tried keeping wickets, then professed specialisation at first slip or short-leg.

I cannot remember being let off classes in order to play cricket. Intra-school matches as well as matches against other schools were invariably played on Saturdays, when classes gave over at noon. Starting around one-o'clock, we would play until dark, with a break for tea. Practice was held at least three times a week, soon after school hours, thus cricket seemed very much part of the school curriculum. Only when the school entered a formal tournament was there any occasion to play cricket on Sundays. Otherwise, along with far-away Christian nations of the world those days, St Xavier's did not violate the sabbath with cricket.

There was practically no competitive school cricket in Patna during my school days, and I cannot remember participating in many inter-school matches. Most schools did not run a regular cricket season and many of my contemporaries in other schools found an opportunity to play cricket regularly only when they came to college. Considering this, it is amazing how quickly they caught up with the few of us who had the advantage of having played the game regularly at school. Even if some other schools provided the minimum equipment, coaching or net practice or match-wicket maintenance was unheard of. Nor did many homes of my childhood, even while permitting the purchase of white keds for boys, consider it necessary to furnish the boys with a pair of white trousers. My own home, with five children of its own to bring up along with a nephew or niece or two, paid more attention to plentiful food and numerous books than to smart clothes. I did not own a pair of trousers until my last year in school—not a pair stitched for me, but a hand-me-down from one of my two elder brothers. Only by outgrowing them in height soon after leaving school did I escape this traditional fate of younger brothers. These first-ever trousers were tended with particular care, worn only for matches, and between matches folded away under a mattress. During the first season this pair was too long for me and I had to roll up the trouser-cuffs and use safety pins to keep them in place. By the third season my legs had outgrown their legs and letting down the cuffs still left my ankle-knobs exposed. Much worse than this public exposure was the secret agony in certain vital regions. Only those who have stooped in a cricket field with tight-fitting trousers biting into the crotch will know what I mean.

White trousers or shorts and white shirts with rolled-up sleeves – never 'half' shirts – used to distinguish the St Xavier's team more clearly than any other element palpable to sight. Father Cleary's insistence that one should look like a cricketer even if one didn't bat or bowl too well made us conscious of the virtues of whiting, liquid or powder, which we applied regularly to keds, pads, even to shirt-collars in an emergency. Then there was the matter of a cap which set us apart even more distinctively. The St Xavier's school uniform has always been white half-shirt, blue tie, and blue shorts, the latter giving way to white trousers in the senior classes. There was also a school cap, not for compulsory wear, which in the early days (1940 and 1941) was a curious affair—a cross between a forage cap and a Gandhi topi, golden-yellow crested on a royal blue base, to be worn with a slant on the left half of the head. Wearing it at any angle whatsoever was not easy, because a brass SX (St Xavier's) emblem was pinned to the left of the peak, and this would invariably pull the peak down unless it was propped up suitably—for example, with half a pencil. These caps had to be bought from the school store and they came in fewer sizes than could match the students' variety of crania. No cap ever seemed to fit anybody and we never wore this outside school, nor often even inside. They can be seen now in class photographs of those years, making us look, at best, like some odd swayamsevak group of the time, at worst like a bunch of juvenile bank-peons. (The old Imperial Bank of India was our nearest neighbour.) This aberration was corrected and replaced around 1942 or 1943 by the more British-style school-cap—roundheaded, with a short peak in front and a button on top, yellow lines running down a blue base. The new cap was readily adopted by the cricketers and it certainly gave the team a distinction that no other eleven in Patna possessed then. One possible result was that whenever an ex-SX boy achieved a position of influence in his college career he managed to institute a cricket cap for his college team. Sometime or another since then, all college teams in Patna have sported caps. Those of us who had read the right kind of cricket literature fondly hoped that some 'cap-awarding' custom would be set up for the school cricket team. It never was, since this item of distinction could be purchased for filthy lucre at the school store Monday to Friday by any one-legged boy who could not even write the scorebook.

The matter of shorts continues to fascinate me. In my youth people won Wimbledon titles wearing floppy trousers, but now neither man nor woman nor beast would like to be caught dead in trousers on a tennis court. Will test cricketers also demand such liberation one day? And what of women cricketers? Already foreign teams seen in action in India have worn knee-length skirts. Will these rise to tennis-skirt length and make the bowling-end umpire's job a little more interesting than it is now? Men continue to function here.

In the absence of inter-school tournaments, intra-school contests and net-practice sessions carried us through the cricket season. Umpiring, coaching, exhorting, admonishing, Father Cleary occupied our cricket afternoons and evenings. His sheer powers of standing must have been unlimited. I can't remember him squatting on his heels or flopping down on the ground in between phases of activity. Sometimes five or six practice sessions would be on, and he would stride from one pitch to another without any symptom of tiredness. He did carry a shooting-stick, especially when officiating as umpire, and rested between overs on it. But more often he used it to demonstrate a particular stroke or draw diagrams in the soil to show some field placing. When he brought this stick out on net-practice days, we knew he wouldn't be batting or bowling that evening. On these days he also wore leather shoes and used these to great effect in stopping balls. He would be talking to somebody at the bowler's end but somehow always knew when a firmly driven ball was racing along the ground in his general direction. In mid-sentence he would turn around and stop the ball dead with the sole of his shoe. This was a trick none of us was able to imitate and perform.

The coaching for any day began when nets were put up, but generally continued long after the nets were brought down and taken away. We would stand around him in the gathering darkness, marvelling as he recalled a bad stroke one of us had made, or a loose ball another had bowled, or how a third while fielding had allowed something to pass by instead of making adequate effort to stop it. Nothing, particularly no lapse, seemed to escape his eye. Yet, when he cited it, he did not do so in order to rebuke, but more by way of reminding us that a lapse is unlikely to recur if the person concerned recognises it as a lapse and remembers it.

Sometimes the coaching would continue in Father Cleary's room, where you were invited almost by divine sanction. There you were made to practise your strokes in front of a long-mirror so that you got an enlarged bowler's eye view of yourself. Anything near at hand – a textbook, a ruler, even a handkerchief – would be pressed into service by Father Cleary to demonstrate a correction, accompanied by a running commentary on the pupil in imaginary action. At the next net-practice session you were expected to carry out these corrections, but it did not matter if you could not do this immediately. The important thing was to have remembered and made an effort to correct your mistake—that itself would please Father Cleary for the time being because it showed that a chink, however small, had been made in your incorrectness. The long-mirror in his room also came in handy to illustrate the anatomy and physiology of bowling, but budding bowlers profited more from coaching on the field. Father Cleary could enact and repeat for emphasis a bowling action in slow motion, all the while uttering instructions on what to look out for. He could stop the action suddenly, freeze it as it were at any chosen point, so that pupils could note a particular alignment of arms, torso and legs in relation to the bowler's endeavour. As for vagaries of the ball in the air or off the pitch, I think his diction and syntax more than any practical demonstration helped to convince us that the ball was the servant of the bowler, employed by him to master the batsman.

A bonus of these private coaching sessions in his room was that you were shown books on cricket you had never seen before and also heard numerous anecdotes. I think he had seen the MCC team of 1933–34 in action, because his eyes would cloud over with treasured memory as he described C. F. Walters hooking, B. H. Valentine driving, Douglas Jardine simply clamping his jaws. But no episode could have been half as exciting as the way it was told by Father Cleary, his voice modulating according to the stage of action being narrated, sometimes dropping to a dramatic whisper. We listened spellbound, later remembered with joy, and hoped that some day we would also tell stories so well—or, the supreme hope of all, that he would be holding latter-day audiences enraptured with stories about ourselves!

It was not only my contemporaries at St Xavier's who were educated in cricket by Father Cleary, but a whole generation of college players and town cricketers who were always welcome to join us at nets and lingered afterwards for the pleasure of chatting with him. Patna winters are even more mosquito-infested than the other seasons, and little swarms would form over every head as we stood around. He showed us how, by humming, a swarm could be brought lower, and then, by ducking away, left suspended over nothing. Many of the visiting players were not known to him by name, other names he got wrong and never got around to correcting – the person concerned would be the last to insist about this – and to some he gave nicknames. And everybody, of course, was addressed as 'son', as freely as everybody called him 'Father'. Calling everybody 'son' was no doubt a priestly privilege, but in his conversation it was almost a speech-mannerism. An occurrence which never failed to amuse was whenever Mr Bhatia—one of the brothers who owned the sports-goods shop named Roy Brothers – came to see him – Father Cleary invariably addressed him as 'Roy Son'.

One of the enduring enigmas of my association with Father Cleary is that I can never make up my mind about how good he really was as a cricketer. While I was in school it did not seem there could be a better or more complete cricketer than he anywhere in the world. My yardstick was, of course, the standard of cricket I saw being played only in my home town. That he did not score a century and/or bag ten wickets in every match he played in Patna cannot be a measure of his abilities. Even if he were capable of such feats, by character and by vocation he would have been averse to attempting them. He played in a match, if not as a man of God, certainly as a preceptor of the game—always playing not so much for his own good or even for the good of his team but for the greater good of cricket itself. I am pretty sure that having chosen to be a Jesuit priest, he abjured any other kind of ambition not connected with his vocation. When the Reverend David Sheppard made or attempted a comeback to England's test team, I remember wondering whether, had Father Cleary aspired to and got the right breaks, he would ever have made it to the Indian test team of the mid-1930s, contesting C. S. Nayudu or S. Amir Elahi for a place. The road to such eminence would have been laid through the Pentangular contests –

would he have played for the Europeans or the Rest? – and through Ranji Trophy matches. People who ought to know in Jamshedpur have told me that during his playing days he could have walked into the Bihar team any time he liked, had he made himself available for selection. I have no doubt that, had he gained wider cricket fame, many of us in St Xavier's would happily have converted to Christianity if only he asked us.

A schoolboy's judgement of a cricketer cannot be of much value, less so when that schoolboy had nothing better to judge by than the cricket played in a backwater of the game. Even here Father Cleary's performance in terms of runs scored and wickets taken was not out of the ordinary. Many of his pupils must have surpassed him. Except once, I never saw him pitted against better opposition than what Patna could afford in those days. This was a two-day match with a visiting side from Jamshedpur, probably the Cricket Club of Jamshedpur, played on the Engineering College ground. I remember the location clearly because I was sitting behind the goalpost at the northern end and one of Father Cleary's drives came whistling over it. He seemed to have no difficulty in dealing with the visitors' bowling (which must have included a future Bihar captain, Bimal Bose, at least) and hit up thirty-odd runs fairly soon before he was bowled. He also ran somebody out at the striker's end from mid-off and leaped to a marvellous caught-and-bowled for one of the four or five wickets he took in this match. This must have been in 1943 or 1944, and he fully justified my conviction at the time that he was the best all-rounder playing then in India. Happily, this belief has never been tested and, since it was never disproved, I may as well hold it till my dying day.

More than actuality, it was the imagination that he filled for me, and there is no place in such realms for judgement. Even mere description is not easy, surrounding him as we did with a halo just above the sola topi in which he played. He must have been about five-foot nine or ten inches in height, and was quite strong without seeming to be so because of the good proportions of his figure. His main skill was as a bowler, but his batting could not have been very much behind. A stylist as the very correct can be, he favoured the front foot and was a strong driver of the ball, but generally forbore from lifting a drive and forbade his pupils from doing so. I remember him cutting the ball square with much force, often in the old manner off the front foot, but cannot recall many legside strokes. If some of the schoolboy batsmen he fostered are any index, he discouraged hooking, barely countenanced the pull-shot, and generally disapproved of cross-batted hits to the on-side. Arguably, if that was what he preached, he practised such discipline himself. Handsome of face and playing from an upright stance, he could well have modelled portraits of batsmanship in action.

I should remember him better as a bowler because I kept wicket to him in my last two seasons at school. It was a job that came to me more or less by default, there being no other aspirant in the school those days. (Later, the school provided several wicketkeepers to the Patna University team, at least two to the Bihar State team, and very recently S. Saba Karim has toured the West Indies with the national side.) It was a job made more onerous by the worry of letting Father Cleary down by muffing a catch or fumbling a stumping chance off his bowling. I did both, quite regularly, but never heard again about them from him because he knew much better than anybody else that I was anything but a born wicketkeeper. He and I worked out a signal by which, when he pulled up his shirt-collar while walking back for his run-up, I would know that the next delivery would be his faster ball and quietly retreat several steps from my already not very close position several yards behind the stumps. This used to be quite fast, from the way my hands stung within schoolboy-size wicketkeeping gloves. Generally I took this right-handed in order to make sure that it stayed – thereby violating a fundamental principle of wicketkeeping, namely, that both hands should be employed – and between overs I sometimes examined my reddening palm (and telling myself, from my reading knowledge, that I should use a piece of raw beef inside, or is that for a black-eye?). Mercifully, the good Father bowled this infrequently, perhaps once every three overs or so, and I was spared permanent damage. Even more rare, perhaps one every three matches or so, was his googly—a real secret weapon, a *brahmastra*, preserved carefully for use only when nothing else would do. Or maybe I only imagined it was rare, because I never learnt to spot it and he may have bowled many without my recognising them. In his tactical tip to legspinners (I aspired to be one for a couple of seasons) he always advised cautious and sparing use of the googly, so that its surprise effect does not dissipate. Also, he warned that apprentice legspinners who get too fond of the googly sometimes lose their legbreak. I seized upon this warning thankfully a few years later to explain away (to whoever cared to listen) my failure to develop into a legspinner. I had learned to bowl a googly first and could turn it on any wicket, but never mastered the legbreak. The few that ever turned did so without any contribution on my part. In this I had sorely failed my mentor.

Father Cleary was mainly a legbreak bowler, but alternated with off-breaks, and bowled both quite briskly. Off an eight- to ten-yard springy and beautifully balanced approach, he bowled practically at medium pace, with the ball snapping up smartly from the matting wickets on which I kept to him. Had his cricket career developed amid more specialised circumstances, he would probably have cut back on speed and flighted the ball more. By the time I saw him he was an all-purpose bowler – for example, he used the practically new ball for our school team – and this was another waste forced upon him by his situation. As the shine went off, two to three legbreaks per over were the usual quota, pitching on the stumps and going away, sometimes fetching snicks which I dropped or slip-fielding team-mates muffed. To my boyhood sense of cricket, his pitching on the stumps was a waste, more so when the catches he provoked were not accepted—why didn't he pitch outside the leg-stump and aim at hitting the stump outright? This, he explained, not in terms of his own bowling but while instructing aspiring legspinners, would be far more wasteful because the batsman had bat as well as pad to deal with the legbreak pitched outside the leg-stump and may not need to play the ball at all. Whereas by pitching on the stumps, the legspinner compelled the batsman to use the bat, whether in defence or in attack, and thus enhanced the chance of his losing his wicket. Watching cricket at higher levels in later years, it has always seemed strange how legbreak bowlers and left-arm spinners assiduously bowl outside the off-stump all day. If they had passed through Father Cleary's hands, they would have bowled at the stumps and got on with the job.

Whatever be the reason, I find it easier to recall the batsmen among my schoolmates than the bowlers. Easily the best of them was Niranjan Ray, who not only owned strokes all round the wicket but could also hit the ball quite hard even while he was in the seventh or eighth standard. He did not finish his schooling at SX and later went into the Navy, but I am surprised not more was heard of his cricket afterwards. A classmate of his, Samar Sengupta, could bat very straight and correctly when he wanted to – which was not often – but was another batsman of potential I never heard of again. Surendra Bahadur Singh (later the topmost surgeon of the Tata hospital at Jamshedpur) could not have surpassed his academic record with the runs he made – so good was he at studies – but he made them with the same fastidious care and correctness with which he wrote his exams. That dashing driver of the ball, Rajatnath Roy, came to us from Hazaribagh and disappeared on leaving school into dairy science studies, probably abroad, instead of developing a defence that would give reliability to his batting. That kind of defence was already part of Kawaljit Singh's batting when he was halfway through school. He would captain the Bihar schools' side and later the Patna University team before he qualified for the Indian Revenue Service.

Among bowlers, the most feared at net-practice was David Singh, left-arm medium-pacer, who seemed always to be bowling at your abdomen-box (which wasn't always worn in school cricket). He could be and was at times quite dangerous with the new ball; he made the old ball so soppy with spit that other bowlers would sometimes protest about having to handle the same ball. My classmate Shunil Roy came from a cricketing family of Ranchi (actually, of Kanke, where his father ran a large farm). He was quite a tricky spin bowler because neither he nor the batsman facing him knew what spin had been imparted to a particular delivery. A more orthodox legspinner was K. G. Rao, but when he went to college in Patna we found he could bowl a very delayed in-swing with the new ball. That did his bowling ambitions no good at all and later he chose the greater adventure of flying planes for Indian Airlines.

Then there were the characters—the loudest of them Anthony Surojit Sen, who would drop his first name when he grew up and become a well-known radio voice in India for many years. In school cricket he bowled very fast but seldom straight, with a spectacular throwing about of arms and legs. Also the owner of gangling limbs was Gautam Bir, and he never forgot to click index-finger and thumb in exasperation when he missed a ball, even while batting. And the most enduring of them all was Sumantra Sengupta, whose company I had from school up to a couple of years in college. He used to bowl the most massive legbreaks in school – even larger than those bowled by Father Cleary – tossing them high up and waiting anxiously for them to land. But he tossed them so high that batsmen got enough time not to let them land at all. So, when a little older and wiser, he turned to wicketkeeping and was Patna University's reserve 'keeper for two successive years—not so much for his competence behind the stumps, but because he was such fun to be with on a trip. Capping all his pleasure-giving accomplishments was his skill as a flute-player. He not only commanded a wide range of melodies; he could also play the flute with his nostrils. When properly primed, he did excellent mimicry of Father Cleary admonishing somebody for hitting with a cross-bat or bowling long hops.

Which returns me to the lingering topic of this chapter and also the remnant of my school cricket. Father Cleary's playing days gave over soon after I left school, but he remained on the scene as umpire and selector for a few more years. For a few more he continued to coach St Xavier's boys, but the increasing complications of an intestinal ailment finally forced him out of any sustained physical effort. I did not watch this decline and thus can easily remember him better on the field than off it.

The brightest such memory is of the day in 1944 when St Xavier's nearly won the Sifton Cup. That a school team should have been competing at all in this tournament had made enough history. This was Patna's only 'open' cricket tournament – that is, open to all teams, not merely to colleges or only to club sides – run on knock-out lines, and it generally fetched an out-station team or two. No school had ever before participated in this tournament, much less reached the final—which we did at only our second attempt. We ventured to participate partly because we could draw upon Father Cleary, also upon another cricket-playing cleric (Father Mackessack), and a lay-teacher (Mr Kennedy) more feared in the boxing ring and on the football field. But also, there was no other tournament then in which we could participate, and I don't think we were at all aware of any presumptuousness in challenging college teams or adult club sides. Our opponent in the final that year was Science College and the match was played on their ground—which to us in those days was the nearest thing to a test ground. We batted first and were out for a little over one hundred, but they did no better and lost about eight wickets for somewhat less. Father Cleary must already have taken five or six wickets when one of the tail-enders – Kiran Mitter, to be exact, who was in the team (I later came to know) more for his enthusiasm than for his ability – made a desperate heave at him and away the ball soared over wide mid-on. The nearest fieldsman – again I remember the name, Sourin Ghosh, whose football was better than his cricket – set off in chase, overshot the mark, turned around and just managed to catch the ball near one of the flag-sticks marking the boundary and ran across the line. In any class of cricket it was a great effort and we began yelling in joy, but a much greater hubbub arose from college supporters sitting under a tree nearest to the spot. They claimed that the catch had been made outside the boundary line. Now the college captain came out and demanded justice of the umpires. The one at the bowler's end, who had nearly joined our applause for the catch, solemnly walked to the spot, came back to consult his colleague, then broke our hearts by declaring the hit to be a six. We did not know how to protest, and, even had we known how, with Father Cleary present we could not have protested. But all fight was knocked out of us, not by the batsman but by that umpire. A few more swipes and the match was irretrievably lost.

Some of my team-mates wept that evening, others uttered foul swear-words out of our teachers' hearing, a few planned to murder the umpire. As I cycled back from the ground in a bunch with Father Cleary, he was already talking about the next season. That day, I think, I grew up a little more, and not only in the cricket sense.

Two years later, when the last 'All-India' cricket team to visit England was announced, some of us thought Father Cleary should have been selected instead of C. S. Nayudu or S. G. Shinde or C. T. Sarwate or all three—such was our faith. With India's political independence approaching, we even thought of conferring Indian citizenship upon him by giving away one of ours—such was our innocence. For all we knew, he had always been a citizen of India.

[1996]

Military Manoeuvres

Not unlike playing for a legbreak only to find it turning the other way, sometime in 1954 I applied for a job at Dehra Dun (U.P.) but found it only at Khadakvasla, near Pune, in Maharashtra. The post was that of Instructor of English at the National Defence Academy (NDA), and interviews were held by the Union Public Services Commission at Delhi. Candidates (that is, civilians) were expected to have had NCC training and experience, but my not possessing this qualification was apparently compensated for by my cricketing background. At least so it was made to appear by the chairman of the interview committee, Professor N. K. Siddhanta (formerly of Lucknow University). He monopolised the interview, interrogating me mainly on cricket – what was my batting number, did I bowl, where did I field, were my glasses any handicap in taking slip catches, etc. – before turning to the other members to say that an all-round sportsman was any day to be preferred over halfbaked NCC officers. I knew straightaway that I had been selected. What I did not know was that I was not destined for Dehra Dun or that I would be meeting several famous cricketers at the place where I would land up.

I had to undergo the usual medical examination conducted by the Civil Surgeon, as was customary for anybody who accepted a government post, and had further to be cleared by an eye-specialist who certified that my defective vision would not prevent me from carrying out the duties of the post for which I had been selected. All this took some time, during which interval the Academy had moved from the foothills of the Sivalik range to a valley in the Deccan overlooked by the Simhagad fort. Rather, what used to be known as the Joint Services Wing, housed temporarily at the Indian Military Academy of Dehra Dun, had gone to its permanent residence.

As a result, with the 1954–55 season not yet over, when I informed the Ministry of Defence that I was now ready to take a train to Dehra Dun, I was instructed to go by whatever means available to me and quite soon to Khadakvasla. I had never heard of such a place before, and it needed some map-consultation and railway route-hunting before I found out that the place was about ten miles away from Pune city.

Those who have seen the NDA at Khadakvasla and marvelled may not realise what fabulous sports facilities are available there for cadets as well as for instructors. Cricket, football, hockey; tennis, squash, badminton; swimming, sailing; riding, gliding; table tennis, billiards—all these were already there in my time, and more must have been added since then. Cadets of course have to follow a given schedule of work and play, but for instructors like me – and especially if they were bachelors – there was far more opportunity for play than for work. Academic instruction was over by 1.40 p.m., so the long afternoon and the whole evening was free to be used for any game one fancied. For me cricket predominated, but there were brother-officers, civilian as well as military, equally besotted about other games. And competence or even conspicuous interest in any game immediately was a point in one's favour as far as the 'management' was concerned. This became obvious to me when, during my second year at the NDA, I was unanimously elected Secretary of the Officers' Mess—a responsibility that had not been entrusted to any civilian before that.

The Mess occupied all but the spectator seating space of the three-storeyed residential part of the stadium. Thus, my room on the second floor could be entered from the gallery behind the stadium over-hang which carried two levels of spectator seating space. I could drag out my own armchair and watch cricket being played on the ground below from just outside the room. At the back of my room was a large balcony which overlooked the swimming pool, beyond which were the tennis and squash courts. It was quite difficult to stay inside the room, when one was not teaching or otherwise on duty. A varied world of sport was verily at one's feet.

One can't talk of the NDA of the mid-1950s without first mentioning Major-General E. Habibullah, then commandant, and drawing whose attention was considered a major achievement among the officers. I did so without planning to, by falling dangerously ill within a month of joining and being removed to the Military Hospital—where he apparently visited me once, though without my knowledge, because I lay unconscious for nearly three days. Subsequently, his attention grew into recognition when he saw I played cricket, and it probably developed into some regard when he found I wrote a little on cricket as well. That last gift has endured the longest because it was he who first put into my head the idea of publishing a book on cricket.

Cricket as well as riding were major passions with the General, and it was widely believed among NDA staff, in or out of uniform, that if one batted or bowled or rode, all other sins of commission and omission would be forgiven. And it was not just abstract interest for the General but active participation. I used to marvel at the energy of this seemingly elderly man when, on many Sundays, he would return from riding to the hounds for breakfast, then be at the RSI ground by ten-o'clock for that day's cricket match. Like the rest of us he brought his own packed lunch, though it was naturally packed more elaborately than ours. We would try and cover up for him when fielding, but this annoyed him no end. When he took a wicket sometimes or held a catch, he would be as pleased as a jawan given a day off from parade.

The NDA calendar used to contain two terms, January to May and July to November, with a passing-out parade marking the end of each term. Pune weather being what it is, it was possible to play cricket for almost ten months from June to March—which may be one reason why Maharashtrians excel at cricket. They simply play more of it than cricketers of any other state. (Maybe it is the weather again, of Bangalore, which will explain the recent achievements of Karnataka in the Ranji Trophy.) On account of that spell of illness I missed the tail-end of the 1954–55 season at Khadakvasla, but was raring to play when I returned in July after the summer break. The stadium wickets were not yet ready for use, nor the practice pitches outside and below road level on your left as you approach the stadium from the direction of the parade ground. So one had to toil uphill and through residential quarters on a nearby plateau and down to an improvised cricket-ground in another hollow in the hillside. The only matting-wicket laid here was used for net practice as well as for inter-squadron matches. Here at nets I had to lay bare my cricket upbringing for a couple of days before, much to my secret joy, I was informed that I should keep my next Sunday free and be available to the RSI team for a Poona League fixture. At least the honour of Patna and Bihar cricket had been upheld—though it remained to be seen how well and for how long.

By then, of course, I had met several people who would add considerably to the pleasure I got out of my cricket at the NDA. First and foremost among them was H. R. Adhikari (Hemu), then a Major and posted as a squadron officer at the Academy. Somebody pointed him out to me at a squadron party and I couldn't quite believe that this short, average-looking man sitting quietly in a corner could be a cricketer who had toured Australia with the India team and only a couple of years ago was vice-captain on India's tour of England. I sometimes thought test cricketers could be identified off-field by a halo around their heads or some other kind of effulgence and would certainly be the centre of conversation at a party. Later, when I got to know Hemu, I realised that no matter how many tests he played or cricket tours he made, he never sought or ever would seek any social limelight. His wife Kamal was a perfect match for him in modesty and friendliness. Had she ever taken to playing cricket, I am sure her batting and bowling would have been exactly the same as Hemu's. Maybe her fielding would have been less spectacular.

Then there were A. K. Khanna (Nandi), a Captain at the time and posted in charge of the engineering workshop, N. B. Sawardekar (Ramesh), a civilian instructor in physics, and P. G. Joshi (Nana), on temporary assignment as cricket coach of NDA. The last-named ran about on a red Jawa motorbike in those days, and many a time I got a ride with him from the temporary Officers' Mess in one wing of the cadets' quarters to the makeshift cricket ground on the hillside. During one of these rides he mentioned that somebody had written nasty things about him in an article in last Sunday's *Times*. I don't think he ever found out (I certainly did not tell him) that I had written that article under my cricket-writing pseudonym of 'Skim'. This was an obituary piece on S. G. Shinde, in which I pointed out that had Joshi not fumbled several catches and stumping chances in England's second innings at the Delhi Test of 1951, Shinde may have run through the opposition again as easily as he had in the first innings. At first hand, however, Joshi's speed and neatness while keeping wickets never failed to arouse my admiration. He took me home once, to a house quite close to the Mula river bank, and showed me photographs and other mementoes of his cricket trips abroad. Nearly all of these were washed away in the dam-burst of 1962 which deluged parts of Pune city.

I must digress for a minute on the matter of that pseudonym. I had concocted it for the weekly column I wrote for a Patna newspaper (for reasons to be explained in another chapter)[1] but in the *Times of India* I would certainly have preferred my own name in print. However, I discovered that among the service conditions at NDA applicable even to civilian staff, one was that should officers write anything for publication, it would first have to be cleared by the administration (including, if necessary and somewhat fatuously, reference to the Ministry of Defence). I don't know if clearance had ever been denied to anybody, but delays could occur, and the requirement was a point of irritation with civilian instructors. This was specially so among my colleagues in the English department, several of whom aspired to write. The most famous writer of them now, Chamanlal Nahal (later Professor of English at Delhi University), had not yet courted destiny as a novelist. Darshan Singh Maini (who retired some years ago as Professor of English at Panjabi University) would, soon after leaving NDA, begin to be widely read for his regular 'Chandigarh Letter' page in the *Illustrated Weekly of India*. K. R. Narayanswamy was then the most published of us all, but he got around the ban by publishing poetry in his wife's name and by signing himself 'Nano' for satirical pieces in *Shankar's Weekly*. I didn't want anybody in the Academy administration to edit or even approve (I didn't think anybody qualified) my essay on the late Shinde, so I sent it off to the *Times* with the request that I be allowed to use my pseudonym. Subsequently, when my old school magazine asked me for a contribution, I wanted this to go in my own name, hence wrote and duly submitted it for clearance. It was cleared within three days. One of the staff officers came over to my desk carrying the thing in a folder, and I thought he was about to explain why it could not be cleared. But he had come personally to

---

1 See my *Autobiography of an Unknown Cricketer*, New Delhi: Ravi Dayal Publisher, 1996.

show and congratulate me on what General Habibullah had scrawled on a note-sheet attached to my typescript.

What the General had written was so flattering to me that I hesitated to show it to any but the closest of friends—for example, somebody like Ramesh Sawardekar. Thereafter, the General took the trouble to read and invariably communicate appreciation of whatever I wrote on cricket. (I am not so sure of his high marks where my playing it was concerned.) Ramesh, reserve wicketkeeper and emergency opening-batsman of our team, was ready to talk or play cricket at any time of day or night. His personal acquaintance with many Bombay cricketers (many of whom were his college contemporaries) and familiarity (because of long employment at NDA) with Services cricket gave him a knowledgeability I very much enjoyed—I never tired of discussing cricket with him. Even without these special possessions he was an immensely likeable and warm person. He and his wife and two young children freely gave of their company, backed up by endless food, whenever I was lonely or tired of the Mess food. Several generations of defence services officers have passed through his hands, in physics or at cricket—a fact which was duly noted by the *Times* in a news-item reporting his retirement in 1979 or 1980.

Of them all I am in most recent touch with Nandi Khanna who has settled down in Delhi. A thread of cricket administration passes through Nandi, Ramesh and me, because I succeeded Nandi as officer-in-charge of cricket at NDA, while Ramesh succeeded me and held this charge for many years. Nandi had by 1955 stopped playing for the Services and concentrated instead on building up his family and career. His wife Meena, apart from being fabulous in looks and cookery, is a pioneer among the women cricketers of Delhi. When I met them first, their elder son Arun was still an infant and used to gurgle away in the backseat while we drove the long way to and from matches in the city in Nandi's Morris Minor. They always carried lunch for me, and quite often I ended up on match days having dinner with them as well. As with Hemu's wife Kamal, Meena seldom missed a match where her husband was playing. I don't know how this affected their husbands' batting, but I was always assured of a variety of home-cooked food during the lunch break. Nandi, incidentally, had made his debut in Ranji Trophy cricket with an unbeaten century (133 n.o. for Services vs Rajasthan) in December 1951. He was still a very good batsman, a formidable driver off the front foot, but what he seemed to enjoy more than batting was being allowed to bowl his entirely personal brand of leg-spin.

These five – Hemu, Nandi, Nana, Ramesh and I – and the General, whenever he was not away on work, provided as it were the reliable core of the RSI team for those two years at Pune. Lance-Corporal Jagadisan, a high utility all-rounder, was another fairly regular participant. Other places were filled by whoever was available from various military units stationed in the city. Some played in a series of matches, some in one or two, and it was the business of Hemu Adhikari and Nandi Khanna to locate and rope them in. Among the irregulars was fast bowler V. Swamy (who appeared in a test against New Zealand in 1955); all-rounders H. T. Dani (another one-test player but otherwise a Services stalwart who later did a spell as national selector), and G. N. Kunzru (whom I had played against once when he was in the Holkar team); a Major Cohen (it was rumoured he had once played for the Rest, though he did not look old enough for this to me); and General Dargalkar (called 'Drag' or 'Dragon' by those of his own rank, and this rank rather than any cricketing eminence qualified him for the RSI team). From the Academy we generally brought along a few cadets in cricket kit who could fill places if required or attend to the scorebook and other such needs. We also contributed an umpire to every match we played. This was our Regimental Sergeant-Major Ayling of the Coldstream Guards, surely the only ruddy-faced if not blue-blooded Englishman to be sergeant-majoring or umpiring cricket matches in the India of the later 1950s. Ayling's plan was to retire from military service and take up professional umpiring in England. On account of NDA backing (augmented no doubt with a word or two in the right ears from General Habibullah and Major Adhikari), he rose through Ranji Trophy matches to officiating at the West Indies–Services fixture (at Khadakvasla, in November 1958). Unfortunately, he fell ill soon after he returned home and died.

I have omitted so far to explain that the initials RSI stand for the Rajendra Singhji Institute—which in Pune meant a club with a cricket ground, swimming pool, facilities for some other games, dining-in and residential facilities, all only for the use of defence service officers and their families. Because we played as a team in the first-division cricket league conducted by the Maharashtra Cricket Association, I used to think that the RSI was a kind of defence services club located in Pune. Long after I left the Academy I came to know that there was an RSI in every large military centre in the country, this being the name given to post-Independence defence service clubs in honour of General Rajendrasinghji, independent India's first chief of army staff. The Pune RSI had not always played league cricket nor did it continue to do so, but for a few years the support of NDA personnel had made possible such regular cricket activity. While the General or Hemu or Nandi were members of RSI by right of service, civilians like Nana Joshi and Ramesh Sawardekar and I represented RSI only in cricket by virtue of our attachment to the Academy. The latter were therefore careful not to use any other facility at RSI because we were not members—not even the swimming pool which, on warm Sunday afternoons, appeared to be full of half-clad bathing beauties. Or so it seemed from third man on the southern side, a fielding position which became unexpectedly popular on occasion.

There must have been ten or twelve teams in the league because we used to have a pretty full season, with the occasional friendly match being arranged. The NDA team (of cadets) also participated, and the RSI vs NDA match on the Academy's own ground in the stadium became quite a family occasion. The RSI generally played at 'home' – that is, on its own ground in the cantonment area – but we played 'away' matches as well. This gave me the occasion to play on Pune's many cricket pitches—Deccan Gymkhana (of hallowed past), PYC (next to which Professor D. B. Deodhar built his house and the lane in front is named Kriketpatu Deodhar Path after him), S. P. College (a cricket ground on its premises, as we used to have in Patna), Club of Maharashtra (now a full-fledged stadium named after Jawaharlal Nehru), Poona Club (which has hosted the very old presidency matches, the less old Pentangular contests, and later in the 1940s Maharashtra's massive run-getting in the Ranji Trophy). Each had a character of its own, pavilions large or small, groundsmen short or tall, and a convention or two peculiar to its past which was kept up even while the framed group photographs faded. Above all, everywhere the game was played in great earnest and most club sides put in a certain amount of net practice on weekdays in preparation for Sunday's match. Players kept their place in a team not only on what they achieved on Sundays but also on their regularity at nets. This to me was the most marked difference between cricket in Pune and what I had known at Patna—the seriousness of application, quite apart from the quality which was consequently much higher.

On or around these much-used grounds I came across well-known names of yesteryear – J. G. Navle, Kamal Bhandarkar, M. V. Patwardhan – the last-named, in fact, played in a match for the Ordinance Factory against us—also players of more recent vintage like Ranga Sohoni and Madhukar Rege. And, of course, the imperishable D. B. Deodhar was not difficult to locate. I actually first met him at a street-crossing, when a traffic light had halted him on his bicycle. Quite unbelievingly I went up to him and asked if he was Professor Deodhar. He admitted he was and readily agreed to receive me if I called at his residence, which I did very soon, and found him more willing to talk about his badminton-star daughters than about his own starred days in cricket. Once I even had the good fortune to see him bat—what a memorable event this was, because who should be bowling to him but C. K. Nayudu! This was at some festival match on the Deccan Gymkhana ground, about which I have written in *Between Indian Wickets* (1979).[2]

Not on that occasion but on another, Colonel Nayudu visited the Academy as a guest and stayed in the Mess for a week or so. We didn't know about his coming. Another civilian instructor, T. U. K. Menon (my departmental colleague and fellow resident) had made it an after-dinner practice to have a game of billiards with me before we went up to our rooms. One evening we found somebody in single occupation of the billiards table, a man of striking appearance who was practising trick shots and succeeding almost every time. He was so preoccupied that he did not notice our arrival, and we watched him quietly until a particularly difficult try and astonishing result made us break into spontaneous applause. Whereupon he looked up with a smile and I instantly knew it was the Colonel. I said so and he graciously asked who I was. When I said I had played against him

[2] See "One Magic Afternoon", this volume.

once in Jamshedpur, even more graciously he pretended to remember, and thereafter we got along famously. Every evening when he was available I would buttonhole and badger him into talking cricket, and he didn't seem to mind at all. Quite a lot of what I got out of him has gone into the making of my first book on Indian cricketers.

Of three adjustments I had to make in order to play cricket in Pune, one was to take (or at least appear to take) the game seriously. Among those I played with regularly – and apart from cadets under our charge, many of whom would play for the Services and one for India (though only once) – only Hemu Adhikari and Nana Joshi were entitled to nurse extraterritorial ambitions and thus had reason to pursue excellence. The rest of us, not excluding Nandi Khanna (who manages even now to play a few friendly matches every season), played mainly for pleasure. Hemu was still a Services regular, would make one comeback in the Bombay Test against the Australians of 1956–57, another against West Indies in 1958–59 in Delhi, after which I really thought he should have gone to England as captain of India's 1959 team. Nana was then in and out of the national side, played for West Zone against New Zealand in November 1955 (at Pune), but was not quite back in consideration for test matches. Both therefore sought to be in good trim, but the wonderful thing was they managed to do this without making us feel small (they were test players but we were not and never would be). They also managed to infect us with the sense that whatever is worth doing is worth doing well. Certainly I had never practised so assiduously ever before, and realised that I would surely have improved my game considerably if I had had such models and mentors around me at Patna. At Khadakvasla I cheerfully went through all the cricket-field exercises the cadets did, and didn't think twice about running a lap around the stadium to finish off for the day. Also, I cut down my smoking and switched to a pipe, but couldn't do much about my eyesight.

That relates to the second adjustment required of me from time to time at Pune, having to do with the weather. I had never played cricket in rain before, thus had no idea what a nuisance it could be to anybody who wore glasses. The first few times it happened to me while batting I tried rubbing the water off with thumbs clad in batting-gloves – which made it worse because batting gloves are by no means clean. So one had to pull off one's gloves, bring out a handkerchief, clean up, put away the handkerchief, pull on gloves again – and all the time wondering if one would last the remaining balls of that over. A star batsman can delay proceedings as often and as long as he wants to, because his reputation entitles him to have everything just right. But a comet batsman like me (who did not shine everyday) could not but feel guilty about causing stoppages. Apart from wiping glasses clear, the taking off and putting back of glasses does cause a momentary break while eyes re-adjust—as any bespectacled batsman will testify. So I had to push, tug and twitch before I felt I was ready to face the next ball, and this wasted a few more seconds. Such an emergency cannot be very serious because I can think of any number of bespectacled batsmen who must have had to bat in rain in England without making too much fuss. And, of course, more recently contact lenses have solved the problem altogether. But one indirect consequence of my travails was that I stopped batting with a handkerchief around my forehead, as I had learnt to do in Patna, not just to keep the spectacle-legs in place but also to prevent perspiration drops falling on the lenses. This can be a most unnerving experience—you play forward to a ball you have seen clearly, then a drop of perspiration changes your lense power in a trice and you find a highly distorted ball, sometimes rainbow-coloured, reaching you before or after you had expected it. In Pune, rather than add to the delays by having to untie the handkerchief with which I would clean my glasses, I stopped tying it on altogether. I had quite forgotten this practice of mine until many years later I saw Zaheer Abbas batting and noted that he was using a handkerchief in the same way. This gave me such an instant feeling of affinity with the Pakistani star that I began to see that he played many of his off-side strokes as I used to!

The third adjustment had to do with the playing surfaces. Before I went to Pune I had batted on turf on not more than half a dozen occasions and thus felt quite at sea at first. I seemed to be playing too soon or too late, and would either pop the ball up in front or have to jab at it belatedly. So I had to teach myself to play back more often than play forward – though the latter had been my customary first move, as it probably is of most matting-wicket batsmen – and generally ended up by playing from the crease. As for bowling on turf wickets, I found that the rolled legbreak I was able to turn on matting hardly deviated from the straight and true on turf. Hence I had to give up all pretense of being a spin bowler and took on the pretensions of a medium-pacer. With the shine remaining on the ball longer than it does on matting, I found that even as second or third change I could swing the ball a little. As a result, I was entrusted several times with the new ball for the RSI.

As stated earlier, the hard core of the RSI team for those two seasons I played in Pune was provided by NDA officers. Hemu Adhikar and Nandi Khanna made the runs; so did Nana Joshi some times, though his main responsibility was behind the stumps; the General provided the dignity; Ramesh Sawardekar and I provided the enthusiasm. What we lacked was bowling, and this lack prevented us from winning as often as we should have. My chief source of delectation at these matches was watching Hemu Adhikari at the crease. As I have written elsewhere,[3] this was a very different H. R. Adhikari from the circumspect ascetic one saw in test matches. For the RSI he cut and pulled against the line or spin of the ball, and didn't refrain from lofting the ban when necessary. But a hermetic defence remained the foundation of his batting and I grew to wonder how he ever got out at any level of cricket, except when he chose to—as he often did for RSI by chancing his arm.

Even before I was nominated OIC (Officer-In-Charge) Cricket, I was already so involved with the Academy's cricket activities that I did not have to bear any extra responsibility when I was, nor, I think, did the cadets regard me as a new imposition. Their rigidly disciplined life made them easy to handle and I, in turn, made no attempt to crack any whip. If anything, I was too easy with them and often forgot that as an 'officer' I should maintain some distance. At least once this lack of distance saved my life or me from serious injury. One of my duties as OIC was to accompany the team when it went to the city for matches. We generally went in a truck, and the officer accompanying them was expected to sit in the driver's cab (this being the only other seat available) while the cadets stood at the back. It was a long drive on the route we

[3] See the chapter entitled "Cover to Cover" in *The Romance of Indian Cricket,* New Delhi: Hind Pocketbooks, 1968.

route we followed, via Kothrud, and I used to get bored sitting next to a wordless driver. So on that occasion I got in at the back and stood chatting with the cadets, when the truck got out of control on a turn going downhill, went off the road with the right front wheel dipping into a large hole in the ground and the truck falling over on its right side. For a few seconds I didn't know what had happened because it was all so sudden. For the next few minutes I couldn't see what was happening, because my glasses had fallen off. By the time things had sorted themselves out, an NDA service officer who happened to be passing by had stopped and taken charge. From what I could make out – I never recovered those glasses – no cadet had come to harm possibly because the tarpaulin top had prevented anybody from being thrown out. By falling on each other, however, some had received knocks and bruises. These cadets were taken away quickly in an ambulance, so was I—because I was quite helpless without my glasses, but luckily had a spare pair in my room. Later I heard that the driver had jumped clear when he found the truck going over on its side, but a friend he had picked up to give a free ride to had had his face and chest gashed at many places by glass shivers when the windscreen shattered. This could easily have been me, if I had conducted myself like an Officer-In-Charge and sat next to the driver. One permanent consequence of this accident was that NDA vehicles carrying cadets were forbidden hereafter to use the Kothrud route into the city and had to go via Pashan instead. Another long-term effect was that for many years afterwards I was scared of riding even buses. Every time a large vehicle negotiated a bend with me sitting inside, I thought it might go off the road and turn over.

Accompanying the team was not an invariable obligation for the OIC Cricket, because this duty rotated among a select range of officers, mostly civilians, for whom this meant a free ride into and back from the city, with enough time in between to attend to personal chores. When I was on duty I had the liberty of dropping the cadets at their match, go on to the RSI ground or elsewhere for my own match, then pick them up on the way back. Not all of them came back because, if a cadet's other record was clean, he could ask for and receive permission to stay back in town for the evening on Saturdays. Sometimes I did this myself (not, of course, when I was on duty)—washing up as best as one could at the clubhouse, then see a film and dine out on Main

Street, and catch the late evening NDA bus back to the Academy. On it would be cadets whom I had permitted to stay back and we would compare notes on how the evening had passed.

Of two high points of my stint as OIC, one was taking the Academy team to Bombay to watch the second test of 1956 against Australia. The provocation for this must have been the fact that Hemu Adhikari had been alerted before the Australians arrived that his services might be required for the India team. This news delighted every cricket-follower in the Academy who, like many others elsewhere in the country, were convinced that Hemu had had a rough deal from the national selectors. Granted that he had failed in the tests in England in 1952 (in two of which he had had to bat at the unaccustomed post of number three in order to spare Polly Umrigar), his 81 not out at Delhi and 31 not out at Madras against Pakistan later that year went unnoticed when the Indian team to tour the West Indies was selected. He was neither called upon for any of the unofficial tests against the SJOC[1] team in 1953–54, nor invited to tour Pakistan in 1954–55 nor to play against New Zealand in 1955–56. So a recall to the three-test home series against Australia in 1956 suggested that the India team was really in need of him. As preparation (mainly for dealing with speedsters like Crawford and Lindwall and Davidson), Hemu got all the Academy pace bowlers to hurl with all their might at him from eighteen yards (instead of the regulation twenty-two) on the concrete practice pitch that had just been laid. This was apparently not enough because, at the first test in Madras, Crawford got him for 5 in the first innings and Lindwall for 0 in the second.

That he performed a little better in the test following at Bombay may have had something to do with the fact that at least sixteen solid supporters were watching—seventeen, in fact, because General Habibullah was also there. I don't know how this kind of expenditure was explained to the auditors, but there we were – fifteen cadets and one officer – spending six days in Bombay to attend a test match, travelling to and from Pune for the purpose, all at government expense. I insisted that all the cadets turn up for the match in full winter 'walking out' dress – Academy blazer and tie, and hat – and myself sported a blazer. I

[1] Silver Jubilee Overseas Cricket.

was anxious that the General should not find anything amiss were he to train his binoculars on the North Stand where our seats were. While we sweated and squirmed (and from the second day onwards I excused the cadets and myself from wearing blazers), India batted poorly until first Manjrekar (55), then Adhikari (33), stood by G. S. Ramchand while the latter hammered out a century. Hemu was going strong until an acrobatic catch by Alan Davidson off Ken Mackay cut him off. Australia's reply soared beyond 500 (Burke 168, Harvey 140, Burge 83), leaving India to play out a day and some hours for a draw. This India managed, with Hemu (22 not out) defending dourly. The cadets and I had played in our minds every ball that he did, and we were quite gratified. Neither he nor we, incidentally, were selected for the third test at Calcutta.

The other highlight was a match between the Indian Military College (IMC) and the NDA. This was an annual fixture, held alternately at Dehra Dun and Khadakvasla. That year was Khadakvasla's turn – perhaps the first time it was being played here – and the Stadium ground was prepared accordingly. But the IMC team arrived along with copious rain, and it did not seem likely that the scheduled two-day match could be played at all. Other concerned officers and I were debating the problem at the stadium on the morning of the match when General Habibullah turned up—in full dress as Master of the Hunt, and riding his favourite horse obviously on his way back from that morning's hunt. Very quickly he sized up the situation and stated his mind pithily: "Do something. These chaps haven't come all the way from Dehra Dun to eff around here", or words to that effect. Within the hour a labour force of about a hundred men and women was commandeered and equipped with buckets and mop-rags. The stadium pitch being sodden beyond human repair, we chose Ground No. 1 outside the stadium where the pitch (meant for a matting-wicket) was relatively dry because it was slightly higher than the surrounding surface. Here the labourers went to work in mopping up the outfield, while the carpentry workshop produced the sawdust required to be sprinkled on the bowling approaches and some other affected spots. By about noon the ground was ready for play. It was decided that the match would begin after an early lunch.

The IMC team contained a couple of players – S. M. Bali and Bhupinder Singh – who had passed out of NDA the term after I joined, but I did not otherwise know what the team's strength was like. The NDA side I knew well and, it being my direct charge, I wanted it to win. The team's wicketkeeper, R. Raghavan, was captain. J. N. Virlley and Kiron Roye opened the bowling, which would later be taken over by off-spinner Nadkarni and legspinner Shivdasani. Among the batsmen I was particularly interested in two freshers, A. K. Sengupta and Yeshwant Bhide, whom I regarded as my 'finds'. Bhide, who came from a cricketing family of Madhya Pradesh, appeared more promising to me—a tall, burly left-hander who drove in front with effortless power. Sengupta, who came to the Academy from Lucknow, two-eyed in stance and predominantly an on-side player, was an opening batsman already long in patience if short on strokes.

I also had to umpire in this match and was thus able to whisper occasional words of encouragement to my team which won the toss and elected to bat. I did my best to hide all un-umpirely joy as, between them, Bhide and Sengupta took the IMC bowling to pieces. Bhide was caught in the deep field after he had scored about 60, but Sengupta persisted until he got his century. It was quite funny to watch their faces as they went on hammering the bowlers. A fresher's life in the Academy during the first term can be quite petrifying because of the instant and unquestioning obedience he has to offer throughout his waking hours. He quickly learns not to have any expression on his face, lest it be misunderstood by his seniors and superiors—and everybody except his 'batchmates' was senior or superior to him. Thus, even while Bhide and Sengupta rattled up their runs, not a shade of feeling showed on their faces, while I imagined that whatever they felt went into the sixes and fours they hit that day.

No matter how carefully the pitch below the matting was repaired next morning, it showed some life when the IMC batted and the Academy spinners bundled the opposition out quite easily. I was naturally quite proud of the victory and the General, who had invited both teams to tea after the game, did not forget to congratulate me—even though, in my anxiety to be fair, I had given several umpiring decisions in favour of the IMC batsmen. My Academy team must have scattered very widely all over the country after its members had qualified as officers because I have met very few of them again in later life.

One other event which merits mention is Maharashtra's match with Saurashtra in the Ranji Trophy which was held at Khadakvasla in November 1956. This, in fact, was the first-ever first-class match to be staged at the NDA Stadium. (Two years later the touring West Indies side played the Services here; cadet A. K. Sengupta scored a century in that match and, later that season, appeared in a test.) Apart from helping a little with the arrangements for the Maharashtra–Saurashtra match – which I could watch from my second-floor doorstep overlooking the ground – I added to my cricket experience in another way. All India Radio were persuaded to put this match on the air. Nandi Khanna and I needed much less persuasion to act as commentators, with Professor Deodhar as the expert. Both Nandi and I did rather well at the microphone – at least so we thought – though we were quite sure that very few people listened in. (One person who had listened was M. G. Bhave, then Cricket Control Board secretary. He singled me out after the match and was kind enough to assure me that he would recommend me to AIR for more matches. Alas, AIR could not hear. Twenty years passed before I did an AIR cricket commentary again.) I was very keen to hear what I sounded like on the job, and my colleague, T. U. K. Menon, who was also a next-door neighbour in the Mess, arranged to make this possible by setting up the department's tape-recorder in his room. Thus I could finish a spell of live commentary and within minutes hear myself, not without self-congratulation, replayed on the tape.

Rain washed out the first day's play and yet the match finished within the next two days. Saurashtra were sent in to bat and collapsed for 83 to the Maharashtra medium-pacer V. B. Ranjane (who later played for India) making his first appearance in the tournament. It became a memorable debut for him because he bagged as many as nine wickets in the match – Nadkarni took the last one – including a hat-trick. Neither Nandi nor I had boned up in advance on previous records, but I came up with some facts and figures from back volumes of the *Indian Cricket Annual* I had in my room. Maharashtra replied with 332 (Nadkarni 125, S. Nyalchand 6 for 83), and skittled out Saurashtra again for 88 by the end of the third day. AIR packed up their stuff the same evening and went home (to Pune), thus depriving two hardworking radio commentators of their remuneration for one day.

That evening the Maharashtra team was challenged to a friendly match by the Academy, to be played on the following day, and it readily agreed. Hemu Adhikari, Nana Joshi and Nandi Khanna were included in the Academy side in order to strengthen it—so was 1, but this must have been by courtesy. Thus, it came about that I had the pleasure of batting against Bapu Nadkarni for nearly two overs. In the second, when I imagined I had got his measure, I stepped back to force him through the covers—only to be deceived altogether and rendered plumb l.b.w.

All this cricket and much more cricket talk was left behind when I left Khadakvasla in May 1957. But, besides happy memories of bat and ball, I carried away some cricket writing, and that will be the subject of another chapter.

[1996]

Fulbright Fielder

In July 1960, when I packed away – for ever, I thought – whatever personal cricket gear I possessed, had anybody told me that I would be playing cricket before another July came round again, I would not have believed him. Yet, before my first year in America was over, I was playing one match every week-end, sometimes two, through the long American summer on the east coast from mid-May to late August. This was repeated the following summer. I couldn't make it three summers running only because I returned home in June 1963. Had I stayed on, I would probably have captained the Fairmount Cricket Club team that year.

I suppose I was lucky that I went to graduate school in Philadelphia, which is on the eastern side of the continent, thus nearest to England and with the oldest connection to British culture. Even luckier was a shipboard conversation in which I was told that, if I telephoned one Mr Hobart in Philadelphia, he would tell me where I could find some cricket in that city. That name I regarded as a good omen, because about the only thing I knew of Tasmania was that all cricket teams touring Australia play a match in Hobart. I called him as soon as I had a telephone in my room (in early September) and he said that, the year's season being just over, I should call him again next April when the following season was about to begin. I did so and within a couple of weeks I had a bat in my hands, was standing on a net-practice pitch and squaring up to face a bowler.

No less lucky was the fact that the man who took charge of me there was Claud Bowen—in fact he and his wife Lois took charge of me and my wife on week-ends during the season. Brown-skinned, stocky and with grizzled hair, Claud's appearance looked quite familiar, though not his accent. As we soon came to know, he had migrated from the West Indies, married an American girl and settled down here; but his grandfather had migrated from India to Guyana, and Claud remembered Hindi being spoken among elders at home when he was a child. He also had vague memories of eating pakora and halwa, but wasn't sure which was salty and which sweet—a matter which was settled when he and his wife came for a meal to our apartment in due course.

From what I could gather before summer came around, in some previous years the University of Pennsylvania itself could muster enough players to make up a cricket team and engage in friendly matches now and then. This had depended on the regular inflow of Indian and Pakistani students who had played cricket at home. Lately, however, there were fewer cricketers among those who had come from the subcontinent and I never found another fellow-cricketer among the Indian acquaintances I made there. I was told that more and better cricket was to be found on the west coast, in the sunnier clime of California, where it had been started in Hollywood by British actors and had spread since then. I spent a moment of regret over the fact that I had not named one of the graduate schools in which the University of California abounds when I was filling up forms for the Fulbright award and naming options among universities.

Sometime late in April or early May 1961 Claud Bowen asked me to come over one Wednesday afternoon for net practice to Fairmount Park. I rummaged among my clothes and found a white shirt as well as an old pair of white gabardine trousers. I had of course brought my blazer along, intended not so much as sporting apparel but winter wear. By happy chance, my cricket cap had remained folded in a blazer-pocket, and this added to my self-confidence. For footwear I chose a pair of tennis-shoes which I had purchased after arrival in America. This was to do duty for me at various games not only in that country, but also for several years after I returned home.

Fairmount Park is a large but tamed forest in the northwestern sector of the city of Philadelphia. I never found out what municipal status was enjoyed by the Fairmount Cricket Club, but it exercised control over one ground and the adjoining house in a corner of the park. Claud Bowen had given me very clear directions about which gate to enter by – otherwise I could have spent the whole day looking for it – and I reached there after changing buses two or three times. I saw a very familiar sight when I entered—three or four people laying down a half-matting inside a tattered net enclosure. Claud had spotted me as soon as I arrived and he introduced me to the others. Without spending more time on civilities, I got down to helping with mat-laying and I think this immediately got me into Claud's good books. He couldn't have known I had done this quite often at home and regarded it as part of everybody's cricket education. As reward perhaps, I was invited to pad up and take first turn at batting. None of the regular bowlers had arrived yet, so I had a fairly easy time playing myself in and could even show off a little with fancy strokes before my turn concluded. It was wonderful to hold a bat between one's hands again, wonderful also to be able to step forward without thinking and drive the ball all along the grass. And to cap these feelings, even before I had taken off my pads, Claud tapped me on the shoulder and said I should turn up the following Saturday to play for the club in its next match. Several matches later – and after a particularly fruitful outing of mine with the bat – I overheard Claud boast to some others what a scoop he had made for the club by finding this 'Indian' cricketer. It almost sounded as if this cricketer was from the Indian test team.

That was how Fairmount Park became my 'home ground' for two seasons in America. The ground itself was quite large, ringed round with trees on three sides. On the fourth, right next to the cricket arena, was a stretch set aside for archery practice. Some time during the afternoon people would turn up carrying bows and arrows, set up large bulls-eye boards and pace out the distances from which to shoot. No wayward arrow ever endangered the cricketers. But occasionally a shapely woman in shorts drawing slowly back on her bow-string would distract some fielders.

The grass in Fairmount Park remained green throughout the summer, though I never saw any watering arrangement for achieving this. Perhaps the winter snow provided enough moisture to be secreted in the earth. The grass was longer as one moved away from the middle, but never thickly or troublesomely so. I expect Claud did some mowing during the week but I never saw him at it. As for rolling the pitch, all of us joined in pushing the roller up and down before every match, and sometimes at the end of the few net-practice sessions that were held. I don't know what other rolling was undergone by the wicket, but it did not behave too badly when matches were played on it. The club had no groundsmen on its staff, so Claud and his young sons must have attended to such chores as needed to be done.

The Bowens in fact lived in the house adjoining the ground. It had a wide and deep porch on the first floor, which doubled as a pavilion during a match and tea was served at the back during the break. Players' wives and girl-friends helped in laying out the tea table. A couple of rooms on the ground floor were used for changing one's clothes and for storing the cricket equipment. Another room downstairs was the club's bar, which I entered only by invitation—generally to celebrate some achievement of the day. The bar was meant for the regular subscription-paying members of the club who used it throughout the year. I was only a cricket member and, as a graduate student, did not qualify for regular membership. Thus, while I could have a beer off somebody else, nobody minded that I could not offer them the same courtesy.

As I got to know other players of my own club, and of those we played against, I came to realise that the ten or twelve teams that played each other in a loosely organised 'league' contained not a single American. The only true-born U.S. citizen I came across was our own Tony Palestini, then secretary of Fairmount Cricket Club more perhaps by virtue of his organising capacities than on account of any conspicuous cricketing ability. He did play on occasion, when we were really short, and did his best to translate baseball habits into plying a cricket bat or negotiating a cricket ball. More often, he would turn up with his plump young wife and even more chubby child and be content to loll on the grass and in the sun all day. That child was a particular attraction for my wife and me – who had left our own behind in Patna – and we loved playing with it whenever we got a chance.

Everybody else playing in these matches was English or West Indian or from India and Pakistan or, very rarely, a white South African. I had expected to meet more Indians than I did but was told that, if they were students, they were engrossed in their studies, and if employed they preferred to while away Saturday afternoons in less strenuous pastimes. The Pakistanis I came across were all employed, and I believe it was easier for them to find employment because of some visa privilege they enjoyed which Indians did not. Many of the West Indians appeared to be temporary residents (unlike our Claud Bowen), who had chosen to try their luck here rather than in England, and had not made up their minds yet. All the Englishmen I met had settled in America and this may have made them more obsessive about continuing to play cricket. They certainly helped the most in supplying equipment – bats, balls, gloves, pads – whoever went home, however briefly, always brought something back for his club. There was a large General Electric concern which employed a number of Englishmen, and their team was invariably better equipped with cricket gear than any other team in the league. General Electric were Fairmount's chief enemy, so there was no borrowing of cricket gear between them, but every year they tried to pinch players from one another.

I have to admit that it was the West Indian factor rather than the British or Indo-Pak element which often decided the fate of these league matches. That is, the side which could call upon some Jamaican or Barbadian bowler or batsman was generally at some advantage over sides which could not—more so, when, because of the roving life of these island people, they turned up where one least expected them. In a match against Paterson, for example, we were confidently bowling out the opposition when a black man in a blue safari suit and dark glasses – who had obviously stopped by to watch the proceedings – was prevailed upon to bat for the home side. This he proceeded to do with murderous effect, hitting everything out of sight for about half an hour or so. He stopped only when his dark glasses slipped off and he happened to tread on them. Another time – in the match against Staten Island, I think – the home team produced a coloured pace bowler who, bowling in suede ankle-boots and with his Panama hat on, made things pretty hot for us for a few overs with his lively speed until he felt thirsty and retired for remoistening, as he called it, of his tonsils. The last we saw of him was playing a guitar in between emptying cans of beer from a six-pack. Both of these dramatic episodes centred around cricketers who were said to have arrived from the West Indies. We used to tease Claud Bowen, our only representative from that realm, for failing to unearth such superstars for Fairmount. But then he had left the West Indies long ago and his current job probably did not keep him in touch with new migrants from his country of origin. What he did produce now and then was the driving power that must have been truly explosive when he was younger and his ankles did not hurt as they did now. Once in my view he nearly broke a bowler's foot even as the latter was following through after having bowled. One season Claud did succeed in persuading two brothers from St Kitts to play for the club but they were both whites and not really dynamic. One of them could not play often enough because he had to moonlight on week-ends to make some extra money; the other was more regular but served us in a quite unsensational capacity as wicketkeeper.

Among the British regulars of my club team were our pace-bowler Dickens, another opening bowler but of less pace named Patterson, and a third and much older man whose name was Cotton or Scotton (probably the latter because he used to be called Scotty). Whether because of their origin in relation to mine, or not, none of them was quite forthcoming without being unfriendly. Dickens, nearest to my age, was the friendliest. Nearly as tall and thin as I, with hair receding from his forehead, he bore some resemblance to the former England fast bowler Frank Tyson and strove his utmost to bowl as fast as he could whenever given the ball. Also, he never forgot to thank you when you took a catch off him in the slips, nor omitted, when you dropped one, to give you a forgiving nudge at the end of the over. Patterson shared the new ball with Dickens when we had a new ball in stock, but claimed that he preferred an old ball to a new one for swinging because, as he theorised, the older ball was easier to control. He was very strong on theory and, for an otherwise reserved and uncommunicative person, could wax quite eloquent on swerve and spin, arm-action and wrist-roll, and other such finer points of bowling. But he was also our main wicket-taker, hence we gave him a patient hearing. Scotty did not get along either with his fellow-countrymen or with us—which was a pity, because he was obviously crazy about cricket. This made him simply hog the batting or bowling whenever he got an opportunity to do so, and this naturally did not win him any friends. Now that I am older I can understand his situation better. He must have been about fifty years old then and, in return for a day's labour in the field, sought to make the most of whatever was available, dreading perhaps that day in the future when he would no longer be able to play. As a bowler, he didn't get many wickets, but neither did he give away many runs. Whenever an opposing pair of batsmen looked like settling down, Scotty would practically demand to be put on—and once put on, wouldn't easily let go. An inveterate smoker, he chain-smoked even while fielding. When his turn to bowl came, he would hand over a half-burnt cigarette to the umpire and take it back after completing his over. The only time he did not smoke was while batting, for which he employed a very effective range of prods and pushes which produced a single off the fifth or sixth ball of the over, which enabled him to retain the strike for several overs at a stretch. When a previous match had denied him the opportunity to bat – because of some unusual opulence in rungetting by those who preceded him – in the next match he would pad up to open without even waiting to be asked. Whereupon some of us would offer to open the batting along with him, just for the pleasure of getting him run out if possible. Quite his opposite was his wife (or the woman who came along with him for every match), a beaming and pleasant person who wrote our scorebook in her neat handwriting and could off-hand tell us our current batting or bowling averages. When not in action in the field, Scotty would skulk near her, puffing away at his cigarettes and muttering imprecations at whoever was batting or bowling.

There was no other Indian in the Fairmount Club team but I made friends very soon with two Pakistanis who played for us in the first year. They got along with my wife as well and visited us at home quite often. For my wife and I this was our first experience of getting to know any Pakistani, and we were fascinated—especially by the contrast between them. To begin with, Nasir was taller and fairer, more given to laughter and general enjoyment of things around him. Short and dark, Noor was moody and caustic, more given to complaining and calculating. When we got to know their origins we began to see why their temperaments should be different, at least in their attitude towards us. Nasir was of Pathan stock from way up northwest, barely knew even Lahore before he came to Philadelphia, had very little interest in India, past or present, thus carried not even a twig on his shoulder about Partition. Noor's family, however, was from Allahabad and they had moved after 1947, when Noor must have been a young boy. He certainly bore grudges against India and Indians, though he did his best not to give vent to any in our presence. We in our turn were careful to avoid what may be called delicate subjects between India and Pakistan when Noor was around. But neither he nor we were trained diplomats, and there would be occasional strains in conversation or of conduct, which was generally dissolved by the happy-go-lucky Nasir. Both of them were employed, but Nasir obviously was better off in America, as he must have been in Pakistan also. He owned a large drop-head automobile which he drove with zest and style, and often picked us up on our way to a match. Always with him, at least for one whole season, was his American girl-friend who made quite a picture at the ground, sitting on the grass under a floppy sun-hat and in short skirts which she decorously tugged at whenever anybody looked. Noor commanded none of these perks of a foreigner in America, and this could very well have strained his friendship with Nasir.

Noor, however, was very much the better cricketer – may in fact have been the best of our lot in Fairmount – though Nasir also had his days of triumph. It was rumoured that when in school Noor had played for the Pakistan Eaglets side. He neither denied nor confirmed this rumour, but conducted himself like the superstar of our team. A typically brisk and quick-footed one-down batsman, Noor did not score as many runs as he should have, when I saw him, because of his lack of patience. The same lack denied him deserved success as an off-spinner who had all the blandishments of flight and turn fit for higher levels of cricket, but he probably also needed better catching support than we were able to offer. He could be quite short with fieldsmen who let him down. And it became painful for all concerned when Scotty and Noor happened to be batting together. Sometimes they would stop in mid-pitch during a run and exchange unpleasantries. I later felt that poor Noor was trying to get out of cricket what life was denying him, and this made him a difficult fellow-player. Even when he had batted or bowled well he could not relax afterwards and responded somewhat ungraciously to any congratulations. In my second season he took it into his head that he should be nominated captain of Fairmount Club, so that, in his opinion, the team's batting and bowling could be properly managed during matches. When he heard that somebody else had been made captain (probably John Dickens), Noor promptly went over to General Electric and offered to join them. Such was his obvious quality as a cricketer that his offer was promptly accepted—though we beat General Electric that year all the same.

That was a good season all around for Fairmount. We not only defeated General Electric but won more matches than any other team and could claim to be league champions of the year. Somehow the absence of a prickly Noor helped us to play better as a team, with only Scotty there as a hazard to fellow-feeling. My scoring more runs than in the previous year made up a little for our losing Noor's contribution while, even more remarkably, Nasir produced several match-winning performances with bat, or ball to earn us unexpected victories. The needle game, of course, was against General Electric, and we knew Noor would be breathing fire and vengeance at it. We even had some pre-match net practice and a discussion that evening on strategy. During these Nasir and I often broke into Hindi (or Hindustani) to press our points of view, and this irritated somebody enough to tell us to stop jabbering in some savage lingo and think instead of what was to be done about Noor, since he would be the main danger on the morrow. Whereupon Nasir and I promptly offered, in English as well as in Hindi, to look after him if he was left to us.

Quite magically, that is precisely what happened. When General Electric batted first, Nasir claimed and was permitted use of the new ball. This gave him early access to Noor, who quite early snicked a catch which I managed to take at first slip. And when we batted, Nasir and I got paired off for the third or fourth wicket and we wasted no time in getting at Noor. When he pitched short, Nasir clouted him cross-batted all over square-leg and mid-wicket; when he pitched up, I drove him long-batted over the heads of mid-off and mid-on. Both of us got out, caught off Noor, but not before we had secured our position in the match. The pleasant thing at the end was that after it was all over, Noor joined our victory celebration and conveyed to me (though not to Nasir) sotto voce that he had made a mistake in joining that bunch of unprintable and again unprintable Englishmen who constituted the General Electric team.

Most of our league matches were played in and around Philadelphia, but some were much further away. My wife and I did not own a car and were wholly dependent on Nasir who cheerfully took us wherever necessary. Then there were 'friendly' games, outside the league fixtures, and one such was a match with Haverford College on their ground. There we were assured that this was one of the oldest centres of cricket (apart from and despite being a hoary seat of learning) in the country, cricket having been played there without a break for over two hundred years. In real terms, as we found out soon, at least one match had been played here every year for two centuries—and this year we were helping to sustain that continuity. The college by no means specialised in cricket and most of its students sprouted fledgling beards in colours ranging between orange and auburn. In the field they struck baseball postures while standing at odd non-cricket positions; but nobody, when they batted, urged them on with rallying cries of 'Batterr-up!' The wicket was on a mound in the centre of the ground, and even the mildly struck ball ran away quickly. The gradient on either slope away from the wicket was enough for a prostrate cover-point to remain invisible to mid-wicket even if the latter stood upright. Nobody actually prostrated himself at cover-point, but I discovered this topographical feature when, after my batting was over, I watched the game lying on my tummy. From there, the wicket appeared to touch the sky-line while the wicketkeeper, batsman, umpire and bowler all seemed to stride the horizon.

I have already mentioned Staten Island – which one normally reaches by ferry from Manhattan – and Paterson, where the local river has been made famous in *Paterson,* a long poem (in 4 vols!) by the modern American poet William Carlos Williams, who also practiced medicine in that town. At the former place we played inside an athletics stadium, and any ball hit for four crossed a cinder track before reaching the boundary. When retrieving, I was sorely tempted to do a record-breaking fifty-metres sprint on that track before returning the ball. As for the match at Paterson, I could not locate the river, hence made no attempt to hit a six into it. Even had I done so, there being no Am. Lit. persons in our team, nobody would have spotted the allusion. Incidentally, an occupational hazard of playing cricket in America was that passers-by would stop and want to know what the heck was going on here. However patiently you tried to explain, when any American heard two 'batters' were on at the same time, he generally gave up trying to understand.

The furthest extremities of our travelling to play cricket lay, to the north, in Hamilton, Ontario (in Canada) and, to the south, in Washington, D. C. I couldn't because of some other preoccupation make the trip to Hamilton, which would have involved crossing a national border and participating in a kind of international encounter. Some flavour of the latter was present when I went to Washington – along with Nasir, Noor and a couple of others from Philadelphia – to take part in a two-day festival match between the U. K. High Commissioner's XI and a Commonwealth XI, which was played on a ground within sight of the Potomac river. I don't know who sent out invitations to players meant to form the latter side, but obviously that agency did not expect all the invites to accept and also turn up. About seventeen aspirants arrived and somewhat brusque queries were beginning to be bandied about when a typically British and no less typically diplomatic compromise was devised. The two-day match was turned into two one-day matches on successive days, with different elevens representing the Commonwealth on different days. About half of those who had assembled for the honour thus played only once. I was among them and grumbled a little because the trip had called for two long drives and one overnight stop. Even if the shared transport costs did not amount to much, a half-share of a motel-room for the night was not an expense I could gladly incur then—and less so when my room-mate for the night was another male cricketer. However, some satisfaction came on the second day when I played, not because I scored some twenty runs without effort and would have got more had I not played on quite providentially, but because when I unpadded and sat down, a West Indian gentleman (diplomat, I was told later) leaned back from the first row to say how much he had enjoyed watching me bat and what a pity I got out the way I did. Those courteous words were enough to keep me cheerful company on the three hundred and more miles back through late night to Philadelphia.

Another season was under way for Fairmount Cricket Club when I left Philadelphia to return home in 1963. I went to say goodbye to Claud and his family. When I visited Philadelphia again twelve years later, it was April, still chilly, and cricket far away. So was Claud Bowen, who had died some years earlier, and the family, which had moved to the mid-West. I did not go to Fairmount Park. Even if somebody else was running the cricket club just as well, it could not have been the same.

[1996]

Part III: Meditations

Prefatory Parsis

In cricket – as in industry or commerce or education or philanthropy – the Parsi community's contribution to India's development in these and other public causes has been utterly out of proportion to the size of the community. They naturalised cricket to Indian soil, undertook cricket missions to England, and fostered the domestic tournament which matured Indian cricket towards international reckoning. And, of course, in modern times they have invariably produced a player or two for our test elevens—Palia, Meheromji, Modi, Umrigar, Contractor, and so on. When Farokh Engineer strides out today to bat or to keep wickets for India, stretching behind him is a long, unbroken line of service to Indian cricket.

Available records do not tell us with any precision when cricket was first played on the Indian subcontinent, but there is evidence to show that the first Indians to play this game were the Parsis when, in 1848, one Mr. Boswell who ran a school inside the fort at Bombay, "initiated young Zoroastrians in the game". They must have taken to the game like fire to wood, because the same year saw the founding of the first ever cricket club of Indians, the Oriental Cricket Club. This was reconstituted two years later and given the more specific name, the Zoroastrians, under which it played matches against local regimental teams. I do not know when the first non-Zoroastrian Indian batted or bowled, nor is it easy to discover whether non-Zoroastrians were institutionally discouraged at this stage from sharing the Parsi predilection for cricket. Accounts of these early days, like M. E. Pavri's *Parsi Cricket* (published 1901) or J. M. Framjee Patel's *Stray Thoughts on Indian Cricket* (published 1905)[1] or Shapoorji Sorabjee's *A*

[1] Much of the information used here is derived from this book, from which notes were supplied by M. K. Das.

Chronicle of Cricket among Parsees all written by Zoroastrians, do not seem to mention other Indians playing cricket. Perhaps, if they did, they failed to distinguish themselves and are thus unworthy of the chroniclers' attention.

The main public arena for this game at the time was the Bombay Esplanade Ground (today's Azad Maidan) and its surroundings were quite different then. The sea licked its chops below where Queen's Road runs at present, hence the Bombay Gymkhana stood, already then in occupancy of its present position, to the *south* of the Esplanade ground. On the northern and eastern boundaries were 'stately buildings' (doubtless none higher than three storeys), while to the west were broad roads and shady trees.

The Parsi cricketer of the day was still oriental enough to dress as he liked at play, and Framjee Patel has quoted this contemporary description: "He went to the wicket with a white band around his forehead, giving him quite the air of the inmate of some hospital, and a still whiter apron dangling from his waist, which was encircled by the sacred thread of his faith. Thus equipped, with patent leather boots and silken trousers, he was a fit study for an artist. The dazzling and deceptive sun he did not mind a bit. No sola topee protected him while at the wicket."

Fast underhand bowling was quickly developed by the Parsis, and was countered in due course by the 'draw or under-leg stroke', for which the batsman lifted his left leg and let the ball pass the bat towards the leg side. Slower bowlers provided variety by bowling the 'tice' – a ball that is dropped nearly at full pitch – or the 'hanging ball', which seemed to stop in the air before pitching or on the ground after pitching. Against such blandishments, some batsmen employed the 'hanging guard', whereby he did not meet the ball with the bat but allowed the ball to come and strike the bat. Forward play had not yet been conceived of, nor the good length ball. Instead, a ball at 'three-quarter' length, was the one to be admired. When he was out, the batsman did not return to the pavilion since he had not come from one. No pavilions existed. Canvas tents set up on the eastern side of the maidan provided whatever sanctuary that was needed.

Early contests seem to have been confined to one Parsi team playing against another, or a Parsi side playing against a garrison team. This will explain the historic importance of the occasion when, in 1877, for the first time an Indian team played against an 'Anglo-Indian' team. By 'Anglo-Indian' is meant Europeans resident or serving in India, whose organised cricket grew up around the two gymkhanas at Bombay and Poona. The word gymkhana today stands for any club which offers some sports facilities to its members, but originally it meant '*gendkhana*' (literally, a room where a ball-game is played), the Indian term for the racquet courts built by Europeans. Thus the Bombay Gymkhana, to begin with, was no more than a racquet court on the maidan.

In 1877, the Parsis (they preferred to spell it 'Parsees' in those days) played this historic game against Bombay Gymkhana and lost. To the Gymkhana score of 168 the Parsis replied with 105 (Dr. Kapadia 28, S. Bezanji 19). This match is sometimes cited as the origin of inter-communal cricket in India, though by strict definition this is the beginning of inter-racial cricket in the country.

Another germination which occurred this year was the desire to undertake a cricket tour of the mother country of cricket. It is difficult for us today to imagine the kind of initiative, confidence and enterprise owned by these men, as yet in their infancy of cricket, who even conceived of such an undertaking. Not surprisingly, the project took nine years to bear fruit. The burden of organising it fell upon A. B. Patel, J. M. Framjee Patel and B. B. Baria. What hours and days and months of calculation and persuasion and preparation they must have expended, the records do not tell us. But on 12 August 1886, the first Indian side to play circket in England set sail. It was the first team of Indians for any sport to go abroad, and it consisted entirely of 'Parsees'. At an eve-of-departure dinner in their honour, Sir P. M. Mehta summed up the tour objective in these words: "As artists go to Italy to do homage to the Great Masters, or as pilgrims go to Jerusalem to worship at a shrine, or as students in the Middle Ages went to the great seats of learning in places where science and philosophy had made their home, so now the Parsees are going to England to do homage to the English cricketers, to learn something of that noble and manly pastime in the very country which is its chosen home."

The team was captained by D. H. Patel, a steady batsman and a fast underhand bowler, who stayed behind in England after the tour was over to complete his medical studies. Other notable members were batsmen like P. D. Dastur, A. C. Major, J. M. Morenas members were batsmen like P. D. Dastur, A. C. Major, J. M. Morenas and S. H. Harwar, and bowlers like D. D. Khambata, B. B. Baria, S. N. Bhedawar and M. Framjee. The last-named was the only over-arm bowler in the side. They played 28 matches, won 1. drew 8 and lost 19. W. G. Grace is reported to have summed up the visit as one which "met with very little success, even against second and third rate clubs". The only win was registered at Normanhurst, the 'seat' of Lord Brassey, where the visitors defeated the local team by an innings and 62 runs. Cricket apart, they received much hospitality from British aristocracy. During the opening game at the 'seat' of the Earl of Sheffield, one member later confessed to have drunk only champagne. The social high point of the trip was a match at Windsor Great Park against the Cumberland Lodge XI, for whom two royal highnesses, Christian and Albert, played. The whole enterprise was duly commended in a British journal in these terms: "The Parsee fraternity is the most intelligent as well as the most loyal of the races scattered over our Indian possessions. For some years past the Parsees have given substantial proof of their affection for our national game, and striven hard, in spite of great climatic disadvantages, to acquit themselves with great credit on the cricket field."

Such commendation could not but fire loyal Parsi hearts to burn brighter and, undeterred by the field record of the 1886 team, a second trip was undertaken in 1888. The organisers this time (P. D. Kanga, J. M. Divecha and D. C. Pundole) were different, only two members of the first team (Morenas and Harwar) joined the second, and just two home seasons separated the first trip from the second. One cannot but wonder whether or not those who were denied a berth on the first tour determined to make a separate trip of their own. If so, they took care to pay due attention to the cricketing abilities (apart from other vital resources) of whoever was invited. The team returned home with a much better record (played 31, won 8, drew 12, lost 11) and even W. G. Grace admitted "there was great improvement on their first visit, when everything went against them. In one thing they showed excellent promise, their consistent effort in playing an uphill match". Financially, however, this undertaking was as large a loss as the last one.

The Parsi team to England of 1888 was led by H. D. Kanga, an accomplished all-rounder who bowled slow underhand but was a free-stroking batsman. In support were N. C. Bapasola, an even more complete all-rounder since he could keep wickets as well; bespectacled R. D. Cooper, a good batsman and the main wicketkeeper; M. E. Pavri, fast right-arm bowler; D. F. Dubash, a steady and elegant batsman; K. R. Erani, another right-arm fast bowler and quick-scoring batsman; D. S. Mehta, the only lob bowler among the Parsis; D. C. Pundole, bowler of slow, flighted off-breaks; D. N. Writer, fast left-arm bowler. Cooper who totalled 952 runs in 55 innings and Dubash with 810 runs in 54 innings topped the batting averages. Among the bowlers, Pavri's 170 wickets placed him way ahead of the others. He took 32 catches as well, only two less than Cooper behind the stumps. This team also fielded better than the last one, and won several of their matches from positions of disadvantage. Fewer names of British nobility were among their hosts, and their notable victory against the Gentlemen of Eastbourne was subsequently eulogised in verse:

THE HEATHEN PARSEES
(A long way after Bret Harte)

Now I wish to remark, and my language is plain,
That for ways that are dark, and for tricks that are vain,
The Heathen Parsee is peculiar, and the same I would like to explain.
It was August the third, and soft were the skies,
Which it might be inferred, the Parsees were likewise,
But they played it that day upon Bournemouth, in a way to open our eyes.
When we had a small game with the artful Hindoo,
It was cricket the same, to Parsees something new,
For they had come all the way from Calcutta to pick up a wrinkle or two.
And the balls that they bowled, with ineffable glee,
And the Yorkers that told, were quite frightful to see,
Till we at Bournemouth looked at each other, and said "How on earth can this be?"
Then the Parsees went in and we gave them a shout,
And pulled up our slacks, for to bundle them out,
But the foreigners were not to be beaten, and that Cooper, he knocked us all out
Then we rose in our places, and said all disgusted,
These Indian races are not to be trusted,

For we thought we had got a soft thing on, and so! We were utterly busted.

Whatever Indian cricket (as represented by the Parsis) did or did not achieve in England, at home the real test in the 1880s was the match-of-the-season against the European (as represented by the British) stronghold, Bombay Gymkhana. The first such Indian-vs-European encounter, as already mentioned, had taken place in 1877. It soon became an annual fixture, the Indian side of it monopolised by the Parsis, and was regarded almost as an international contest. The non-Parsi sectors of Bombay cricket took some time to organise. A Hindu Cricket Club was formed in 1878, but not until 1884 did the 'Hindoos' play their first representative match against Bombay Gymkhana. Subsequently, Sir Permanand Das Jivan Das made a handsome donation and the club was renamed the P. J. Hindu Gymkhana, the name it bears today in Bombay as well as in Poona. The Muslims formed their first club in 1883, but called it the Mohammedan Gymkhana only in 1893. A few years later it assumed the present name Islam Gymkhana.

Turning their attention inland after those two forays abroad, the Parsis helped to establish inter-regional cricket connections by undertaking trips to principal cricket centres in 'upper' India. These, at that time, seem to have been Patiala, Aligarh, Allahabad and Muzaffarpur. The Parsis participated regularly in annual festivals organised by the Maharajah of Patiala at his 'seat' or at Simla. At Allahabad there is record of a match played by the Parsis as far back as 1891. Muzaffarpur in North Bihar has very little cricket today, but was then the headquarters of British indigo planters. Their resources were equal to their defeating Lord Hawke's team in 1892, but the previous year a visiting Parsi side overwhelmed them by nine wickets. On the same trip, possibly, the Parsis ventured as far as Calcutta in search of cricket, but found no 'baboos' among their opponents.

Of these centres in 'upper' India, Aligarh was the only one which could field a hundred per cent Indian and a wholly non-Parsi team against visiting sides. This great nursery of Muslim cricketers comprised the students, past and present, of the Muslim Anglo-Oriental College at Aligarh, which would later become the Aligarh Muslim University. They held their own against touring

Parsis and themselves visited Bombay in 1903, losing only one match (to the Old Elphinstonians by 23 runs) and beating the Parsis on the home ground by 196 runs.

The pre-eminence of Parsi cricket, established beyond dispute in local competition, was reaffirmed at a higher level on at least three occasions when touring sides from England played in Bombay. G. F. Vernon's team of 1890 obtained a narrow first-innings lead (97 to 80), but M. E. Pavri (7 for 34) bowled the Parsis into a winning position when the visitors were bundled out for 61 in the second innings. A crowd estimated at twelve thousand, enormous by standards of the day, watched while the home team lost six wickets in getting the runs necessary for win—the first win of an Indian team over a team of visiting cricketers from England.

Perhaps in recognition of this achievement, the Parsis were granted two fixtures against Lord Hawke's team in 1892. In the first match, the Parsis enlarged upon a first innings lead of twenty runs (93 to 73) to reach a total of 182 (topscorer Bapasola 52) at the second try. Again it was M. E. Pavri (8 for 54) who insured victory for the home team when the visitors were all out for 93. In the return fixture, however, Lord Hawke's team won narrowly by seven runs.

The Parsis vs Oxford Authentics match 1902 produced a lot of runs and yet another triumph for the home champions. The Authentics batted first and recovered from early lapses (caused by the accurate bowling of A. H. Mehta, 6 for 97) mainly through a determined innings of 111 by R. H. Raphael to reach a total of 311. The Parsis replied strongly with 406, borne to this elevation by D. D. Kanga (116) and H. D. Kanga (66). This partnership between the Kanga brothers put on 157 runs. Then pace bowlers A. H. Mehta (3 for 59) and M. D. Bulsara (3 for 36) got working to cut the visitors down to 124 in the second innings, leaving the home team only thirty runs to make to win—which they did for the loss of two wickets.

A benchmark was carved in 1892 when the first 'Presidency' match was organised in Bombay as a more developed form of inter-racial contest already inaugurated by the historic match of 1877. By 1886 the various Parsi clubs had got together to form the Parsi Gymkhana and (though not under this cognomen) undertake those two tours of England in 1886 and 1888. In

1889 they challenged the Europeans represented by Bombay Gymkhana in fair combat. The Parsis batted first and mustered 87 runs; the opposition surpassed it to make 125. The Parsis did a little better at their second time with the bat and totalled 95; they did a great deal better with the ball and had the ninth Bombay Gymkhana wicket down for 54. The last batsman clouted a ball away to leg, ran one, then sauntered back down the pitch thinking that the stroke had gone for four—and was thrillingly run out when the ball was retrieved before he could regain the safety of his crease. The Parsis thus proved the point by two runs, and the idea of an annual fixture between them and the masters was born.[2]

Although the 'Presidency' team sought to give wider representation to all cricketing Anglo-Indians of the Bombay Presidency, in effect the team comprised players drawn from Bombay and Poona cities only. These fixtures were held twice a year, one at either city, and this arrangement enabled Poona to grow into an important cricketing centre. Already the Poona Gymkhana, founded in 1891, provided a nucleus for local Europeans addicted to cricket. Now the Presidency matches added an annual event that was of sporting as well as social importance. The first Presidency match, at Bombay in 1892, ended in a draw. It has gone down in history as the 'Fire Engine Match', not because of any incendiary episode during the game but because fire-engines were called in before play could begin to drain out the water from the rain-soaked outfield.

Perhaps it was the persistent exclusiveness of the Indian side in these presidency matches that compelled the inter-racial character of this institution to develop in an inter-communal direction. While Aligarh had been fostering Muslim cricketers in the last decade of the nineteenth century, the Hindus mainly of Bombay were showing unmistakable signs of having developed adequate cricketing skills with which to challenge the Parsi hegemony. Names such as those of the hard-driving batsman G. K. Telang or of the crafty slow bowler P. Baloo were associated with the best in native cricketing talent of the 1890s. When the

2 If not the term 'masters', something similar was allegedly used by Ranji when, in 1898, he seemed to disapprove of Indians playing cricket against Englishmen in India.

Hindus were awarded a fixture against the visiting Oxford Authentics team in 1903, they managed an honourable draw after being outclassed in the first innings. The interesting feature of the Hindus eleven for this match is that it contained five outstation players—three from Madras, S. G. Seshachari (wicketkeeper), T. D. Narayana Rao and M. Subbarayalu; Shivlal from Kathiawar; and Rajalingam from Kamptee, near Nagpur.

A theoretical exercise indulged in by J. M. Framjee Patel in 1904 reveals the extent to which cricket had spread in the country at the beginning of the century. There was talk, at the end of the Authentics tour, of sending a 'combined' Indian team to England in the summer of 1904. The Parsi Gymkhana held a number of meetings and began collecting funds by public subscription. But the tour did not materialise, partly because enough funds could not be collected, and partly because some leading (Parsi?) players were not available for the trip. Framjee Patel proposed the following team for the tour:

K. S. Ranjitsinhji or Dr. M. E. Pavri (Parsis), Captain; K. M. Mistry (Parsis), all-rounder; P. Baloo (Hindus), slow bowler; R. P. Meheromji (Parsis), opening batsman; A. H. Mehta (Parsis), fast bowler; Ali Hasan (Aligarh), medium-pace bowler; S. G. Seshachari (Madras), wicketkeeper; H. D. Kanga (Parsis), batsman; B. Jayaraju (Mysore), batsman; Ahsan-al-Hak (Aligarh), batsman; G. D. Telang (Hindus), batsman; D. D. Kanga (Parsis), wicketkeeper-batsman; Shafkat (Aligarh), slow bowler; M. D. Bulsara (Parsis), fast bowler.

All seven Parsis were from Bombay, unless Captain Mistry had already joined as A. D. C. to the Maharajah of Patiala. All three from Aligarh were Muslims; Ahsan-al-Hak was in fact an Afridi from the North West Frontier Province and later played for Middlesex. Of the four Hindus (excluding Ranji), only two were from Bombay. Altogether, this is the first ever pre-figuration of an 'All-India' team to be sent abroad.

The team that did go to England in 1911 gave concrete shape to this concept. The original sixteen contained three from Patiala, six from Bombay, three from Aligarh, and one each from Madras, Bangalore, Delhi and Kashmir. Two withdrawals were filled by players already available in England, Prince Shivajirao Gaekwad (Baroda) and M. P. Bajana (Cooch Behar). Community-wise, the breakdown was six Parsis, six Hindus and four Muslims, led by a Sikh (the then Maharaja of Patiala).

The presidency matches between the Europeans and the Parsis were opened to admit the Hindus in 1895 (?), and it thus became a Triangular Tournament. Seventeen years later it became a Quadrangular when the Muslims joined in 1912. The Parsis duly won in the year of inception but were champions only twice more until 1929. The Europeans, only slightly less localised than the Parsis whose human resources were confined to Bombay, won the championship four times during the same period. The Muslims – who were called the 'Mahomedans' in this tournament – made a glorious entry by defeating the Europeans in their very first match in 1912, but had to wait until 1924 for their first championship success. The Hindus won for the first time in 1919, four times more until 1929, (the tournament was suspended between 1930 and 1933) and once more in 1936—six times altogether, while the Mohamedan's successive wins of 1934 and 1935 brought their tally to three.

In 1937, the 'Rest' side (conceived by A. S. de Mello and consisting of Eurasians—the Anglo–Indians and Indian Christians) was admitted, making this national tournament a five-sided contest. The Pentangular confirmed what the Quadrangular matches had already revealed, namely, that the Parsi predominance of Indian cricket had passed for ever, and that the resident Europeans never really had a chance once all Indian communities took to cricket. Neither the Parsis nor the Europeans ever won the Pentangular. Individual Parsis have continued to excel at the highest levels of Indian cricket, offering occasional reminders of what the community has contributed to the making of Indian cricket. If the Bombay Cricket Association had been more conscious of history and less vulnerable to patronage, they would surely have named the new cricket stadium after a Mistry or a Pavri or a Kanga or a Warden.

[1976]

An Early Cricket Writer

How many of those who play or watch or write about Ranji Trophy cricket know that Ranji was not only our first cricketer of renown but also among our first cricket-writers? He played very little cricket in India and wrote almost nothing about Indian cricket, but *The Jubilee Book of Cricket* by K. S. Ranjitsinhji, published by William Blackwood and Sons (Edinburgh and London) in 1897 occupies a permanent place at the top of our cricket writing averages.

Dedicated "*by Her Gracious Permission to her Majesty The Queen-Empress*", the publication was issued in three separate editions. The first was the 'Edition De Luxe', in Crown Quarto, printed on handmade paper and handsomely bound in buckram. It carried 22 photogravures and 85 full-page plates. Limited to 350 copies, each of which was signed by 'Prince Ranjitsinhji', this was priced at £5 5s. One imagines that most of these copies were given away. Having inscribed his name on each copy, would the Prince have cared to sell his signature?

Secondly, there was the fine paper edition in Medium Octavo, with a photogravure frontispiece and 106 full-page plates on art-paper, priced at 25 shillings.[1] This edition is the one usually seen in India, in the possession of old libraries or in family collections.

Then there was the popular edition in Crown Octavo size, with 107 full-page illustrations, priced at six shillings. This ran into at least six editions and there was at least one poem written about it in England soon after the edition was released. The poem began:

> To buy it all the people press.
> With a despairing eagerness ... etc.

---

[1] One copy at the Kanga Cricket Library in Bombay carries a printed slip with the monogram of the Sussex County Cricket Club, indicating that this was originally a presentation copy. But the name of the donor is absent.

About two-thirds of this 465-page book discuss the theory and practice of the game, as understood by Ranji, with profuse reference to contemporary English exponents. The rest of the volume is taken up by chapters on Public School Cricket (by W. J. Ford), Oxford University Cricket (by Thomas Case), Cambridge University Cricket (by Ford again), and on County Cricket (by various writers).

These four chapters would be of no interest to Indian readers, and could not be of much interest even to today's British readers.[2] Ranji concludes the book with a chapter on Cricket and the Victorian Era, wherein he develops the theme: "The rise and fulfilment of athleticism, until it has become a most important aspect of British life, has been one of the marked characteristics of the Victorian era." As this sample sentence shows, Ranji's batsmanship may have been idiosyncratic but his prose style was very much in the great tradition.

Not much in the book reveals the secrets of Ranji's success as a batsman. But there are five full-page photographs which, even in the fixity of late nineteenth century photography, show him as somehow quite different from the leading batsmen in English cricket of his time, whose photographs are also available in the book for comparison. The photograph on page 197 which illustrates the Ranji leg-glance is fit to be embossed on the Ranji Trophy itself. The legs are crossed, the bat aslant, the right hand low and preparing to hypnotise the ball into changing direction—and sending 'A. E.' and Cardus and A. G. Gardiner into raptures. He explains the stroke on the opposite page: "Different batsmen play the stroke in different ways. Some draw their feet close together, some turn considerably, and some get right in front of the wicket. Personally I move my left foot across the wicket towards point, face the ball with my body from the waist upwards, watch it on to the bat, and despatch it at the last moment by a quick turn of the wrist. The great thing is to have the bat from the start in the line of the ball, so that in the case of a mistake in timing, the ball hits the bat and not the leg ... People often say to me, 'That leg-stroke of yours is very risky. If you miss the ball you must be out leg-before.' Quite so; but one would be out pretty frequently, clean bowled, if one missed the ball. So it

[2] These were omitted from the popular edition.

does not make much difference whether or not the legs are in front of the wicket."

Neville Cardus has said somewhere that "play back or drive" was the main principle of Ranji's batting. Four out of the five photographs of Ranji in this book show him playing back. In some other book I recall seeing a photograph of him launched into a drive, both feet off the ground. That must be a very rare instance indeed because much of what one reads of Ranji's batsmanship suggests he played more often from behind the crease than before it. As he himself asserts, "I believe tremendously in backplay" (p. 174).

Ranji's exposition of the game begins, characteristically, with a chapter on fielding. "Good fielding is as helpful as bad fielding is noxious," he says. "To a certain extent it turns bad bowling into good, and makes good bowling better" (p. 9). He claims that the fielding at Raj Kumar College (where he went to school from 1882 to 1888) was not only better than their batting or bowling, but was superior to that of an average English public school eleven of that time. This is a situation that surely declined ruinously as batting and bowling developed in India. Ranji could not have anticipated this, but his stress on good fielding is an example that no Indian coach should ever neglect to reiterate.

The next two chapters are on bowling and on batting. The chapter on bowling confirms a view I have held for long that batsmen analyse bowling better than bowlers can, just as bowlers can analyse batting better than batsmen can. Their own skill they employ without needing to comprehend it, but it is vital that they study and understand their natural enemy. They teach their own craft better by demonstrating it than by expounding it. Ranji himself concurs indirectly when he says, "Young players should always be encouraged to bring their imitative faculties to bear upon cricket. They should be advised to watch good players, and to absorb into their own play everything that is good in that of others ... On the whole, I think more cricket can be learnt by watching good performers than in any other way" (p. 158).

The chapter on bowling has two valuable and unique sections. The first is a series of thirteen field settings for various types of bowling, with alternative positions suggested for a particular state of the cricket. Nothing so thoughtful and elaborate has been offered, as far as I know, in a cricket book again. The second interesting feature – which immediately follows the above – is a brief account of an imaginary innings by a typical eleven, narrated from the bowling side's point of view. Each batsman is introduced in terms of his strength and weakness, then we are told how the bowler plans to get him out. The batsmen are given names, which facilitates narration. To quote a sample: "As the wicket is good the left-hander (medium-pace opening bowler) cannot get much break on the ball, so he determines to feed Stockwell's off-drive judiciously. He first gives him a couple of straight good-length balls, then a beauty to drive on the off, which flies past extra-cover to the boundary. Then he bowls one rather wider and rather faster, at which Stockwell tries the same stroke, mistimes it, and sends the ball spinning straight at third-man's head. Third-man gets his hand in the right place, but fails to let them yield to the ball. Consequently it bounces out of his hands on to the ground. Hard luck on the bowler! Stockwell steadies himself after this and will not pick another 'wrong 'un" (p.130). As a briefing on tactics, such an account is far more effective than a formal discussion. My only complaint is that Ranji did not write about an actual match and comment on its tactical points.

The chapter on batting is naturally the largest. It is also unnaturally correct and conventional, when one recalls that in watching its author's own batting, in the words of Cardus, "you turned from the known world of law and order to the world of the occult." The general principles recommended by Ranji are irrefutable. Every now and then, there are incomparable asides. Thus, while discouraging the jab or dab (he actually uses the phrase "slipping the ball") through the slips, he reflects: "In its worst form this is commonly known nowadays as the 'if-stroke'. Originally it was called the 'but-stroke', after its great exponent, the Sussex wicketkeeper; but some wag suggested that it should be called in preference the 'if-stroke', because if you hit the ball you are nearly sure to be out" (p. 182). Or, on the importance of judging the ball's flight: "A yorker does not exist absolutely: its existence depends upon some mistake made by the batsman in judging the flight of the ball. This is rather enigmatical—it smacks of metaphysics; but the practical aspect of the statement is that, no yorker is ever bowled which by proper timing might not be turned into a full-pitch" (p. 177). Or, in recommending moderation and relaxation: "A man who is engaged in heavy brain-work, such as writing a book on cricket or trying to matriculate at a Cambridge college, cannot expect to be at his best in the cricket-field" (p. 228). And, of course, there are any number of pithy statements, almost epigrammatical in their force and truth: "By continual practice the artificial actions of cricket become second nature" (p. 152); "Batsmen, besides learning the strokes, must study the relations of various strokes to the wickets" (p. 203); "Playing with a straight bat is to batting what good length is to bowling" (p. 209).

Smaller chapters on captaincy and on umpiring, then the final chapter, complete Ranji's longest innings with the pen. The volume is not easy to come by these days in India. Even if a modern cricketer were to lay his hands on it, he may not find the leisurely prose and courteous argument easy reading. Most of the names mentioned would also be unfamiliar to the Indian reader, unless he is well-read enough to remember that Lord Hawke (shown cutting on p. 223) brought a team out to India in 1892, K. J. Key (also shown cutting, on p. 287) toured India with the Oxford Authentics in 1904, and F. S. Jackson (shown forcing the ball to leg on p. 293) not only made a cricket trip to India but returned later on a gubernatorial assignment.

Many of the illustrations, however, are faintly comic. Action photography had not yet matured, and most of the photographs show famous English cricketers of the Victorian era frozen in various awkward attitudes of batting or bowling or fielding, waiting for the photographer to release them from the obligation of having to stand still until the camera had done its work. Only to the connoisseur there are compensations which make a search for the book worthwhile even in 1976.

[1976]

Cricket by the Book

Among many factors that distinguish the game of cricket is one by which its great exponents are remembered for much longer than those of any other game. The reason is easy to locate: cricket and cricketers get written about and read of far more than any other game and its exponents. As a result, cricket has a large reading public for whom a famous cricketer plays on and lives long after he has actually stopped playing and even living. Before the advent of television in this country there was a phenomenal and growing number of persons who watched or listened to or read about cricket, in English and in our many other languages. I used to wonder, at that juncture, why, as compared to the watchers, listeners and readers, so few in India wrote on cricket and even fewer published books on the subject. That situation persists.[1]

Yet, the history of such publication, though sparse, is quite old, because the first book on cricket by an Indian which is also the first book on Indian cricket appeared nearly one hundred years ago. Had it not done so, the honour of being the first Indian author of a cricket book would have gone five years later to one who was the first Indian to have won international fame as a cricketer. We may not always remember but another Ranji Trophy could quite appropriately be instituted for our champion cricket writers. Kumar Shri Ranjitsinhji was not only out first great batsman but also among our first cricket writers. He played very little

[1] *Editor's Note:* With characteristic modesty, Sujit Mukherjee has failed to mention his own significant contribution to the literature of Indian cricket. He is the author of three widely acclaimed books *The Romance of Indian Cricket (1968), Between Indian Wickets* (1976), and *Playing for India* (second edition, 1987), with a fourth, *A Couple of Wickets* in press. *Seminar* 371, July 1980. [The last was published as *Matched Winners* by Orient Longman in 1996.]

cricket in India and wrote almost nothing about Indian cricket, but his *The Jubilee Book of Cricket* was published in 1897 by William Blackwood and Sons and issued in three separate editions simultaneously.

Compared to such opulence, M. K. Patel's *History of Parsee Cricket*, printed at the J. N. Petit Parsi Orphanage Captain Printing Press and published in 1892,[2] is a modest, even minimal, effort—more a booklet than a book since it ran to only 65 pages. It belies the claim of being a 'history' by turning out to be a summary account of the cricketing achievements and aspirations of Bombay's Parsi community.

According to the title page the author, Manekji Kavasji Patel, was a teacher at the Fort High School and the material was prepared for a lecture delivered at the Framji Cowasji Institute (Bombay) on 10 December 1892. The occasion for the lecture was the forthcoming match, twelve days later, between the Parsis and a team of Englishmen led by Lord Hawke which toured India during 1892–93. But the inspiration for the lecture was surely the match held two years earlier between the Parsis and another team of English visitors under the captaincy of G. F. Vernon. The Parsis won that match by four wickets.[3] In fulfilment of the expectations roused by M. K. Patel in his little book, the Parsis again defeated the English tourists in December 1892, this time by 109 runs.

Such match-winning authorship would be embodied in two more early books before it became very rare in Indian cricket. M. E. Pavri, leading bowler of the Parsi team which visited England in 1888 and who figured in that victory over G. F. Vernon's team in 1890, published his *Parsi Cricket* in 1901. J. M. Framjee Patel, who captained the victorious home team in that match, wrote a more substantial work and published it in 1905 under the title *Some Stray Thoughts on Indian Cricket.* As the title

---

2 I have seen not the book, but a photocopy is in the possession of Ramachandra Guha; he found the book in the Yale University Library.

3 With reference to the visiting team's match at Calcutta, Vasant Raiji has mentioned in his *India's Hambledon Men* (1986) that the first known cricket publication from India is the compilation, *Calcutta Cricket Club Matches 1814–54;* but he gives no date of publication.

indicates, the game had extended by then to other Indian communities and this Parsi cricketer-cum-author was willing to look at it in wider perspective.

He states in this book that after an English team, styling itself the Oxford Authentics, had toured this country in 1903–04 (and lost two out of their 19 matches, the Parsis again defeating a visiting side), plans were made to send a so-called 'combined' Indian team – that is, a combination of various communities – to England in the summer of 1904. The plans did not materialise, but Framjee Patel proposed a team that consisted of seven Parsis, three Muslims and four Hindus, to be captained by either Prince Ranjitsinhji or Dr Pavri. When a similarly constituted combination did visit England in 1911, it was called an 'All-India' team. Country-wise, the breakdown was six Parsis, six Hindus and four Muslims, led by a Sikh (the then Maharaja of Patiala). Outside of newspapers, no duly descriptive or evaluative accounts of the matches on this tour are to be found.[4]

From then until now, newspaper reporting has formed the bulk of our cricket writing and this is likely to remain so, for some time to come. There are, of course, more sports magazines today than there were 20 years ago. Two kinds of outlets are thus available to the aspiring writer. A distinction may emerge some day between the daily cricket chronicler (that is, during the season) of newspapers and the weekly or monthly cricket articulator (in and out of season) of magazines.

Whatever the difference in the nature of such writings, the roles of these writers are not difficult to interchange because they hold fulltime jobs with the newspaper or magazine concerned and are thus more or less obliged to write. Because of this obligation they may not always enjoy writing what they do. But they are undoubtedly the most widely read of our cricket writers, and it is through their columns, features and articles – all forms of transitory publication – that the growing and changing history of our cricket is being recorded. Some of these journalists have also sought to enter the more enduring repository of books. The easiest way to do this is to rehash in book form what has already been served up in daily despatches. Rajan Bala did this for the 1968–69

4 Very short descriptions and the score sheets can be seen in the volume *India–England Cricket Visits, 1911–1946*, ed. S. K. Roy (1946).

double tour of India by New Zealand and by Australia in a book predictably titled *With the Kiwis and the Kangaroos* (1970). Kishore Bhimani's account of India's 1976 tour of the West Indies is based on notes he made (possibly also on some articles written during the tour) while he was there to fulfil radio and television assignments. The book is called *West Indies' 76: India's Caribbean Adventure* (1976).

After producing two books describing matches he never saw – three of India vs West Indies and three more India vs England, all on foreign grounds in 1971 – Sunder Rajan took the precaution in *The Hat-Trick* (1974) of getting four colleagues to write for this volume eyewitness accounts of the first four matches of the 1972–73 home series with England. The fifth match was seen and reported by Sunder Rajan himself, but I can't believe that he or any of the other four wrote their pieces only for this book.

That most esteemed of South Indian cricket columnists, S. K. Gurunathan, probably never wrote a book other than the largely statistical *Twelve Years of Ranji Trophy*. What he gave to our cricket, instead, is a much larger and continuous gift—the *Indian Cricket* annual which has grown from a book of a hundred-odd pages in 1947 to the 750-page 43rd 'edition' of 1989. I prefer this to the *Wisden* any day, because while I can read with interest every page of *Indian Cricket* I can't say the same of the other publication.

Gurunathan's younger contemporary N. S. Ramaswami, squandered a good opportunity when he decided not to toil and sweat for writing a substantial history of Indian cricket but to produce, in some hurry, two lighter works—*From Porbandar to Wadekar* (1975) and *Indian Cricket: A Complete History* (1976). The latter is no more complete than any history can be within 140 pages of a slim paperback in crown size. The first book is badly titled – Porbandar is more of a place name, and is more famously associated with somebody other than Maharaj Natwarsinghji – and rather dully written considering Ramaswami is quite a stylist in his own fashion.

None of these sports journalists followed the lead given long ago by Berry Sarbadhikary in his *Indian Cricket Uncovered* (1945), where he not only made many painful disclosures but also addressed himself seriously to the question of how the conduct of cricket in India could be improved so that its practice could also become better. Much less serious in intention, Raju

Bharatan's *Indian Cricket: The Vital Phase* (1977) tells so many untold stories that the reader cannot but wonder at this author's ubiquitosity. Also, Bharatan cannot resist making puns, even very bad ones.

The other unsurprising writer of a cricket book in India is the cricketer himself. We could leave him out of our consideration here. For one thing, he writes only about himself; for another, he almost never writes any other book; for a third, he almost never writes even the first book. My real objection to the usual cricketer-author is that if he were not already famous as a cricketer, no publisher would be interested in what he wrote. That is, a well-known cricket player's autobiography is not so much a book as it is another innings he plays—though not with bat and ball. Only when relatively unknown cricketers write their autobiographies or professionally unrelated persons write on cricket can their books be regarded as books and not as non-cricketing extensions of famous cricket careers.

As for the few cricketing biographies that we do have (of C. K. Nayudu by 'Eskari', of Vinoo Mankad by Sudhir Vaidya, of Vijay Merchant by Vasant Naik , etc.), these have turned out to be such slight works that they are hardly remembered as books.

One shift in emphasis we may note in this connection is that while our cricketers of an earlier era (like Professor Deodhar or Mushtaq Ali or Vijay Hazare) wrote their autobiographies after they had retired from action, the modern trend so triumphantly exemplified by Sunil Gavaskar is to write a book in mid-career. In two notable instances, however, what I have called match-winning authorship earlier, came a cropper. First it was Mansur Ali Khan, the younger Nawab of Pataudi, who published *Tiger's Tale* (1969) soon after he returned from having led India to our first test victory as well as series win abroad (in New Zealand) in 1969. Just over a year later he was deposed from captaincy.

Ajit Wadekar's career was blighted more terminally after he published a book. To cash in on his three successive series-wins as India's captain, he was persuaded to tell his story to K. N. Prabhu who wrote it up on Wadekar's behalf as *My Cricketing Years* (1973). Before another year was over, Wadekar had failed both as captain and batsman on our 1974 tour of England and announced his retirement before he could be dismissed from that post. Pataudi at least came back for a few tests as player and also captained India again; Wadekar did neither. As for Prabhu, perhaps our finest cricket columnist, because his understanding of cricket matches his prose style—he has yet to write (or publish) a book on cricket that is entirely off his own bat.

I don't know whether Prabhu has loaned his pen for anybody else's book, but the fact that the profession of cricket ghost writing has not developed in India may be one reason why we have produced so few cricket books. We may note that a new variety of ghost writing appears to have given body to that book on Gavaskar published by Macmillan (India) in 1984. Though the name of Dom Moraes is given as author, there is a guest editor's note among the book's prelims, and it seems that the text was largely written by T. G. Vaidyanathan—who, as his occasional pieces show, is quite capable of writing a book on Gavaskar and another on Dom Moraes. Moraes, of course, is a cricket writer who became a poet; he had published *Green is the Grass* (1952) at the age of 13 or so.

I wish I knew more about another kind of cricket-inspired writing which hasn't yet been attempted in English (that is, in India) but which appeared in Bangla quite some time ago and must also have found a place in our other languages as well. I am thinking of fiction centred in cricket which, in representing the more sporting aspects of the game, cannot but reflect upon the social situation of those who play it. My favourite writer in this context is Moti Nandi, an accomplished writer of non-sports fiction as well, who used to be the sports editor of *Ananda Bazar Patrika*. His writing of sports fiction became nationally known when two of his football stories got published in English translation.[5] Another widely appreciated short novel about a girl swimmer named Koni (an English translation appeared in *Imprint* magazine around 1978) has been made into a successful film. Subsequently, Nandi has written at least three novels, each of which has a cricketer as protagonist, but these have not yet been rendered into English.

Another writer of cricket fiction in Bangla is Manabendra Bandopadhyay, who is by profession a teacher of comparative literature. His *Khel Samachar* (1986) is a short but richly contrived novel which tells of the formation of an imaginary Indian National

---

5 Moti Nandi, *Striker/Stopper*, trans. Mihir K Das, Sangam Books, 1976.

Cricketers Association (for short, INCA; like me, Manabendra is a member of INCLA, which stands for the Indian National Comparative Literature Association) in between an Indian team's return from a victorious tour of Pakistan and the opening match of a home series with England.

The technique used by this author can be sampled from this sequence, comprising the first section of the novel: (a) sports review from Akashvani, Delhi; (b) newspaper report; (c) four news items, one of which mentions INCA; (d) advertisement announcing a new cricket magazine; (e) three more ads, all featuring test cricketers; (f) excerpt from a cinema magazine gossip column about the cricketer Ulhas Patil and the actress Shyama Khosla. Such apt fictionalising of what normally appears as newspaper material has not been attempted before in Bangla fiction about cricket.

No survey, even the present cursory one, of cricket writing by Indians would be worth its salt if it failed to take into account the authorial efforts of Vasant Raiji. Neither a sports journalist nor a cricket autobiographer (not even a teacher of comparative literature!), last year he published his eighth effort—which makes him the most productive of our cricket book writers or makers (he has compiled and edited some of them).

A former Ranji Trophy cricketer and Pentangular reserve and a chartered accountant by profession, Raiji must also be the most versatile of amateur writers on cricket. After a book each on Ranji, Duleep (with Vijay Merchant and others) and Victor Trumper, he edited the handsome *Ranji Centenary Album* (1972). After editing another character sketch, that of L. P. Jai, Raiji has celebrated important occasions with appropriate books—thus, 50 years of our national championship in *The Romance of the Ranji Trophy* (1984); one hundred years after our first cricket voyage to England in *India's Hambledon Men* (1986); the golden jubilee of Bombay's more hallowed cricket ground in *CCI & the Brabourne Stadium* (1987).

His latest book, *C. K. Nayudu* (1989), is subtitled 'The Shahensha of Indian Cricket' and the author believes that C. K. was the greatest cricketer born on this subcontinent. The more recent of his books are tastefully produced and contain many rare illustrations and unusual reports or items of information that Raiji has retrieved after diligent research. He must be the envy of all cricket writers in India because he can write on whatever takes his fancy and he has no difficulty in getting published.

Cricket writing in India has still to achieve many other dimensions than the one which reports cricket matches. We don't yet have a comprehensive history of Indian cricket that tackles the subject at macro as well as micro levels. Nor do we have authors who can use cricket as the springboard for other enquiries. We learnt to play cricket from Englishmen and other sahibs; we may still have something to learn from them about how to write books on cricket. The Australian entrepreneur Ted Docker, in order to write *The History of Indian Cricket* (1976), must have spent countless hours poring over old newspaper files and not relied on other accounts for the basic information he needed. Perhaps he was not knowledgeable about Indian cricket, hence had to get back to such sources and thereby managed to dig up facts and events not many of us knew or remembered.

Richard Cashman, another Australian but a university lecturer by profession, happily undertook the research which enabled him to enlarge a seminar paper into a 193-page book, *Patrons, Players and the Crowd* (1980). This is a pioneering study of those who play, watch or support the game in various ways. Even Scyld Berry's *Cricketwallah* (1982), based as it is on the 1981–82 MCC tour of India, gets away as often as it can from the actual cricket, to tell his readers about Ranji's Nawanagar, about the manufacture of cricket bats in Jalandhar, about club cricket in various Indian cities. I suppose I ought to add Mihir Bose's *A Maidan View* (1986) to these examples because he has been living and working abroad for many years. His book certainly has enough of that outsider's view with which many foreigners are able to look at India afresh. Each of these books is a welcome departure from the rather humdrum kind of cricket book that has until recently been written in India.

However, now that a 'tau' among our social scientists has written a book on Indian cricket, there is much cause for jubilation.[6] More than in its country of origin, cricket has come to occupy an area of our national life at so many levels that it is not enough if only cricket reporters and test players are to examine such conspicuous presence.

[1990]

6 Those interested may see Ashis Nandy's *Tao of Cricket*, New Delhi: Viking, 1989.

The Cardus Complex

In first-class sport of any kind, only a few play while many watch. The players change periodically, but the spectators do not seem to. Those players whose careers are over remain for a time in the talk and minds of spectators. Then they fade away. Perhaps by that time the well-known players of yesterday have joined the anonymous ranks of today's spectators.

The game of cricket is distinguished by the fact that its great exponents are remembered much longer than those of any other game. The reason is easy to explain: cricket and cricketers seem to get written about and read more than any other game and its exponents. As a result, cricket has a large reading public for whom a famous cricketer plays and lives long after he has stopped playing and living. Even in a relatively underdeveloped – economically as well as cricketwise – country like India, a phenomenally growing number watch or listen to or read about cricket. I have belonged by turns to the watchers, the listeners (and, with the advent of television, the viewers), and the readers. But the really exclusive group, the elite as it were, are those who write about cricket. Having joined this group, I prize my membership dearly—chiefly because it has taken such a long time to get there.

Let me quickly disclaim any aspiration to be equated with those distinguished names which appear in bye-lines of national newspapers all over the cricketing world. These are names of writers who make or break cricket reputations, predict victory or defeat in test matches, and in general mould public opinion among cricketgoers. Mine is a more humble station with much less onerous obligations. I re-live with relish far-off events and battles long ago by writing about them, and fondly hope that there are readers who share my passion for looking backward.

I have watched better cricket than I have played, and have read about better matches than I have watched. As a result, the game and its players appear to me as a continuum in which the ancient left-hander Colonel Mistry becomes a contemporary of the recently retired Ajit Wadekar. The little that I have written persuades me that those who are playing today can be watched, applauded, discussed, but cannot be written about with lasting pleasure. Instead, those who cannot be seen at play any longer seem to inhabit the mid-air above my desk, ready to materialise the moment I bring pen to paper.

Young readers may protest that my attitude is no different from that of all middle-aged men who persistently find the past more worthy than the present. Granted this past-mindedness, I should like to claim that there is need for a kind of cricket-writer who chooses to write about players of the past so that these players – but for whom the game would not have reached its present state of development – are never forgotten by cricket-lovers. A century or a hat-trick or three catches at third slip are made of elements which cannot be retained except in the eye's mind, cannot be celebrated except in the written word. The spectator is by definition a slave to the immediate. Today he praises to the sky the very player he will cast to the dogs tomorrow. The sports journalist, without wanting to be like the instant-happy spectator, cannot afford to be very different. He too has to change with the passing day, has to move from one match to another, from one test series to the next. Those he has once removed from the headlines he may not again award space to even in small type. Hence the need for another kind of cricket-writer who writes not because he must but because he loves to.

We are told that in the world of literature there are many aspiring novelists and poets who turned critics when they failed as novelists or poets. This must be largely true of cricket-writers, whose vocation is a kind of endless wish-fulfilment. That is the real pleasure of writing about cricket, of being able to sit in judgement over those whose equals one could never have been. All cricket-followers are addicted to this indulgence, and the successful cricket-writer is one who can feed this appetite so that it grows by feeding.

I wish I were an eminent enough writer to be able to recall the first piece I ever wrote and to expect my readers to be interested in such trivialities. I myself got tired ultimately of the scrapbook in which I used to paste cuttings of everything I had written. Much of it was in one of Patna's two English dailies, the *Indian Nation,* for which I slaved in a highly informal capacity while I was in college. I used to file reports on local matches without any guarantee that these would be published. But whatever was published would be paid for—by the inch, calculated on a so much per column rate, minus the headlines. I grew to detest large headlines, because this meant my report would be pruned, and I developed a complex style with involved sentences, giving as little scope as possible for the sub-editor to prune. Then there was the problem of reporting matches in which I had played—perhaps kicked a goal, which was rarely, or hit some runs, which was more often. I recall undergoing agonies of calculated modesty, and wonder how many sports reporters have had to undergo this experience.

In due course I was granted a Sunday column, for which I concocted a byline spelt *SKIM* out of the initials in my name. This writing I found far more to my taste mainly because I didn't have to rush straight from the ground to a desk. Also there were no given limits to the scope of my weekly piece. After having paid lip-service to some recent happening, I could roam at leisure over past, present and future. Also, by writing about any sports event in the world I could pretend I was kin to any sports journalist in the world.

Thanks to this column, I was put on the sports panel of the local AIR station and broadcast many sports reviews of the month. This was yet another kind of education. AIR conventions are pretty rigid about allowing free expression of opinion, and I had to play hide-and-seek with a programme executive who had a highly trained mistrust of candid comments and honest judgements. Another hazard was that 'Sports Causerie', as this item was called, invariably followed the national news in English. The last thing I heard before opening my own mouth was Surojit Sen or Roshan Menon churning out good news along with bad as if neither mattered very much to them. More than once I found myself imitating their tone and rhythm, although I had neither floods or epidemics nor inaugurations or installations to report on.

The first sports article I ever published in an out-of-town journal was, oddly enough, something in the *Men Only* magazine and, no less oddly, was more about football than about cricket, the burden of my argument being that it should be possible as well as desirable to write as lyrically about football as Neville Cardus does about cricket. In those days this magazine was available every month at Wheeler bookstalls, and it was certainly not bought for its reading matter on sports. A six-guinea cheque arrived long before the article did, and, having no bank account of my own, I had to hand it over to my father who proudly deposited it in his account. But I could never show him the article itself, because it was placed uncomfortably near one of those bare-bottomed beauties who used to grace every issue of this journal.

Memorable as this happening was to me, no less quoteworthy is the editorial mention I earned in this particular issue; "...Mr. Mukherjee sent his literary offspring to the Editor of *Men Only*. He did not include stamps for return postage, these being unobtainable, and so, when his *opus* arrived at this office, we were faced with the harrowing alternative of publishing it, or sending it back to India at our own expense. Fortunately for Mr. Mukherjee, the office stamp-tin, which had once contained fifty Players, did not, at that moment, contain any stamps. Which is why you will find, on page 48, an article, 'Football Literature', which came to us all the way from India on the very night we were discussing a similar topic at the Cambridge Union."

All over the English reading world, I imagined, every reader must be turning immediately to page 48 after reading this editorial. Alas, I never met many. In fact, I met only one person who had read this article without my having to lend him one of the three copies I bought with money borrowed from my father.

The most satisfying appearance in those days, at least to me, was in the pages of *Sport and Pastime* of Madras. It was a weekly journal, hence publication was generally not very long after the letter of acceptance came. On publication, the copy could be freely shown to near relatives as well as to friends. *Sport and Pastime* invariably paid for contributions, hence I could afford to buy extra copies and present them to persons I wished to impress. Also, invariably, the magazine published suitable photographs along with the text. What wonderful transformation my ill-typed copies underwent when they appeared on the much-beloved pages of *Sport and Pastime!*

After about half a dozen of my articles on cricket had got published up to 1953 or so, I began to dream of writing a book on Indian cricket—especially of a kind that had never been written before. None of the books available then made satisfactory reading, so I knew what my book would not be like. It would not be like Dom Moraes' *Green is the Grass,* which requires being present at every test of a series. Nor would it be like Berry Sarbadhikary's *Indian Cricket Uncovered,* which calls for 'inside' information of a sort that would never be available to me. Autobiographical accounts like those of Deodhar or C. K. Nayudu or Rusi Modi were by definition out of my reach. And I had no desire to compile statistics or rehash newspaper accounts of matches I had not seen.

I had read all of Naville Cardus – and, when I became a wage-earner, bought all his books[1] – and thoroughly imbibed his style and temperament, especially his infinite capacity for seeing the pastness in the present, also his ability to sketch cricket players as if they were human beings first and test cricketers second. An equal favourite with me was Ray Robinson who writes like a good opening batsman, secure in defence but quick to punish the loose ball. He structures his books better than any other cricket writer I have read. Much later I got to read and enjoy Ronald Mason who has pointed out to me that he and I must be unique in the fact that both of us write literary criticism as well as about cricket. These three are writers I read and re-read with undiminished pleasure, and if my own writing imitates, reflects and echoes them, I am guilty of a sin most cricketers are heir to—namely, modelling their own batting or bowling on some hero of theirs.

I think I write mainly in order to re-discover Indian cricket. In the act of writing our cricket past becomes clear and real to me. Born to a race of idol-worshippers I am very conscious of the fact that it is the worshipper who lends life to the idol, which would cease to exist if he ceased to worship.

The bulk of the material for my book was collected, written up and revised during the two years I spent at the National Defence Academy in Khadakvasla, near Poona. The magnificent sports facilities available there sustained an atmosphere in which there

---

[1] Including the rarely seen *English Cricket* reissued in a special edition by Collins in their 'Britain in Pictures' series, and excluding *Good Days* which I borrowed from M. K. Das and never returned.

was much talking as well as doing of sports. Distinguished sportsmen visited the Academy every now and then, while national-level players and athletes of the defence services get posted there. My bachelor apartment on the third floor overlooked the swimming pool on one side, the cricket pitch on the other. It was possible to catch a snooze in my own bed between innings or cool off quickly with a swim after a long day's fielding.

Apart from what the Academy had to offer by way of cricket talk, Poona city was well-stocked with persons who had participated as performer or spectator in the eras of cricket I wanted to write about. Professor Deodhar could be met any day either in the PYC clubhouse or at his own home in Kriketpatu Deodhar Path, a lane in the Deccan Gymkhana named after him—surely a unique municipal tribute to a cricketer. Kamal Bhandarkar was coaching then at Ferguson College, while, Narse Nagarwala was available some evenings at Poona Gymkhana. I was introduced once to J. G. Navle but failed to get him to talk cricket to me. Every Sunday, when I played in local league matches, I was likely as not to come across a former Maharashtra cricketer whose career might have begun in the Pentangular days. On the Academy staff itself were Hemu Adhikari and Nana Joshi while at least twice Colonel Nayudu visited us and graciously permitted me to buttonhole him for long after-dinner chats. Thus I was able to pick up assessments and anecdotes ranging from at least 1915 to 1955.

The Academy Commandant of those days, Major-General E. Habibullah, was a great devotee of cricket. He thoroughly approved of the fact that besides teaching English I was capable of playing cricket with the cadets. He had heard that I had pretensions to be a cricket writer. When I completed the first draft of my book (by then I had left the Academy and returned to my college-teaching job in Patna), I sent him one of the three copies I had typed, painfully, with two fingers on at least five different typewriters. About two months later I got a letter from General Habibullah which fairly inflated my ego. It said: "I would say that this is the first book of its sort about Indian cricket ... I took the liberty to ask the great Duleep about it. He read it and liked it very much indeed. His only comment was that, in spite of everything, it is essentially in the line of Neville Cardus ... (Your) work is certainly an important addition to cricket literature and will, I feel sure, receive the appreciation it deserves from all cricket lovers." He also suggested that I try my luck with a British Publisher first, and gave six names and addresses.

That was in early November 1957. During the next nine years, my manuscript must have travelled more miles than any other manuscript of the time. One copy crossed and recrossed the black waters at least four times. Frederick Mueller actually read it before turning it down; so did George G. Harrap. A literary agent called Curtis Brown Limited tried on my behalf but with no better result.

The other copy I used for sending to Indian publishers. Jaico Publishing House offered to read it if I could obtain a foreword from an 'important cricket personality'. Asia Publishing, after correspondence over a year, agreed to read it but returned it in much less that time. I thought *Sport and Pastime* might serialise it, but they said S. K. Gurunathan was already doing a similar project for them. I tried the Maharajkumar of Vizianagram, Sardar Surjit Singh Majithia (then President, Cricket Control Board), and finally Kumar Shri Duleepsinhji. He replied promptly: "I am very shortly leaving for a holiday and am not in a position to read your book and write a foreword. If you will write to me in November, I may be in a position to go through your book and write a foreword." I waited till November (1959) and sent the manuscript to him. A month or so later he died suddenly. Whoever went through his papers was good enough to return the manuscript to me, along with a letter apologising for Duleep's not having had time to do me the favour I had sought. I took this as an ill-omen, put away all three copies of my as-yet-unpublished opus, and decided not to spend any more postage on it. When I left Patna more or less for good in 1966, I presented a copy to my old school library, along with all my cricket books. I was about to join a university department at Poona, and I thought I should put cricket reading and writing behind me for ever.

Sometime in late 1967, on a train journey, I happened to buy a few paperback translations of Indian fiction published by an Indian firm I had not heard of before, Hind Pocket Books of Delhi. I was so pleased with the whole idea – English translations of novels in regional languages, printed reasonably well, priced at around three rupees – that I wrote off a letter of congratulations to the publishers. A few mutually appreciative letters followed, then I enquired if they would be interested in my translating a contemporary Bengali novel like Samaresh Basu's *Bibar*. They replied they were aspiring to publish only standard writing (Saratchandra and Rabindranath were mentioned) and on standard subjects because they were on a noble mission. Whereupon I pointed out that among twenty-odd titles released by them already were books on birth control and business success and the like. I concluded by asking whether, since their range of subjects was commendably wide, they would publish a small book on Indian cricket.

Almost by return of mail they asked to see the manuscript. In about three months' time they wrote they would publish it, following up with a contract and an advance-on-royalty cheque. I was so dizzy with delight that I never stopped to think that the material was rather out of date now. Even if I had realised this, I wouldn't have dared to tell my newfound publisher, lest he change his mind. Within a year of my having written a rather snide letter, the book was out in print.

On later reflection I was a little sorry that the publisher had changed the title I had given, *Between Indian Wickets,* to something of their choice, *The Romance of Indian Cricket.* I was also somewhat revolted by the front cover, on which a calendar-pretty batsman is playing a stroke not known to decent cricket. And I was most unhappy about the way some lines had been removed from my preface – in which I had acknowledged my debt to Cardus and Robinson and Mason – and used as blurb material. But these were minor discomforts amid the euphoria I lived in for many days afterwards. The manuscript I had conceived, composed, nursed, then practically strangled and buried, had at last seen the light of print.

My second book has been much easier to get into print. By then I had taken the precaution of joining a publishing firm. The third book has been the easiest and the most gratifying because the initiative came from the publishers, those hardy souls who took on my first manuscript and made me an author of a cricket book. The only condition I made this time was that I should be allowed to use the title I had wanted for my first book, a title borrowed un-ashamedly from Ray Robinson.

Whenever I get a chance I thrust my books at cricketers and cricket-writers I admire. My only regret is that I shall never know if Neville Cardus ever read my writings. The nearest I ever got to him is an adjacent page of the *Playfair Cricket Monthly.* But the Cardus complex continues to haunt me. About a year ago I had the privilege of making the acquaintance of Vijay Merchant, while sitting next to him on all five days of a test match at Delhi. Inevitably I presented him with a copy of my first book and asked him for comments. About a week later I received a letter from him wherein, after saying things which made me feel that the pains I had had to undergo, not so much of writing the book but of getting it published, had been well worth it – I cannot resist quoting a sample: "I find it very interesting and I was able to follow every incident quoted by you very clearly because nearly all of them were within my knowledge. You have brought them out with an exactitude which is indeed remarkable" – he also admonishes me gently for using flowery and descriptive language not always suitable for a simple and straightforward game like cricket: "Language of the type you have used may befit a man like Sir Neville Cardus, but somehow for others it neither seems necessary nor advantageous."

I assure Vijay Merchant that the next time I write a book on cricket, my enchantment with Neville Cardus may have diminished somewhat, and I shall then use a language as simple and straightforward as Merchant's bat.

[1976]

Cricket in the Mother-Tongue

The laws of cricket are available in Calcutta these days in more than one Bengali publication. I should imagine this would be true of other Indian languages especially in regions of the country where cricket has a large and literate following. Therefore, until they are equipped to read and comprehend English, countless youngsters get acquainted with the written laws of cricket in whatever language their mothers speak.

To those familiar with the phrase 'played under MCC rules', it may come as something of a shock to realise that the MCC have so far omitted to rule that the laws of cricket do not lose their legality when not inscribed in the English language. The question of the language of these laws has never really been regarded in this light before. Cricket has followed the imperial wake of the British as naturally as the English language has, and we are all familiar with the phenomenon that serious practice of the game has remained confined to the Commonwealth countries and successfully survived the decay of the Empire. But is there some subtle but unseverable connection between learning English and learning to play this English game? How otherwise has cricket-playing been accompanied by English-speaking in so many climates for long?

The matter obviously deserves investigation. I see possibilities of a brave new minor sub-branch of English studies sprouting at some red-cement university in Britain, and anxious young men who had despaired so long of making a breakthrough in English Literature study or English Language research flocking to attend post-graduate diploma courses in "The Teaching of Cricket in a Foreign Language". A new kind of Rhodes Scholarship (to honour Wilfred, not Cecil) will be instituted to enable native teachers of English from all over the Commonwealth for refresher courses which will naturally include two hours of net practice morning and evening on alternate days throughout the academic session. Some enterprising departmental head will adapt an American innovation and budget for a 'Cricketer in Residence' every year, with honoraria for incumbents on par at least with what is offered by Lancashire League clubs. Vijay Merchant and not Ravi Shankar will be invited out on lecture-tours; Kennington Oval and not Stratford-on-Avon will form part of the pilgrimage. And soon we shall have that irresistible seal of approval embossed upon this new humanistic discipline when the first Ph.D. thesis is completed on "The effect of non-aspirated consonants on the off-drive of left-handed batsmen."

India will, of course, provide the richest material for field-work in this direction. The necessity of playing cricket in English has not yet been questioned in this country, not even by the most rabid pro-Hindi or pro-Tamil brickbat-chucker or tar-brush wielder. Yet the language of Indian cricketers has seldom been only English. Was it not Sir Leonard Hutton (then plain Len) who was upset while batting against India when he heard fieldsmen saying things he did not understand. Other divisive elements apart, has not the Indian test eleven always been more vulnerable to internal dissension than any other test side in the world merely on this account—that two Indian cricketers can speak to each other in a language which is as incomprehensible to a third member of the Indian side as it is to all members of the opposition? Thus, it was hypothetically possible during our last tour of England for Bedi and Madan Lal to say uncomplimentary things about Vishwanath's batting form to his face with poor Vishy understanding not a word of what the other two were saying. Such a situation would not be possible in unilingual sides like the Australian or the English or the West Indies. In fact, I have often wondered how cricketers in these teams let off verbal steam without endangering their careers. The time may come when an Indian cricket team going abroad will require, in addition to the usual contingent of Deputy Manager and Assistant Treasurer and Chief Masseur, a brace of interpreters, one each from North and South, to enable our bowlers to converse with our batsmen.

Every region in India has its own cricket patois, as any Bengali knows who has watched a test match at Madras or a Maharashtrian who has been to a Calcutta Test. Especially in the cheaper seats, where English does not function as a link language, an outstation onlooker can find it most disconcerting that he is unable to participate in the ceaseless chatter interspersed with loud expletives which relieve the monotony of watching test cricket. Certain pleasures of being on one's home ground are available to the Indian spectator but not to his counterparts in cricket grounds abroad—the dubious joy, for example, of abusing to one's heart's content some distinguished visiting cricketer fielding on the boundary line and he grinning back in delight because he thinks his presence is being appreciated. But our barracking, irrespective of who the target is, is almost invariably in English. As on parliamentary occasions, English seems to lend itself suitably to concerted shouting in public.

Other aspects of regionalisation of the language of Indian cricket may be sampled while listening to a radio commentary or in reading a newspaper account. Between a Hindi broadcast and a Bengali broadcast (these being the two languages most familiar to me), I have found the Hindi more convincing—perhaps because the verb is always so conspicuous in a Hindi sentence and an action described in Hindi becomes more effective because of the seeming preponderance of verbs. (Which, however, is precisely the reason why I find it difficult to enjoy Hindi poetry.) Both languages, however, bring an artificiality to cricket commentary in the way they insist on using the honorific inflections *(aap* and its consequences) when narrating the deeds of cricketers whom we refer to in far more familiar terms in our normal speech. Whether it is Rajni Patel or Brijesh Patel, the radio will invariably make them do *kar rahe hain* in Hindi and *korchchen* in Bengali.

As for cricket-reporting in the regional languages, ever since I started reading Marathi newspapers I have been fascinated by the determined coinage of cricket terminology which has taken place in this language. One wonders how and when this currency began, and whether these terms are actually used by Maharashtrian cricket-fans when they talk about cricket. To uninitiated eyes like mine, the scoreboard in a Marathi newspaper, full of *trifala* and *payechit,* looks like a prescription of Ayurvedic medicine; and when a bad performance is denoted by *ghasarle* and explained in terms of deficient *kshetrarakshan* or proficient *madhyamgati golandazi,* I feel I am reading an account of some forgotten Maratha war. I wonder if any other Indian language has regionalised cricket to this extent. No wonder Bombay has won the Ranji Trophy eleven times in a row.

Bengal has not won the Ranji Trophy again since that sole triumph of 1938–39 when the team was full of 'domiciled' Bengalis like P. I. van der Oucht and S. W. Behrend, T. C. Longfield and A. L. Hosie, who undoubtedly played their cricket in English. Who knows whether Bengal may not regain the championship when not only the laws of cricket are rendered into Bengali, but the very language of Bengal's cricket becomes Bengali.

And this brings me to my final speculation. English teachers in India will have fresh cause to moan when cricket laws are translated into all the regional languages, thus making the English teacher a little more irrelevant in India. But does not our English teaching situation contain a lesson for our Board of Control for Cricket? It is widely stated in public (and sometimes even believed in private) that the accumulated futility of our education system, especially at higher levels, may be traced to our misguided use of English as the medium of instruction. *Ergo,* once we have adopted the regional languages as media of university education, our education system will inescapably revitalize itself and start producing Nobel Prize winners (or runners-up, or at least quarter-finalists). May not the same argument be applied to our suggested development in cricket? We have not developed as we should have because, contrary to our national genius for regional predilection, we have been playing cricket in English. *Ergo,* let us change over to cricket in the mother-tongue and we shall, within a few years, produce a team capable of defeating not only England, West Indies and New Zealand but also Pakistan.

[1976]

Paigah Nawabs Vs Vazir Sultans

The Moin-ud-dowlah Gold Cup invitation tournament was not held this year. With the tour of Pakistan in the offing, the onset of the cricket season was packed with Duleep Trophy (inter-zonal) matches as well as the Irani trophy match (Ranji Trophy champions vs the Rest of India). These provided the basis for selection of the India team to Pakistan, and players were generally not available for friendly contests elsewhere. Not for the first time, thus, Hyderabad citizens were denied a privilege they have enjoyed for over half a century. This privilege consists of being able to watch, for a week or ten days every year, all the leading Indian players of the time. Hyderabad has held a test match only once, but, because of this tournament, the city has hosted every test cricketer of the land—sometimes, of foreign lands as well.

It has always been an invitation tournament. That is, you could not simply wish to play in it or qualify to do so by competing; you had to be invited. And that, too, not on as an individual but as a member of informal teams that were put together for the purpose of taking part in what is meant to be a festival of cricket. That is the real privilege enjoyed by Hyderabadis. Dour players of test cricket let down their hair, as it were, in these matches and enjoy themselves—and, in doing so, offer enjoyment of the sort that is seldom to be found in cricket occasions of higher import in India. Here, too, alas respect for professionalism is growing.

This tournament is named after the donor of the trophy, Nawab Moin-ud-dowlah, a name not unknown to foreign cricketers as well, at least during the 1930s. When the MCC team led by Douglas Jardine toured India in 1933–34, it played against a Moin-ud-dowlah's XI at Secunderabad (the younger but Siamese city twin of Hyderabad) and was forced to yield first innings lead in a drawn encounter. Two years later, another Moin-ud-dowlah's XI overwhelmed Jack Ryder's team of Australians by an innings and 115 runs. And yet another Moin-ud-Dowlah's XI, in January 1938, defeated Lord Tennyson's team by six wickets. The home teams on all three occasions were, of course, nearly Indian test elevens. That was the prestige commanded in cricket by this Hyderabad nawab in those days. When he invited, nobody dreamed of declining,

Though the tournament itself dates back to the 1920s (according to some chroniclers it is as old as 1911), the gold cup got associated with it only in 1930. That year an unexpected combination of exigencies, cricketesque as well as political, pitched Hyderabad onto the cricket map of India. Until then, this princely state ruled by the fabled Nizam had regarded cricket as no more than a part of 'English education', which was made available to the well-born who attended Jagirdar College (really a high school) in Begumpet or Nizam College in Bashirbagh. The fact that the MCC team under Arthur Gilligan which visited India in 1926–27 (but played no official test matches) had no fixture in Hyderabad will show that cricket here did not yet command visionary patronage or tested competence.

The MCC tour of this country that was to have taken place during the 1930–31 season was cancelled – suspiciously well before it was due – by the British Government of India after Mahatma Gandhi launched his Civil Disobedience movement. Gandhiji himself, while not averse to cricket as such, did not approve of the Bombay Quadrangular – then our only cricket tourney of some national standing – because it was played on inter-communal lines (among the Europeans, Parsis, Hindus and Muslims). As the cricket season approached that year and civil disobedience intensified, it became increasingly clearer that the Quadrangular matches would not be held and the 1930–31 season would be a barren year for Indian cricket.

By some happenstance (which no historian of Indian cricket has yet explained)[1] around this time, Nawab Moin-ud-dowlah made public his desire to donate a solid gold trophy if a cricket tournament of some import could be arranged in Hyderabad.

---

1 My own guess is that Nawab Moin wished to out do another nawab, Behram-ud-dowlah, who had started a largely local tournament in the city in 1926. This was beginning to draw players from outside, and the 1929 final saw many cricketers of national fame in action.

We do not know who took up this challenging task, but invitations went out very soon mainly to other princely states all over non-British India—and nawabs and rajahs vied with each other to collect the best elevens they could put together by fiscal and other means. Consequently, not only did the 1930 Moin-ud-dowlah Gold Cup tournament bring to Hyderabad nearly every cricket player in India capable of representing the country, but also two legendary English cricketers.

For the presence of the latter, due credit must go to the Maharajkumar of Vizianagram, known otherwise, as Vizzy to anybody familiar with India's cricket history. The year before he had put together a Vizianagram XI (which included D. B. Deodhar from Poona, P. Vithal from Bombay, C. K. Nayudu from Indore, L. Ramji from Kathiawar), to participate in the Roshunara tournament of Delhi, but his team lost in the semi-final. In 1930 he planned to collect an even stronger team. He was in England that year during the summer and the cancellation of MCC's tour of India that winter may have given him the idea of going around the country with his own team, augmented by a few foreign players. It is alleged that he ventured to sound Don Bradman, then on his first tour of England, but was politely refused. So did leading English players who were approached. Vizzy had better luck when he tried veterans, and returned home triumphantly with assurances from Jack Hobbs and Herbert Sutcliffe. That is how these two legends, became realities for a few days in Hyderabad.

Even without these two, the Vizianagram XI was a strong team, including, as it did, grand masters like D. B. Deodhar and C. K. Nayudu, established players like J. Nasomal and Ghulam Mohammed from Karachi, and others who would soon make their mark in Indian cricket—all-rounder Mushtaq Ali from Indore, wicketkeeper Dilawar Hussain from Lahore, legspinner C. S. Nayudu from Nagpur. It reached the final without much trouble and Nawab Moin's resources were stretched to the utmost to put up worthy opposition. His team depended on Wazir Ali, Amar Singh and Ram Singh, and it was led by Prince Ghanshyamsinghji of Limbdi.[2] He had hoped to procure some

2 He would be nominated vice-captain of India's 1932 team to England, which included several others among those who appeared in the 1930 final of this tournament. And of those remaining, some went to England on the 1936 trip.

leading Bombay players and it is rumoured that the services of a no less leading film actress of the time were utilised for this purpose. Whether on, account of her or not, L. P. Jai, R. T. D. Jamshedji and N. D. Marshall came from Bombay, wicketkeeper J. G. Navle from Poona. They could not, however, prevent the Vizianagram XI from winning the gold cup in that inaugural year.

Moin-ud-dowlah was a 'paigah' nawab and lived in Hyderabad itself (a city founded in the fifteenth century), but the matches used to be held in the adjoining nineteenth-century cantonment called Secunderabad. (The notorious incapacity of the British in transcribing Indian names must have produced 'Secunder' from 'Sikander'.) When the golden jubilee of the tournament was celebrated in 1980, some matches were played on the Secunderabad Gymkhana ground to honour the past. But major cricket matches moved away long ago to Fateh Maidan (which now boasts a fully covered cricket stadium) in Hyderabad and much nearer to one of Nawab Moin-ud-dowlah's properties. Because of this change in centre of gravity, some crowning individual feats in the tournament have developed double aspects. Thus, in the old days, C. K. Nayudu's clouting a ball from the Gymkhana pitch into the Plaza Cinema premises was a record. But more recently, Kapil Dev has challenged this on Fateh Maidan by lofting an off-colour break from Shivlal Yadav onto the stadium roof.

Now, as then, there are no spectator facilities at the Gymkhana ground. These had to be provided with colourful canvas, tall bamboo and strong rope, when the tournament was held—provided not by the tournament organisers but by local patrons of the game who were eminent enough to issue invitations to spectators of some standing. At ordinary matches Nawab Moin-ud-dowlah would be driven up in his Rolls-Royce, have it parked strategically, and watch the proceedings from the car. But for the tournament, a large and resplendent shamiana was erected and furnished with two or three rows of cushioned chairs of graded height. Those who sat lowest – that is, in the first row – were axiomatically the highest in status. Guests stood, not on the order of their coming, but sat according to their standing. The cricket being played before them was generally interesting. Should interest flag occasionally, there were solid as well as liquid refreshments arrayed at the back. One did not avail any of these oneself, but waited until it was offered, then waited further while it was fetched.

Alongside would be perhaps an even larger and no less resplendent shamiana, equally full of distinguished presences. These were the guests of Maharaja Kishen Pershad Bahadur, prime minister to the Nizam. Besides seating comfort, food and drink, his guests were offered an extra enjoyment. They were encouraged by their host to lay bets—on who that day would score the most runs or bag the most wickets, and so on and the winner was promptly paid off at draw of stump, and in cash, by the Maharaja himself.

The Vizianagram XI from Banaras won the first two finals. The next two were won by the Freelooters from Bombay, led by the Maharajkumar of Alirajpur. The latter's bid to win it for a third time was foiled by the Retrievers from Patiala, led by the then Yuvraj (crown prince) Yadavendra Singh. Though the Bombay team was strengthened this year by (Sir) Learie Constantine and L. Ramji, Lala Amarnath hit a rapid 157 and confirmed to locals the reputation he had made overnight at Bombay against Jardine's team by scoring a test century on first appearance. There was a long break in the tournament from 1937 to 1961, until the Hyderabad Cricket Association took over and revived it. By then, of course, the Nizam's kingdom had dissolved and Nawab Moin-ud-dowlah had departed.

While he was alive, the Nawab attended to his player-guests personally and was an unusually complete host to cricketers invited to play in the tournament. To and fro rail travel was naturally paid for—by first class carriage, once the preserve of Englishmen and other Europeans. Players were put up at his garden-palace in Bashirbagh, and transported back and forth during matches in limousines. The sponsor of each team was responsible for fitting his players with blazer and cap, but the Nawab enquired about each team's self-sufficiency in cricket kit and clothing, so that deficiencies could be made up immediately. A local clothier named John Burton & Co. employed extra hands during the tournament for this purpose. Some players, it is alleged, would arrive with only the clothes they were wearing but leave Hyderabad with a reasonable wardrobe for the rest of the season.

When the Moin-ud-dowlah tournament resumed in 1960–61, merchant princes and industrial royalty had replaced the maharajahs and nababs and rajkumars of old. The typical contenders of today are the State Bank of India, ACC (representing the Associated Cement Company of India), Vazir Sultan Colts (sponsored by Vazir Sultan Tobacco, the leading cigarette-manufacturing concern in Hyderabad), Russi Mody's XI (organised, by the Managing Director of Tata Iron and Steel Company in Jamshedpur) and such others. These industrial and commercial houses not only support such a tournament by participating at their own expense. They also employ cricketers and offer them careers that will continue even after the players have stopped playing. And when they play for the gold cup in Hyderabad, they do their best to glitter.

[1980]

The All-ness of India

Had we become independent in 1857, would India have qualified to play test matches by 1900? Indian teams consisting only of Parsee cricketers toured England privately in 1886 and 1888 and didn't perform too well. So, when another tour was being planned for the summer of 1904, the organisers favoured what they called a 'combined' Indian team. The tour did not materialise but the proposed team was made up of six Parsees (K. M. Mistry, R. P. Meheromji, A. H. Mehta, H. D. Kanga, D. D. Kanga and M. D. Bulsara), four Hindus (P. Baloo, S. G. Seshachari, B. Jayaraju and G. D. Telang) and three Muslims (Ali Hasan, Ahsan-al-Hak and Shafkat Mohammed, all from Aligarh) Ahsan-al-Hak was actually an Afridi from the North West Frontier Province (NWFP), while Baloo was a Hindu by courtesy. He was a *chamaar* and didn't eat lunch with his caste Hindu team-mates when he began playing for Poona's Deccan Gymkhana club. For leading this team, the choice lay between the Hindu prince K. S. Ranjitsinhji and the Parsee doctor M. E. Pavri. Obviously, if not quite an end-of-the-century democratic alliance, at least fairly early in that century, a cricket coalition was thought to be more suitable for tackling the opposition.

This and other such combinations performed well enough against English teams abroad (1911) and at home (1926–27) to gain credit with the Marylebone Cricket Club (MCC). Fifteen years before India became an independent country again, its national team played against England at Lord's in 1932, to be followed by similar contests during 1933–34 in Mumbai, Kolkata and Chennai. These cities answered to different names then, so did the Indian team. The eleven was nominated 'All-India' for reasons never clearly stated by whoever gave the name.

Even the team which toured England in 1946 was dubbed 'All-India'. From what or where did this all-ness derive as far as the country's cricket was concerned? Was it a composite of the Pentangular tournament, that highly successful 'panchsheel' of Indian cricket which, in its fully evolved form, pitted against each other teams representing Hindus, Muslims, Parsees, Europeans and The Rest? That can't be the answer because the self-styled Europeans of India (mainly Brits, Scots and the Irish, perhaps a few Welshmen as well; hardly any French or Germans, Danes or Italians) resolutely used this category to keep themselves apart from Indians outside working hours. They couldn't really have aspired to wear India colours; for that matter, not many were able enough to win them on merit alone. The one and only time an Indian team was heavily represented by Europeans was in the second unofficial 'test' against A. F. R. Gilligan's team at Calcutta beginning on 31 December 1926. Seven Europeans and four Indians (C. K. Nayadu and R. J. Jamshedji, Wazir Ali and Nazir Ali) made up the eleven which lost this match. Yet, at an earlier 'test' that same month in Mumbai, an Indian-only team had easily held its own against the visitors.

To go back to the Pentangular for a while, it became a five-contestant tournament only in 1937. Held always in the then city of Bombay, from being a Triangular (among Europeans, Parsees and Hindus) contest in 1907, it became a Quadrangular when Muslims joined in 1912, and remained so until 1937 when several communities got together to put up a team expansively called The Rest. How expansive that description was can be gauged from the fact that for a couple of years, two brilliant Ceylonese batsmen, S. S. Jayawickreme and M. V. Sathasivan, played for The Rest. They may also have appeared because the Inter-university Board then was one which embraced India, Burma and Ceylon. On form, one or both of them could have been selected for an India eleven. The all-ness of Indian cricket thus crossed the Palk Straits. But the question of any batsman or bowler from Ceylon (now Sri Lanka) being invited to play for the All-India team somehow never arose.

A much-forgotten aspect of the Pentangular is what started as an inter-racial contest (Europeans vs Parsees or Europeans vs Hindus or simply *Gora* vs *Kaala*, even if many Parsees were as fair-skinned as the Europeans) was transformed by ever-increasing native Indian participation into an inter-community tournament. In his *History of Indian Cricket,* Ted Docker has quoted a letter-writer of the 1920s to the *Times of India* who assured, "If ever India is to win communal unity, it will be on her cricket fields..." Certainly, the good example was followed in other parts of the then India, sometimes as inter-community matches (as at Karachi, Aligarh, Ajmer), sometimes as invitation tournaments (at Delhi, Cooch Behar, Secunderabad). By the 1930s, all of India was getting into the game. Whether that helped to better inter-community relations or not, it certainly improved our cricket.

What it could not do was to reduce our capacity for wrangling. Each time an Indian cricket team was selected to play the official test matches of 1932, 1933–34 and 1936, some quarrel or the other invariably broke out just as often over who was selected as over who was not. Iftikhar Ali Khan, the first Nawab of Pataudi whose name anybody knows, once wrote in the 1941–42 annual number of that short-lived magazine, *Crickina:* "Let us imagine for a moment that all branches of our cricket are managed on scientific lines, and that we have a galaxy of talent. We are then confronted with the task of selecting a representative Indian side. How are we to proceed? Are we to follow the 1932 and 1936 style? If we do that, we shall have to try and please each community, each province and association, and we shall also have to please the rich patrons of the game. By the time we please all of them, we shall have succeeded in ruining the team, and we shall then start thinking of the people who will sit on the inquiry committee at the end of the season!"

Did Iftikhar Ali Khan feel all these compunctions when he accepted the captaincy of the All-India team of 1946 to tour England? He had fallen ill during the 1934 season in England, played practically no first-class cricket there or in India since then, yet allowed himself to be anointed leader of a side most of whose members he probably knew only by name. Certainly, he could not have made much effort to ensure that the best available team was selected. Otherwise, how could the claims of up-and-coming youngsters like D. G. Phadkar, Fazal Mahmood, Imtiaz Ahmed, as also of established players like H. R. Adhikari and Ghulam Ahmed have been ignored?

The Pentangular tournament was discontinued in 1945, perhaps out of apprehension about the 'communal' feelings it could arouse. Mahatma Gandhi was among those who disapproved of this form of cricket. Already, however, a far more inclusive national tournament had started in 1934 with the Ranji Trophy, donated by Maharaja Bhupinder Singh of Patiala, which "was to be competed for annually by the Provincial Cricket Associations of India". Though originally meant to be an inter-provincial competition, its format left ample room for the entry of other kinds of cricketing combinations. Thus, in the first year of the tournament, teams representing the army (which fielded nine sahibs and two natives), Central India (but also Central Provinces & Berar), Northern India (but also Southern Punjab), Western India (but also Gujarat and Maharashtra) were contestants, apart from the city of Bombay and the kingdom of Hyderabad. Over the years, other combinations (like Delhi & Districts, Rajputana) formed and re-formed, more provincial sides (like those of Bengal and Bihar) joined, as did other state teams like those of Baroda and Nawanagar. In addition to geography – spreading from NWFP to Madras, Gujarat to Orissa – history also stretched to include princely states alongside units of British India. More than by combination of communities, it was this coupling of history with geography that justified the All-India name. Of the 16 members of the 1946 side, seven were drawn from British India, nine from 'Indian' India, with the Nawab of Pataudi lending the last touch of royalty to an Indian cricket team. All other rajahs and *thakore*s and *nawabzada*s and *rao sahib*s since then who have hung around Indian cricket were called so only out of politeness. After some years, they even lost their stipends.

The community-wise breakdown of the 1946 team was 10 Hindus, four Muslims, one Parsee and one Christian. That it was led by a Muslim was quite without precedent—unless we take into account S. Wazir Ali's captaining the team in two unofficial 'tests' against Jack Ryder's team of Australians which toured India in 1935–36. All-India won both these matches convincingly and Wazir Ali may have thought he should be in the running for captaincy of the 1936 team to England. In cold fact, he was used to keep C. K. Nayudu out of the running, even though C. K. had led India in our first-ever test match (by courtesy of those two fine gentlemen if not great cricketers, H. H. Porbandar and K. S. Limbdi) against England at Lord's in 1932, and in three tests that followed in India during 1933–34. Not a two-nation but a three-nation view of Indian nationhood was then being sponsored by the British in India. Other than Hindus and Muslims, the so-called princes were being tutored to inherit if not India, at least Indian cricket.

That must be how M. K. Vizianagram ('Vizzy') was smuggled into the team in the only capacity he qualified—not as bowler or fielder or batsman but as captain. Apparently, the selection committee preferred him over Iftikhar Ali Khan! Not for nothing had Vizzy got that shabby structure put up at Ferozshah Kotla and named it the Willingdon Pavilion.

The All-ness of India was drastically altered by Partition and Indian cricket, Aligarh westwards, lost many Muslim cricketers – some already established in first-class cricket, some about to in the near future – who migrated to Pakistan or chose to stay on there. Among its numerous deprivations and aberrations, however, Pakistan has gained substantially in cricket from what happened in 1947. Within five years, it was able to defeat India in a test match in India; we have yet to return the compliment though more than 50 years have passed. On its very first tour of England in 1954, Pakistan achieved a test victory in England; we achieved this only on our eighth tour. On these and many other counts, Pakistan's record in international cricket is superior to that of India. The most telling proof of this was seen when Kerry Packer's agents chose several Pakistani cricketers but none from India for his *tamasha* involving the best players in the world.

Looking back from 2000, we may wonder whether or not an All-India team on pre-1947 lines would have performed better than India or Pakistan teams have done separately since then. I am not sure it would have. If nothing else, the tradition of selectorial squabbles would have affected player performance. No matter how many good players are available, unless a fair and wise selection committee can choose the best possible eleven, how would test matches be won? The necessary fairness and wisdom have not always been evident on either side of the border. But, somehow, Pakistan has been able to generate match-winning performances even from unknown and untried players. That is the secret of their success.

What India has achieved, even after losing the All-India label, is an all-ness that should serve us well at present and in the future. Despite the predominance of Bombay, then of Delhi, and now of Bangalore, other regions keep making inroads. When a Bengali opens our batting, an Oriya the bowling, with wickets being kept by a Tailangi, the all-ness of Indian cricket remains secure.

[1999]

Other books by the author

The Romance of Indian Cricket. Delhi: Hind Pocket Books, 1968.
Playing for India. New Delhi: Orient Longman, 1972; revised 1988.
Between Indian Wickets. Delhi: Orient Paperbacks, 1976.
Matched Winners. New Delhi: Orient Longman, 1996.
The Autobiography of an Indian Cricketer. New Delhi: Ravi Dayal Publisher, 1966.

A Passage to America: The Reception of Rabindranath Tagore in the United States, 1913–41. Calcutta: Bookland, 1964.
Directory of Dissertations in English and American Literature by Indian Scholars. Calcutta: Indian Association for English Studies and Orient Longman, 1968.
Indian Essays in Americam Literature (jointly edited with D. V. K. Raghavacharyulu). Bombay: Popular Prakashan, 1969.
Translation as Discovery and Other Essays on Indian Literature in English Translation. New Delhi: Allied Publishers, 1981; new edition, Hyderabad: Orient Longman, 1994.
The Idea of an Indian Literature: A Book of Readings. Mysore: Central Institute of Indian Lanbuages, 1981.
Some Positions on a Literary History of India. Mysore: Central Institute of Indian Languages, 1982.
Forster and Further: The Tradition of Anglo-Indian Fiction. New Delhi: Orient Longman, 1993.
A Dictionary of Indian Literature I: The Beginnings to 1850. New Delhi, Orient Longman, 1999.

Translations by the author (all from Bangla)

Bewitching Veil (A long poem by Monindra Roy). Calcutta: Bengali Literature, 1967.
The Naked King and Other Poems (A selection of poems by Nirendranath Chakrabarti; translated jointly with Meenakshi Mukherjee). Calcutta: Writers Workshop, 1975.
The Book of Yudhishthir (A study of the Mahabharata by Buddhadeva Bose). Calcutta: Orient Longman, 1986.
Three Companions (Three long stories by Rabindranath Tagore). New Delhi: Disha Books, 1992.
Modern Poetry and Sanskrit Kavya (A long essay by Buddhadeva Bose). Calcutta: Writers Workshop, 1997.
Gora (A novel by Rabindranath Tagore). New Delhi, Sahitya Akademi, 1997; reprint 1999; 2d. edn. 2001.

Related titles from Orient Longman

Great One-Day Internationals
Gulu Ezekiel

Matched Winners
Sujit Mukherjee

Patrons, Players and the Crowd: The Phenomenon of Indian Cricket
Richard Cashman

Playing for India
Sujit Mukherjee

The Dictionary of Cricket
M A Pervez